NOT ONLY CHESS
A Selection of Chessays

Other Books by
GERALD ABRAHAMS, M.A. (Oxon), Barrister-at-Law

LEGAL

Law Affecting Police and Public, Sweet & Maxwell (1938)
Law Relating to Hire Purchase, Eyre & Spottiswoode (1939)
Law for Writers and Journalists, Herbert Jenkins (1958)
According to the Evidence, Cassells (1958)
The Legal Mind, H.F.L. (1954)
Police Questioning: The Judges' Rules, Solicitors' Law Stationery Society (1964)
Trade Unions and the Law, Cassells (1968)
Morality and the Law, Calder & Boyars (1971)

POLITICAL THOUGHT

Retribution, W. H. Allen (1941)
Day of Reckoning, W. H. Allen (1943)
World Turns Left, W. H. Allen (1943)
La Mediocrazia Contemporanea, A. Giuffrè, Milan (1956)
Lo Stato Come Societa Commerciale: E La Irresponsibilita Dei Ministri, A. Giuffre, Milan (1957)

FICTION

Ugly Angel, Eyre & Spottiswoode (1940)
Conscience Makes Heroes, Eyre & Spottiswoode (1945)
Lunatics and Lawyers, Home & van Thal (1951)

PHILOSOPHY AND SOCIOLOGY

The Jewish Mind, Constable (1961)

CHESS

Teach Yourself Chess, E.U.P. (1948)
Technique in Chess, Bell (1961)
La Tecnica en Ajedrez, Bruguera, Barcelona (1965)
The Chess Mind, E.U.P. (1951) Penguin Books (1960)
Test Your Chess, Constable (1963)
Pan Book of Chess, Pan Books (1965)
Handbook of Chess, Arthur Barker (1965)

BRIDGE

Brains in Bridge, Constable (1962)

TRAVEL

Let's Look at Israel, Museum Press (1966)

NOT ONLY CHESS
A Selection of Chessays

Gerald Abrahams

London   George Allen & Unwin Ltd
Ruskin House   Museum Street

First published in 1974

ISBN 0 04 794005 0

Set in 10 point Times Roman type and printed in Great Britain *by*
Page Bros (Norwich) Ltd, Norwich.

PREFACE

Fifteen years ago Naboth, the British chess player, enjoyed a small vineyard; half an hour each week on the Third Programme; 1000th part of BBC hebdomadal time. But the Tyrant desired the plot, and took it away from us.

We were told that chess was insufficiently significant to justify the grant of a 1000th portion of wireless time. Clamouring for use of our plot, they said, were topics more calculated to stimulate the British listener; Third Programme topics like Incest Amongst the Incas, and the history of heterosexuality in Bulgaria. We chess players could not compete.

From that small vineyard, however, I have preserved a few of my own vines, including some that were being planted, and some that were about to blossom, when the bulldozers came.

I present them here, together with some printed pieces and some unprinted pieces; some melodies already heard, some melodies so far unheard.

There is a variety of topics here, but chess gives them a certain unity. Chess is a subject with which many are acquainted. But even for those who are unacquainted with real play there is much that can be told by way of description, much that they may find fascinating in accounts of life and thought outside the edges of the board.

I write, therefore, of more than chess for those who are not only chess players, including those who are not players at all. In chess there is a world of intellectual values. Myself have found on the chess board not only an arena of competition but a field for speculation relevant to many other topics in which I have been absorbed. A sort of world view emerges in the mind of the self-conscious chess player. *Such a view I endeavour* to present here.

I am indebted to my good friend and fellow chess player John Beach, for valuable advice and help at proof stage.

CONTENTS

CONTENTS

Part One

IN THE CHESS ATMOSPHERE

1 Chessboard Meditation

I was watching a friend of mine in action at a recent tournament. Let us call him Bill, if only because his name is not Bill. Bill is a man of pipes. I rather envy him this, because pipe smokers, having small chattels to toy with, are less apt to make hasty moves or any of the finger-fehler that are committed by abstainers, or cigarette smokers, or cigar smokers, or, let me add, orange eaters. Benevolent powers have provided playthings to engage their otherwise idle, nervous, hands.

My friend Bill rejoiced in his pipes, and, while he was constructing an impressive King's side array of aggressive force against a lean and hungry looking non-smoker, his hands were happily busy, as pipe after pipe was filled, lighted, puffed, emptied, cleaned, refilled—and wrong ones frequently inserted into his mouth. In that way he exorcised blunders from his play. As for the pipes, they seemed to me, as in pathetic fallacy, to be gloating. Happy playthings. But fallacy, alas, was there, and pathetic. Later, it seemed hours later, a desperate, bluffing, Queen's side Rook intrusion, organised by the irritating non-smoker, had diverted Bill somewhat from his benevolent dragon parade, Bill had been caught, as I have heard it expressed, on the horns of two stools. He was very uncomfortable and, as his hungry opponent, not calmed by smoke clouds, greedily devoured pawn after pawn, I saw Bill assume a melancholy aspect—and I saw that the pipes were still.

Later, after his resignation—though he was not yet resigned to it—I found the man staring at the board with glazed eyes. Beside him the strewn pipes, and tobacco tins, and pipe-cleaners, lying there unplayed with, suggested to my mind (as marbles conjured by Buzfuz) abandoned toys; in this case the epic toys of the

11

children of Hector or Baldur, or other defeated and slain hero, while the infants, grouped (as for the cameras) with their mother, were failing to understand that Daddy had really left home this time; that what used to be was not, and was no more to be; that what might have been, what should have been, had somehow evanesced into the shades of the unachieved; into the unfuture of unhistory.

That, I thought, moving, as I meditated on the tragic Bill, from the order of melancholy epic into sad semantics and the psychology of misery, that is the meaning of grief. That he had lost a point was not the point. (I will add that winners, anguished by the missing of some convincing brilliancy, are more easily comforted.) Bill was looking, through the scattered pieces, at the King's side attack that had gone, though not vanished; and he was yet unreconciled—would for long be unreconciled—to the fact that the shade had slipped through his extended thought-arms. So one deserted mourns the lost, though living, lover. That attack was still real to a mind battling against the invading realisation that the attack was unreal. "Woe for those that are lost yet not forgotten." The woe is in the mind of the non-forgetters. From the conflict of the vivid memory with the resistant reality comes the forced armistice which is sorrow. Then words, and laments, are only stomatic efforts to distract concentration, and mechanically to relieve the mind of pain. Therefore it is more charitable to let a chess player tell you how he lost than to gloat with him when he tells you how he won. But even if you assist in the assuagement of sorrow, you will never cure him of regret.

At this point, let the pundits call me Humpty-Dumpty for the uses that I assign to words. Sorrow emphasises, by reluctant acceptance, the goneness of what has gone. Regret dwells on the persistent reality of what might have been."Saddest of all words." The versifier who said that (Bret Harte) was a better psychologist than the poet Tennyson was when he wrote "wild with all regret." By that line, reason is sacrificed to rhythm: for regret is not wild. The thought that what might have been has, in fact, not been, does not deprive the might have been of reality, in the way that the sorrowful acceptance of some present anguish exorcises the spectres of the past. Regret stays sadly and quietly with the mind;

dwelling on unactual realities, "while memory holds a place in the distracted globe."

To many chess players this experience is real—is at once acute and chronic. When the old campaigner Morry was asked by a spectator: "What is that player thinking about?" he replied: "He's not thinking, he's regretting." But the person referred to was living in a real world: the world in which he moved the other Rook; the world in which he did not foolishly capture the Pawn, or foolishly refuse the Pawn, as the case may be. And as the rules of chess apply in that world, and as in that world one sees always what it was in one's capacity to see, that world is sounding with melodies that are not less melodious for being unheard by the vulgar.

Moving firmly from the elegiac to the metaphysical, let us recognise that something in the chess player makes the most philosophic of them unphilosophic in his attitude to his own results. (And how philosophic have been other philosophers?) In particular, the average good chess player does not accept as valid a rigid distinction between the "actually is" and the "never was." He does not accept, in other words, the unreality of possibility, including the possibilities of the past. To the logician the whole issue is too easy: true or false. It is just untrue to say: "I moved the King's Rook," when in fact you moved the Queen's Rook. And if you say: "But what if I feel as if I had moved the King's Rook?" he will reply, if he is a modern: "From a false proposition, all absurdities follow." But the chess player will not be convinced, for he has lived in a dimension of reality which professional philosophers ignore or pretend to ignore. His regrets accompany him in a dimension of thought which even the idealists find hard to recognise.

To the philosopher who works on the conceivable shapes of a world stated in barren words, possibility means either a degree in statistical probability—which will be made significant or insignificant by the future events—or it expresses a degree of ignorance, which more learning will abate. The distinction that matters to him is between "this is the case" and "this is not the case." "May be" he will tolerate for a time; but "could have been" is to him, *ex hypothesi*, unverifiable; is therefore meaningless.

The expression "possible world," in the chess player's sense, is, to the logician, the creature of an invalid modality—especially anathema to the schools that know not modality in any case. But let these thinkers become unhappy chess players; perhaps they will not then condemn the chess regretters as paranoiacs with hallucinations or, worse to them, mystics with invalid metaphysics. Nor will they, in any case, try to communicate these vituperations to the players, for it is hard-headed proletariat and bourgeois who make up a majority of the chess world, and who speak of what they should have done as if it were more real than what they did; and they speak so, without awareness of the difficult and derogatory philosophic epithets to which they are exposing themselves.

Most taking of all words: it might have been. I do not know whether the philosopher Bergson was a chess player. Nor do I know what percentage of chess players is aware of the Bergsonian philosophy.[1] But if ever I meet Bergson in the shades, I'll tell him that the chess players of the world know the real meaning of The Reality of Time. I do not refer to *Zeitnot*, which is time mechanised and formalised, and only a clog to the creative spirit. I refer to the richness of time, with all its possible dimensions which are the dimensions of possibility. Bergson's fountain of potential creation is the real world. The backflow of actuality and the actual past is as relatively unimportant as the actual result, which only matters in the tournament—and, in a Swiss tournament, only in the most sophisticated way.

But even if my fellow chess players resent my ascription to them of a French philosophy, in days when the French are notably inexpert at chess, and chaotic in philosophy, they will not quarrel with me if I say that they are aligned on the side of the angels in the spiritual cold war. Let him admire the Russian masters as he may, the chess player who thinks about it will not accept (even in exchange for an invitation to Moscow) the determinism of the Marxist materialist. One feels that Tchigorin, the real Russian father-figure, would have none of it. When the chess player says: "I should have won: judge me by that," he is

[1] One connection between Bergson and Chess is that Norbert Wiener, pioneer of Cybernetics, and so of the electronic chess player, assumed that Bergson's account of Time (*durée*) was a practical concept.

contributing commissariat to the children of light. For when he declares that what happened did not express his real self, he is implying an adherence to the school of Free Will, as well as a belief in the essential self (as opposed to the accidental self), such as the existentialist compiler of results would reject out of hand.

"Chess players of the world unite: you have nothing to lose but your pawns." Stopping only to hazard the conjecture that Sartre and Karl Marx were probably very bad chess players, I assert with some confidence that every true chess player believes in the freedom of the mind, and believes too in a will-power, or an aggregate of forces equivalent to will-power, which, being harnessed, would enable him to see well, do well, think well and create new ideas. What chess player has not rebuked himself for Acedia, even if he does not know the word?; has not regretted that he did not play with a pipe for a moment and look around? Then he *would* have done what he *could* and *should* have done. What player has not experienced the sense of effort as one says: now let me see the sequence from P × P, P × P; Kt × P, Kt × Kt, *et seq?* The effort, to a tired mind, is like getting out of bed on a cold morning, or taking a cold bath because one believes that it is good. In chess there is effort of this kind, and, if will-power is not a scientific description, at least let it serve till a better expression comes along. With effort goes a sense of freedom and awareness of choosing—creativity in some degree. The philosopher chess player, therefore, can never be worse than critical-realist. And if he dwells on the wonderful way in which the chess mind grasps a long process in one act—sees in one *Gestalt*—he may even be tempted to idealism.

In chess there certainly seems to be choice. I have even seen Buridan's ass at the chess board, so equally balanced as to his desires to make specific moves that he has lost on the clock. Usually there exists in the mind some rational determinant, some line of thought that led to the choice. If further thought could have revealed a bigger perspective, then the player blames himself: "Why didn't I take a second glance at my back row and play P–R3 before P–K5?" He will not blame the error on an hypnotic opponent (though that has been done) nor will he believe that there is any sort of subterranean determination, that his unconscious make-up compelled the error. If he thought that, he'd be inclined to give up chess. If, after years, he finds that he is still making the same type of error, for no assignable reason, he may resort to a psychiatrist. This person may well say: "Your errors are determined; they are the consequences of a bad technique of breast-feeding on the part of your early nourisher. What they amount to now is the manifestation of the death-wish. To which the tortured one may well reply, "Yes, I have a death-wish: will you please drop dead." Then he will return to his board and his regrets.

The chess player will not accept that he lives on a plane of mere behaviour. As I wrote in 1926, before the existence of modern existentialism, and when I had only the vaguest notions of behaviourism, "every chess player has, in his chess pieces, a ready made distinction between ideas and the material order." The chess player, I say now, cannot be an existentialist, cannot be a pure materialist, an accidentalist with no essential purposes.

But this philosopher chess player of mine (whom I used to think of as the successor to Plato's Philosopher-King) is, unhappily, not the best of players, for evidently he has distracting thoughts, and, as we have seen, more to regret than those who lose less. Moreover, I have come to suspect that in chess, as in other walks of life, those persons prosper who hold a minimum of metaphysic in their minds, a minus quantity of music in their souls. Desperate bad losers, who play to kill, and slave-drive their seconds to analyse the variations in the ending or for the next game, these don't regret, these hate. But we many, who, losing much, console ourselves with the thought that we are more than chess players, we can enjoy philosophic meditation over the game up to a point. Up to what point? Till you take up pipe smoking? At that stage there is still hope. To the point when the King's Knight takes on a looking-glass appearance and invites you to fight. That's too far.

Perhaps the point of no return is reached when you decide that your life has been a badly played opening, with many chances missed, followed by an ingenious middle game in which you still might have achieved something at certain apices of departure; and that now you've got to struggle to get something out of the ending. Please reader, never play badly enough to find yourself using the chessboard as a source for that melancholy analogy. You'll be asking yourself next whether your life would not have been better spent had you refused to play chess. That's worse than regret. That way Bingo lies. To save you from that fate, I say to you (perhaps against my doctrine) that such a question cannot be asked because your mind, being a chess player's mind, is not constituted to ask it. As Wittgenstein put it when he forgot the translatability of beliefs: *Wovon man nicht sprechen kann: darüber muss man schweigen* (This is unspeakable: on this topic we must be silent).

2 Sportsmanship and gamesmanship in chess

Years ago, in a chess brains trust, the question was asked whether chess players are good losers, and the answer was a unanimous negative. Speaking as one who, to say the least, is very good at losing, yet has not during the most anxious adjournment ever hired an assassin (or, worse, an assistant) I feel qualified to investigate this question and the wider, possibly different, one: whether chess players are sportsmen or, on the other hand, gamesmen. But let me say, *en passant*, that I and other players make no claim to sportsmanship for not having hired an assassin or an assistant. We don't do these things, simply because we are too arrogantly self-reliant to summon outside aid or to tolerate the feeling that we have been adventitiously assisted.

But *tempora mutantur, et nos* (or some of us) *mutamur in illis*. There was a time when it was thought wrong to look at one's position during an adjournment. That was taking advantage. But now, in so respectable an enterprise as a match for the Championship of the World, it is taken for granted that the adjournment is a time for hard analysis. This fact can even influence the timing of moves. More strikingly, it is permissible for each player to have a second, or several seconds, in order to assist him in his analysis. Assassins—not yet; assistants—in plenty. They are allowed (it is believed) to discuss the game with their player, even while the opponent is thinking. It is still, however, not the thing for a player to seek aid while his own clock is running. Nor is it thought proper to make trial moves on a pocket board while the actual (unadjourned) game is in progress. Over forty years ago a player of world-class was penalised in a continental tournament for that kind of conduct. There

18

is still a theory that the test of chess ability is the *extempore* play
that goes on during playing hours. But "around the game,"
so to speak, the test is one of reinforced endurance. The most
popular liquid at tournaments is midnight oil.

If asked: "Do you call this a game?" my answer is: "Don't
be silly, whoever told you that it was a game?" And if I were
asked whether I blame professionalism (whether official, or dis-
guised, as in Eastern Europe) I would answer "No." For my part
I have observed concession and sportsmanship—whatever that
is—among professionals, and the opposite among amateurs. So I
would not agree that the professional has caused any great change
of attitude. Economic motivation may bring caution to players,
but not meanness. Among amateurs and professionals alike, the
first-rate performer is usually (I do not say invariably) magnanimous. Pusillanimity is more likely to be found among those who,
as the psychiatrist put it, are quite right to feel inferior because
in fact they are inferior. But what I would suggest to my imaginary
questioner (about the notion of "game") is in the form of counter-
question. Let him show me, in these days of coaching and prepara-
tion, when averages of performance have risen so much—and
in some cases even standards have risen—let him show me any
game at all, from push halfpenny to polo, that can truly be called
a game.

This, I hasten to add, does not mean the irrelevance of sportsmanship. On the other hand, the keener the fight and the more
vital the result, so much greater is the merit that attaches to
sportsmanship; therefore it should be more greatly prized.

But sportsmanship is not an easy idea to grasp. When Lord
Harding described it as "not complaining in defeat, not gloating
in victory," he was, if I may say so with great respect, describing
some external appearances, not the real thing. He was describing
something that can be the consequence of an acquired, trained,
but disingenuous politeness. By all means don't gloat—most
chess players are too conscious of good fortune when they win
to do that. And by all means don't moan—that's harder advice.
But I won't judge your sportsmanship by these tests. We are
dealing with ethics not etiquette.

What to my mind constitutes sportsmanship is illustrated by

something that happened to me. This was when an opponent whom I knew to be a moaner and a gloater, and against whom I had a big advantage (so that he was entitled to feel miserable), drew my attention to the fact that I had left my clock going. He could have sat tight and let my clock run. And even if someone explains that he was too conceited to want to win that way, I'll still call him a sportsman. After all, your materialist psychologist can reduce all the generosities to self-love if he tries hard enough.

If sportsmanship means anything that is ethically significant then it means a measure of generosity. One is playing a small boy in a simultaneous exhibition and he is resigning because he does not know how to make the saving move, which is P × P *en passant*. He doesn't know that particular move. A generous opponent shows him. That is not to say that the player who does not show him is mean or unsporting in any positive way. After all, if the boy doesn't know the game properly he deserves to lose. On the other hand, the exhibitioner—I almost wrote exhibitionist—wants to win, if possible, by his own good play. He accepts his opponent's errors, but he does not want to win by his opponent's ignorance of a rule.

In chess we do play the rules. Nevertheless, we deplore players who try to use the rule book in order to get onto the scoreboard results that are not the objective results of play. Most of us do not like to win on the clock—even though the clock is a part of the game. We feel that the victory was not achieved by moves and moves only. A player who refuses to win on the clock is being more sporting than can be reasonably expected, is being quixotic. In contrast that minor master was very unsporting who—when his opponent, having forgotten to stop his clock, was walking about pending his turn to move—sat draped over the board in apparent thought waiting for the flag to fall. He was not obliged to inform his opponent of the omission. To have done so would have been sporting, generous. Not to do so would be to behave without generosity. To take positive advantage was mean, and is correctly described as unsporting. It is a question not of manners, but of degrees of generosity.

There is scope in the application of the rules.

There is a rule in chess that a sealed move must be unambiguous, or the game is forfeited. The reason for the rule is obvious. One could seal R–B5 and occupy the adjournment working out whether one meant QB5 or KB5. Yet errors are easy to make. I myself (in describing files) frequently write K instead of Q, and vice versa. Players, being awarded a game through this rule, have been known to refuse the gift. On the other hand, all those players would accept victory on the clock if it came their way. The distinction is this: let me win in the play subject to the time rules, but not by the rule book. The rule book should not be used, and for the most part is not used, as a chess piece, though I have heard that it has proved its utility as a golf club.

Another occasion for generosity in chess occurs whenever in a team match a good player has to adjudicate in collaboration with a weaker player representing the opposing team. Suppose the weaker player does not see the best line open to him. The sportsmanlike player will show it to him. I would say that the man who doesn't do so is behaving more than negatively—he is behaving badly.

At this stage let me stop and ask what we are discussing. We are talking about something like justice, are we not? or, rather, the equitibly coloured justice that we call fair play. We are talking of the judge who advises the jury to ignore an incautious utterance by the prisoner, and so gives him a sporting chance.

Without entangling myself in semantic combinations, let me suggest an analysis: you can be sporting; you can be non-sporting; you can be unsporting. The positive virtue has two opposites. You can be good, not good, or positively evil. You can be sporting, ethically indifferent, or mean.

When Charles Lamb gave the name Battle to the whist player who "relished the rigours of the game" he was depicting a type not sporting and not unsporting. The lady was keen and non-sporting—not mean, not generous. But Mrs Battle would not be my favourite female chess player. Among chess players there is an awareness of the truths of the board that is (almost) inconsistent with overawareness of the scoreboard. Therefore chess should encourage positive sportsmanship. On the whole I think it does.

When it comes to bad losing we have, as they say, something

else again. I have often thought that had I been a really bad loser I might have won more games. (Does bad losing make one better at winning?) The factor of desperation can cause a man to play harder. In the 1930s, among the chess players from the backward countries, I quite frequently observed that a desperate unconcealed desire to win and a horror of defeat accompanied, perhaps enhanced, great ability. Not at the highest levels, but certainly in the middle reaches of talent. Also I have encountered men who were bad losers when young and now are great players and good losers. It is not that they have become polite. Success has brought a sense of proportion—even a sense of humour.

Of bad losers there are a few chess players, I think a very few, who are naïve extroverted types and who simply hate the opponents who defeat them. Perhaps that hatred explains the spiteful, ungenerous, conduct of those who make their opponent return to the playing room in order to find that the sealed move is "resigns." This is a situation where bad losing has become unsporting. I think that the player who does this particular trick will do other villainies.

Of those who, while behaving properly, yet hate their conquerors, I would say that they are insufficiently conceited. They are jealous of the ability of others—and that is, surely, the clearest possible confession of inferiority. But the normal good chess player—if that is not a contradiction in terms—has no hate at all for an opponent. Indeed, he has no opponent at all, except his own limitation. That is what he is always playing against. And if he is upset at losing, his anger, or distress, or bitterness, is directed at himself. He should have won if he hadn't had a moment of blindness or overexcitement. He should have seen that danger— he should have taken that precaution. He, himself, with his ability, should have had no difficulty here. As for his opponent, he may express these views to him, because a lot of people require an audience, even when they are talking to themselves. In fact audiences are quite often the simple excuses for soliloquies. One may be impatient with an opponent for not agreeing that he should have lost, or for not convincingly demonstrating that your variations could be refuted. But as for hating him—not at all. In repose, one is sorry for him that he has had the misfortune to benefit from one's own failure to be adequate or to produce a masterpiece. Poor devil—he won. But I am the villain for causing him to do so.

Let it be remembered also that a game of chess can be a big mental involvement. The tentacles of the mind are stretching out into many directions of possibility. When the possibilities suddenly disappear and a hideous actuality supervenes, it takes time for a player to realise that what has actually come about is now the state of reality. It is as if something has been amputated and the feeling is still there. In that moment of experience the player releases some tension in expressed self-reproach. Is he, on that account, a bad loser? Possibly, but I do not regard him as significantly worse than the polished person who shows no feelings to the world. In any event if the normal chess moaner is a bad loser, I, who am reported a good loser, will not condemn him as a bad sportsman.

Chess players, on the whole, should be good sportsmen, because they play a game in which there is no bluff and no self-deception. Such are the adjudicators I have spoken of who work for a true result. The man who has immersed himself in chess is not likely to be so unvaluing of the game as to judge only by the formal result—the point on the scoreboard—or to value such results only. As we have seen, he rarely accepts bad results as true indices to his own merit. Evidently this man will not want to get results by sharp practice.

Is there, then, any gamesmanship in chess? Only so far as chess players fall below the normal moral average; and if they do that, why are they interested in chess? I have seen personal hostilities and displays of spite, and I have seen two grandmasters hammering at each other's clocks in the hope of dislodging the flag. That was excitement and a childish extroversion of regret. Of the externalia that may aid victory, jaunty attitudes (one-up-manship) are part of some player's personalities rather than methods adopted *ad hoc*. They are in the same category as the pipe smoked by the Midlands clergyman which he filled with brimstone so that it emitted fumes calculated to make Satan get behind him. This pipe, which shrivelled my oranges in their skins, gave the venerable player as much pleasure as it gave pain to his opponents. It adventitiously won him a lot of games.

In contrast, cold-blooded gamesman-planning is rare. But I have one pretty example. At my first British Championship effort, in 1929, a friend of mine—who is a magnificent analyst and celebrated in the chess world—found himself in a very bad position. But there was a way out. Given that his opponent (a very strong player) did not see the threat, it was possible, with a series of sacrifices, to achieve stalemate. But he had to include in his play a clearly inadequate move, which would inevitably warn his opponent. After all, one plays chess on the assumption that the opponent sees everything. (That is why the word "trap" is not a good chess term.) But my friend devised a psychological trap. He sat and looked at the board with a despairing face until he was well and truly in time trouble. Then he fumblingly made the crucial moves. His opponent, tempted to a little gamesmanship himself, was playing very quickly. Quick came the erroneous capture. Even quicker came the series of sacrifices and, while the flag was tottering, stalemate supervened. Now could he have improved on things in the following way: touched the piece, taken his hand away, and let himself be compelled to move the piece at random? No, he had thought of that, but dismissed it as sharp practice.

(Diagram 2.1: 5R2, 1p2r1kp, 3p2p1, 3Pb3, 4P3, 1r2B2P, 8, 5RK1. Time control at move 40.) At move 31 Black has played R–Kt6, a good move, because, if either Rook guards the Bishop, R × B wins. White thinks, and with the scheme burgeoning, plays:

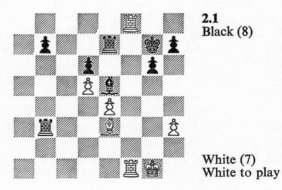

2.1
Black (8)

White (7)
White to play

32	B–Q2	R–Kt6 ch
33	K–R1	R × P ch
34	K–Kt1	R–Q6
35	B–B1	

Leaving himself less than half a minute on his clock.

35	...	R–QB2
36	B–Kt5	

Finger staying on his clock; and Black falls for it.

36	...	R–Kt6 ch
37	K–R1	R × B
38	R(1)B7 ch	R × R
39	R × R ch	

Forcing stalemate or perpetual check.

3 Psychiatry, lunacy and chess

During a Hastings tournament a well-known immortal player asked of another, possibly better but less immortal, player: "How is it that I see everything necessary for victory, yet incur defeat?" The reply was: "Ask a psychiatrist."

I agree that chess players should be aware of the existence of psychiatrists even if their knowledge of them stops (wisely) at that awareness. In being aware of psychology in its modern phase, one is aware that there is more to the playing of chess than pure intellectual apprehension; if only because there is more to pure intellectual apprehension than pure intellectual apprehension. In search of that *ignotum quid*, the experience of chess affords a line of inquiry. If there is pure intellect, chess is one of its manifestations, like mathematics (which is a different, but also pure mental operation). The chess process cannot, even by the acutest Russians, be reduced to an epiphenomenon of some phase of social evolution. Tchigorin may or may not have given something to chess; Karl Marx gave nothing.

The social-economic determinist contributes nothing to chess because he is a determinist, whereas the chess player gives every evidence of free choice. Therefore Sociology delegates the proof of chess causes to the schools of psychology, and the question for us is: what can Freud or the Freudians, with their degrees of determinism, contribute to the understanding of the game?

Clearly the psychiatrist should find interesting material among the chess masters, who have, from time to time, sent their representatives into the best asylums. But so far as the analyst of games is concerned, there is no evidence that lunacy has ever affected the form of a player's play, short of actually stopping him from play. Thus Steinitz is said, albeit on doubtful authority, to have played with the cabined Morphy when the latter was suffering a persecution mania; he reported that Morphy was as good as ever. (Certainly Morphy played splendid chess when already ill.) I am reminded of a story told me by Mieses, who was director of play at that San Sebastian Tournament (1911) which was won by Rubinstein. During the play Rubinstein was obsessed with the feeling that a fly was walking across his scalp. As there was no fly, Mieses took the great master, at the end of the tournament, to a leading psycho-neurologist at Munich. The Teuton expert examined Rubinstein carefully and said, with Teutonic crudeness: "My friend, you are mad. But what does that matter? You are a chess master!"

That neurologist might have been interested to know that fifteen years later, when Rubinstein was giving way to an extreme agoraphobia, his chess had lost nothing of its merit; and it is believed that, on leaving a mental home many years later, he was still capable, subject only to fatigue factors, of great chess. Again, there is no evidence that Torre, when his mental breakdown was supervening, played other than the brilliant chess for which he is remembered. Nor did the incipient dementia of Steinitz bring about any change in his clarity or his systematic approach to the board. [Znosko-Borovsky thought that Steinitz's dementia was a pose—a technique of helplessness.]

Compendiously, there does not appear, in the play of chess masters who are mentally afflicted, any manner of move from beyond the borders of lunacy to distort or enhance their actual play. Their eccentric conduct, such as the fads of Nimzovitch ("My opponent is threatening to smoke"), takes place at a different level from their intellectual operations.

Yet Freud has sought to demonstrate to the world that the rigid distinction between neuro-physical conduct and thinking is a hard one to maintain. Nor should chess players find all his contentions strange. Thus Lasker, great player and great student of the human mind, made many criticisms along the lines of conduct and character. He criticised Mieses, for example, in terms of impatience and lack of confidence, to which he attributed that brilliant player's overaggressive style. (The schools would have used the phrase "inferiority complex.") Consider also the

psychological phenomenon of the master Tarrasch, perpetrating
an oversight, through lack of effort, against the player, Yates,
whose entry he had opposed. He overlooked a quite easy to see
sacrifice at his K3. His hostility, or his pride, may have inhibited
a proper effort. The chess world is content to adopt a phrase
coined by Tarrasch, himself a medical man of great ability—
amaurosis scacchistica or chess blind-spot—to describe errors of
this type. To him this was a failure of concentration rather than a
subliminal intrusion. In a strange echo of Tarrasch's thinking, we
find Emanuel Lasker attributing hypnotic powers to Tarrasch, and
requesting that he be allowed to play against that opponent in a
separate room. He did not suggest more than a general heavy
influence, diminishing the adversary's will-power. Theoretically,
it is conceivable that a hypnotist could induce a sensitive opponent
to make the specific error that he finds desirable for his purposes.
The question arises whether a player, by some auto-hypnotism
operating among his memories, becomes inhibited from specific
moves or induced into specific manoeuvres. (Diagram 3.1:
5rk1, pb2q1pp, 1p1bp3, 3kt1p2, 3Kt4, 1P1BP3, PB3PPP,
Q4RK1.)

Hamburg 1910

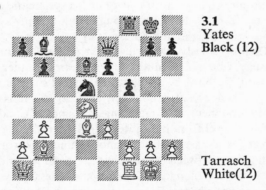

3.1
Yates
Black (12)

Tarrasch
White(12)

White, Praeceptor Germanorum, is employing, against his young
British opponent, a bad plan.

In answer to Black's 18 ... P–B4 he plays 19 R–B1 (Kt–B3
was desirable) and is surprised by 19 ... Kt×P!. This is a
winning move.

There followed:

20	P×Kt	Q–Kt4
21	K–B2	(if 21 B–B1 Q×Pch; 22 K–R1 Q–B5 is
		overwhelming)
21	...	Q×KtP ch
22	K–K1	B×P
23	B–K2	P–K4
24	Kt–K6	B–Kt6 ch
25	K–Q1	B–B6
26	B×B	Q×B ch
27	K–B2	Q–K5 ch
28	K–Q2	Q–Q4 ch
29	Kt–Q4	P×Kt
30	B×P	P–B5
31	P–K4	Q×KP
32	R–B4	R–Q1
33	P–R4	B–B7
34	resigns	

The line of thought suggested by Tarrasch's error brings us to the leading important psychiatric statement on chess, Dr Ernest Jones's famous lecture on Morphy, in which he emphasises the confidence of Morphy's play and early personality.

The word confidence is a bell ringing through Dr Jones's thoughts. To Dr Jones, be it explained, factors like confidence and its opposite are not only relevant to effort, but are causes of changes in the mind under the level of the conscious present, behind it in time, below it in memory. Confident good chess takes place at a normal emotional zero, continuous with abnormalities and anxieties above and below the line.

He regards as relevant the fact that chess is a war game, and all but suggests that the chess player recapitulates chess history in his development. He cannot think that chess players are concerned with chess history, of which most players are abysmally ignorant. (Including Dr Jones, when he speaks of chess played by William the Conqueror.) What he fails to appreciate is that chess to the real player is a science as war is a science, and that pugnacities and defensive reactions in chess, as in a well fought war, are totally subordinate to objective data, objective possibilities and impossibilities. Dr Jones describes Morphy's chess as the product of a mind whose energies were harmoniously sublimated. Morphy's breakdown he attributes to a feeling of guilt aroused from the subconscious when men like Staunton and Harrwitz made him aware of hostility. Then the ever-hostile father-image, which was successfully conquered or assuaged in periods of triumph amid popularity, re-emerged to depress and harass the conscious mind. Significantly, however, Dr Jones has little success in his effort to trace any psychiatric consequences in Morphy's actual play. He is aware that Morphy, in his mental home, played against Maurian some of his finest chess.

Digressing from Dr Jones, for a moment, let me observe that those who remember Capablanca, whose style—or styleless directness—was so reminiscent of Morphy, will remember his great confidence; students of the games from his great period, will feel the confidence of the player continuously manifest. They may also remember the set-back to confidence in the tragic first game against Alekhine, when it was borne in on Capablanca that he had become lazy, and was opposed to a dynamic, ener-getic creator of ideas. Against that creature of controlled neurosis and disciplined megalomania, he was not able quickly enough to reassert the quality of his own once supreme powers. He was not sufficiently integrated for the effort required in order to achieve his old effortlessness. Later on, it became clear that he had lost confidence. Hence the remarkable occurrence at Avro, in 1938, when he lost to Botvinnik, through making, at an admittedly higher level, the kind of error of aggression that Corzo had made against him thirty years before; and he succumbed to a combina-tion not unrelated in type to that with which he had then won.

It is clear from many examples that conduct and character are relevant to chess indirectly, through their relevance to any account of physical or neural, effort; for all mental effort implies some physical effort, though we are only conscious of it in fatigue, in illness and under the effects of age.

What has psychiatry to add to this? I would recommend all players to read Dr Jones's essay. Let me explain that Dr Jones is the great English exponent of Freud, though I suspect that his relationship to Freud is rather that of a Darwinian (like Weiss-man) to Darwin, or of a Marxist (like Stalin) to Marx.

Freud was the thinker who completed the translation of psychology from a study of conscious purposes into a study of behaviour. Without falling into the later dug Watsonian pit, where thought is the use of habit words in the epiglottis, and down the nose (as in America), Freud sought to establish that thinking is behaviour, and that there are factors in thinking other than the logic of the expressed thought. There is a background of phantasmal thoughts, the chaos of apparently random associations which dwell and occur in memory, and which obtrude in the course of the directive thinking which is conscious concentrated thought. His demonstrations, however, seem only relevant to the low level of thought that is the normal of everyday life.

It is beyond my scope to explain the machinery of repression and discipline, the contrast between id and super-ego and the other concepts with which Freud has mapped some regions of the mind. Suffice to say that he has achieved in a degree for human consciousness what Darwin did for human biology, by showing its roots and its origins; using the abnormal to explain the normal, which is continuous with it, as Darwin used the ape in order to give a better understanding of the human. Certainly it is established that there are mental forces and stresses, generated among repressed memories and suppressed wishes, which emerge in dreams, and giving rise to errors, which manifest themselves in mental disorders, and which (as Coleridge knew long before Freud) give inspiration to poetry and other creative arts.

The question for us is whether—in such a field as chess, an objective disciplined science to which only the objective board is relevant—the unconscious can give a quality, or pattern, or an inspiration to the vision and planning of the player, that would be recognisable in the game in the way that the random associations of the poet are discernible in "La Belle Dame" of Keats, or Coleridge's "Christabel."

Chess, be it emphasised, is a science, if only an incompletely articulated science, like medicine or engineering. The chess position can be opaque to mental effort, or translucent. When opaque, it is treated by different players differently—that is what is often meant by style. But always the effort is to see as much as possible, to do as much as possible, to the limits of one's ability, which limit is one's only opponent.

This situation and this effort, however, are quite different from the intellectual situation and efforts which are the arts. In the arts the control is by the free mind, creating among the possibilities latent in the material, an experience of the poet on the couch of his Muse.

The sources of poetry can be investigated. So analysts like Spurgeon can tell us from what sources Shakespeare drew the sounds of dying music, the disintegration of cloud-clapped towers; from what forests Blake conjured his tiger; in what woods and caverns Coleridge found the mysteries of Christabel. But these are the realms of poetry, which participates in dream land. It is a far cry from Kubla Khan to the study of Botvinnik endeavouring to exploit the Caro-Kann.

Unhappily Dr Ernest Jones was insufficiently equipped as a chess player to essay such a research for chess, as anyone will realise who reads his rather elementary (I would go so far as to say fallacious) classification of Morphy's play in terms of a useless distinction between aggressive and defensive, which he seems to equate with the even less useful distinction between combinative and positional. If those distinctions ever could be useful (which is doubtful) they clearly cannot be useful in studying Morphy or Capablanca, or any really great chess virtuoso.

Dr Jones knows some of the history of the game, and he uses it ingeniously (as Jung might use the history of a myth) to help with an account of the place of chess in the psycho-neural constitution. Chess is an old war-game—a war substitute—a canalising of pugnacity. Chess canalises or sublimates the ever-present hostility of the male (he says nothing, though perhaps he could say something, of female chess players—he wrote before the advent of Vera Menchik) to the father image which dominates his subconscious; the conquest of the King is a gratification of that hate, involved as it is with the homosexual urge that the psychiatrist attributes to all of us: and generates an anal-sadistic satisfaction—which seems to have nothing at all to do with *Sitz-fleisch*.

So be it. I am prepared to concede that pugnacity, simple or obscene, may generate energies which chess absorbs. But show me an anal-sadistic idea on the board which I can classify as a type of combination. This Dr Jones only essays once, and I quote:

Morphy was master of all aspects of the game in such a high degree and was so free of mannerisms and peculiarities of style that it is not easy to single out any peculiar characteristics. Chess, it is true, like all other games, is replete with unconscious symbolism. [I interrupt Dr Jones in order to say that when I defend the Ruy Lopez I get no time for imaginary bull fights.]

One could, for instance, comment on the skill he showed in attacking the King from behind, or in separating the opposing King and Queen; the latter, by the way, is illustrated in the first of his games ever recorded, which was played against his own father. But [continues Dr Jones, abandoning this promising attack] such details are not to our purpose; for pre-eminence in chess depends on a broad synthesis of exceptional qualities rather than on skill in any particular device or method.

He goes on to describe Morphy, innocuously, as "confident." Let me only say on this that the details that Dr Jones gives and refrains from giving are very much "to our purpose." Must one be a pederast at heart in order to mate a King from the rear? Or to take one's opponent aback? In the game between young Morphy and his father Alonzo Morphy (number 1 in Maroczy's collection) was there any better way of getting an advantage than the doubling of the pawns at f7 and f6, so as to lay the King open to attack and prevent other pieces from easily participating on the King's side? The purpose of the play was to disintegrate the defence in a degree; that was the effect achieved by aggressive play against an imperfect defence. (Diagram 3.2: r4rk1, pp3p1p, 1b1q1p2, 3p1B2, 2ktP4, 5Kt2, P4PPP, R2QR1K1.)

It is worth emphasising that Dr Jones does not pursue this line of thought further. For some reason, which may be psychiatrically explicable, he drops it like a hot brick. The censor pushed it back below the threshold.

But before we part from it, let me say that it is more important than absurd. The essential doctrine of psychological determination is that even directive thinking is never free, and that this is evidenced by the intrusion into thought of the phantasies. Thus

B

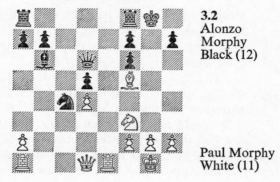

3.2
Alonzo
Morphy
Black (12)

Paul Morphy
White (11)

White has, cleverly, opened the Black King's defences.
There followed:

19	Kt–K5	P × Kt
20	Q–Kt4 ch	K–R1
21	Q–R5	K–Kt2
22	Q–Kt5 ch	K–R1
23	Q–R5	P–KR3

(Father Morphy, in Maroczy's opinion rightly avoids a draw by repetition. This "at a voluntary level.")

24	R × P!	Kt × R? (Better is Q–KB3)
25	P × Kt	Q–QB3
26	P–K6	K–Kt2
27	P–Kt4	Q–B6 (intending Q–KB3)
28	P–Kt5!	Q × R ch
29	K–Kt2	Q–B3 ? Panic (K–Kt1 wins)
30	P × Q ch	K × P
31	P × P	R × P
32	Q–Kt6 ch	K–K2
33	Q–K6 ch	K–B1
34	Q × P ch	R–Kt2 ch

35	B–Kt6	K–Kt1	41	B–B5	P=Q
36	P–R4	P–Q5	42	P–R7 ch	R × P
37	P–R5	P–Q6	43	B–K6 ch	R–B2
38	Q–Kt5	R–Q1	44	B × R ch	K–R2
39	P–R6	P–Q7	45	Q–Kt6 ch	K–R1
40	Q–B6	R(Kt2)–Q2	46	Q–R6 mate	

I defy anyone to explain any aspect of this play in terms of any psychological abnormality.

errors in spelling reveal what was really in the mind. If I write "their" for "there" the determinist is not happy to account for it by the circumstance that I have already written a lot of legitimate "theirs" and that my hand became a trifle habituated. Probably, they say, my super-ego was disturbed by the id because my whole undertaking was misconceived from the standpoint of a harmoniously integrated personality.

The best analogy I know to Dr Jones's effort is to be found in an essay by the late Dr Susan Isaacs—the wife of a quite good chess player. She examined an enuretic little boy in order to find out his anxieties—those of his parents being obvious. She gave him a set of trains to play with and the little boy arranged these with the engine between the coaches; this he insisted on. From this aesthetic preference Dr Isaacs induced, as present in the infant's mind, designs upon herself which would earn the lad laurels among the juvenile delinquents, and entitle him to a scholarship in any good industrial school. In the mental world so delineated, by Dr Jones and Dr Isaacs alike, the Muses of play (and with them the science of chess) enjoy no independence, and thought is only allowed the illusory appearance of a limited functional freedom against which the subconscious mind and the psychiatrist are in active and constant protest.

Let it not be thought that, in saying this, I ridicule the legitimate claims of psychiatry. The subconscious, or unconscious, is a demonstrable constituent of our being, even though, as P G Wodehouse delightfully puts it, "We didn't. happen to know that it was there." If it were possible to show in chess players some idiosyncrasies of play, and trace them to unconscious causes, the results of the research would be instructive and delightful. Why, for example, does one blindfold player (that is, in effect, an ordinary player seeing ahead) have difficulty in keeping track of Knight moves, and another in keeping track of Bishop moves? Why does a certain combination reveal itself to the inward eye of one good player and not to another? What inhibition or obsession obfuscates the mental retina?

I see no reason why emotional disturbances or stimulations should not become associated in a player's memory with specific manoeuvres that he has executed, with plans that have failed or succeeded, with oversights that he has suffered. There memory is adding to technique, though not changing the nature of chess vision. If a good player fails to see what Tarrasch failed to see against Yates, it may be explicable in terms of laziness or pride. Need it be linked with a specific lesion in the emotional-intellectual unity which is the mind in action? I do not accept that this kind of explanation is needed in order to explain chess errors, but I do not deny the scope for research. I suggest that the lesions that matter to actual play are specific events in the mental continuum, and are not usefully classifiable under general or specific anxiety forms. But these investigations will have to wait until Reuben Fine becomes as good a psychologist as he is a chess player. Certainly Dr Jones has made no convincing contribution here and Freud never contemplated the undertaking.

Meanwhile, I prefer to hold that the disciplined mind which is equipped for chess has, *ex hypothesi*, so completely emancipated itself from the physical, and the level of conduct and habits—even mental conduct and habits—that its activity is completely free and objective, the only limitation being that of its functional efficiency. The pugnacity of a player stimulates him, but gives him no ideas, only urges him to discover them; the orchestra of the endocrines arouses him but does not provide him with a chess melody.

Whether that is the whole truth or not, we are insufficiently equipped to be able confidently to say. What obviously is true at this stage is that chess has more to offer to psychiatrists than psychiatrists have to offer to chess.

4 Chess players on the larger board

There was a time when the British Colonial Office was occupied by a very high-class bridge player (unhappily no longer with us). That fact may be as politically relevant as the fact that his predecessor was an extremely tall man. But the precedent may have given chess players to wonder whether the country would be better, or worse, governed if there were good chess players in high office. One feels that in the past they could not have made things worse.

Certainly no good chess players would have made some of the terrible mistakes that have proved so ruinous to this country and to Europe. Any competent chess player could have worked out the military probabilities of the 1930s (and later) with tolerable accuracy. But it is small comfort to chess players that Adolf Hitler overvalued tactics and ignored truths of strategy. Too many good chess players were sacrificed in those wild campaigns. Nor is it good comfort to reflect that first-class intellect is not for politics—nor politics for intellect. Most intellectuals would still like to "have a go."

But in Britain chess players have not been lacking in chances. Admittedly chess was never a must in our forces and higher Civil Service as it was in the Empire of the Czars. Nevertheless, one Prime Minister has been a reasonably good chess player. I refer to the late Mr Bonar Law. Not the worst of players—not the worst of ministers. In his House of Commons he was vastly overshadowed, as a player, by the late Sir Watson Rutherford, who was among the strongest Liverpool players in the days of Amos Burn, when that great master was training giants.

On the other hand, Bonar Law was classes above Sir John Simon, as he then was. Indeed, Simon, for all his achievements, in the law and in politics, was ridiculously bad at chess. Nor can

37

it be said that had he devoted more time and energy to chess he would have been better. He devoted abundant time and energy to it. It was his only vice. We owe him, incidentally, a good phrase: "Chess is a cold bath for the mind."

In talking of Simon I am reminded of a story told me by the late Mr Meikle, a strong Lancashire chess player, better known as the father of some great rugby forwards. Meikle was on the same boat as Simon, crossing the Atlantic just before the First World War. Sir John had roped Meikle into a consultation match by radio with a German liner. With Meikle at the helm the game went tolerably well. But one day Sir John was in the radio cabin when a move arrived from the opponent. He looked at it. "Oh, that's easy," said the great man, "no need to trouble Meikle," and he gave the operator the answering move—as it happened, the only move that could lose a won game. Meeting Meikle on his way down he told him what he'd done. Meikle made gestures of wild despair, and Sir John's long legs carried him quickly back to the wireless room, where he found that the operator had treated the message as a coded priority. Thereafter the Germans won. Two decades later Simon was Foreign Secretary when Germans were projecting attack. No Meikle was on his staff.

Simon was bad at chess. But his lesser contemporary at Wadham, the late Sir Richard Barnett, who had an external appearance that could have been used by any caricaturist as a specimen of the huntin', shootin' and fishin' species—he was indeed a great Bisley marksman—played a polished and clever game of chess, when at his best. Looking at him, I was reminded of the odd fact that one of the very best chess columns in Britain was, unexpectedly, created in *The Field*. (What more improbable niche could have been found for Steinitz?)

On the subject of Simon it must not be thought that lawyers— whose task, as Disraeli put it, is to illustrate the obvious, elaborate the self-evident and expatiate on the commonplace—are necessarily bad at chess.[1] I know at least one very interesting lawyer

[1] The lawyer must diagnose his client's case, giving it a classification, among classes which are not always distinct. He must see ahead, in the sense of anticipating answers to his questions or his pleas. But the range is not distant. Nevertheless, he can find himself supporting claims and defences with insight, to the degree of imagination. Yet I will not say that Disraeli was wrong.

chess player, and I would also mention that high in British chess have stood, at some time, T H Tylor, the Balliol Law Don, Professor Wheatcroft, at one time Master of the Supreme Court, Professor Rupert Cross, the blind jurist of Magdalen, and Mr Roome, who at the moment of his untimely death, was a brilliant Treasury Counsel. Further, among great international names, Morphy was a lawyer. It must be admitted that he was a chess player first. Alekhine held a law degree. Tartakower was a qualified lawyer; so was Bernstein—and there are many others.

In the more general field chess players have their representatives on some high levels of intellect. Old Philidor was a musician; and the modern Russian Taimanov is a high-ranking concert pianist whose name I have seen at the top of a Russian musical bill. Lasker was, a considerable mathematician; Tarrasch a good medical man. Staunton was a scholarly analyst of Shakespeare; Buckle, champion of the City of London, took time off to write the monumental *History of Civilisation*.

Quae regio in terris nostri non plena laboris?

In modern Yugoslavia the leading authority on the physics of engineering was for many years that great chess player Vidmar (third in the London Congress of 1922). His contemporary and friend, Dr Treybal, was a Judge in the Czecho-Slovakia of Masaryk. In Russia Ilyin Genevski combined the roles of master chess player and leading revolutionary. (He got the surname Genevski from his exile at Geneva.) His unpolitical contemporary Levenfisch was, in his day, a pioneer of glass engineering. The more than once world champion Botvinnik was decorated by his government for good work in electrical engineering. His first challenger, Bronstein, has stooped a little for his government in the press: but is mainly significant for the fact that if you ask a Russian: "Who was Bronstein?" he does not need to say "Trotsky."

Much more of a list could be made in the intellectual fields. The thought occurs, however, that the great politico-economic spheres do not accommodate many players. Exceptional is such a phenomenon as Von Kolisch who, being befriended by one of his admirers, who happened to be Rothschild, became a millionaire. I am not aware of any other good player in that rare category—

certainly none that has got there directly or indirectly through chess. In Russia, chess players are aristocracy, but not government. A Russian general, speaking with bated breath, confided that He (Stalin) took great interest in the game, and was undoubtedly a great master—but that, as a matter of fact, he never played. I have told elsewhere how I threw out a subtle suggestion about his strategy, having in mind that, had he been good at chess, he might have cooked up something better than the combination of the Molotov–Ribbentrop pact—which eventually cost Russia 25 million men. Safer perhaps is chess.

But to revert to the implied question with which I started: why there are no good chess players in the front ranks of politics. One or two lines of thought occur to me. Good chess players are severe thinkers. They perhaps would not find it easy to enter into the give and take of party politics, and to excite themselves about trivial issues. If I may speak from my own experience, when I stood as a parliamentary candidate I very much enjoyed my own oratory, but I confess that I could not raise enthusiasm in debating the merits of issues in domestic economics that interested the housewives and the trade union wallahs—issues, moreover, on which I could see both sides.

In politics one requires either a platform power—and that is not much use without a platform—or the smooth polish which is the skin of the "guinea-pigs" on the board of our joint stock state. In any event, chess players tend to accumulate in the classes that sell their brains, not their personalities.

Whether chess players would improve the political world as it is now I do not speculate. Given an honest chess player (and chess players, among other intellectuals, are not *eo ipso* virtuous), one would have a person who could not be bluffed by threats and who would not judge by results. There is brilliant repartee on the chessboard; but no debating points. And the good player beats the bad player. That has not been true of politics since the short period from Talleyrand to Metternich.

In modern politics salesmen are required—advertisers who know nothing of the inner logic and workings of what they advertise. But they plan campaigns. Chess players, therefore, would either be very good politicians or very bad. At this moment

I know that there is a strong county player on the opposition back benches, but he has offered no parliamentary gambits, and sits with others to analyse the endings of debate.

We know that musicians—even recently—have found politics unharmonious. As Clemenceau said of Padereswki's Presidency, "*quelle chute.*" Would a chess player in politics also be falling?

A more melancholy thought for chess players arises from the observation that there are no grandmasters in the Praesidium of All the Soviets. They haven't even got good chess players in the Government of Israel. Here's the final proof surely that the forces of chess are, in some way, unfitted for the control of affairs on the larger board.

Can it be that chess is high bourgeois in an age that has liquidated the higher levels of the bourgeoisie? Has chess failed socially? Hardly failed—it hasn't been tried. But as a matter of brute fact, the social accomplishments of politicians in the Western world consist (according to class) in golfing and grouse shooting, which they claim (perhaps rightly) to be less antisocial than chess. What though I disagree, yet can I see what they mean.

Nevertheless, I hold that the Government of Cuba set a great example to civilisation when they bestowed on their chess genius Capablanca the title: Ambassador Extraordinary and Plenipotentiary General from the Government of Cuba to the World at large.

That magnificent piece of protocol will only be excelled if the United States and the Soviet Union combine to send Bobby Fischer and someone like Mikhail Tal to play celestial chess on a satellite, and so give to this cosmic activity some recognition of its cosmic significance.

The reader will now ask: what significance is this? and I can't tell him.

Warfare and Chess
Chess is described as a war game: and both activities have evolved into objective sciences. Should we, then, expect the generals to be good at chess? That, I suggest, would be *non sequitur*, if only because few of them are good at war. Optimistic

czars recruited chess ability. Petrov and Jaenisch were military engineers. But there seems to have been less chess ability at the higher levels.

Of the spectacular captains, Sam Loyd has attributed some amusing chess to Charles XII and Lasker has filed a claim for Napoleon, arguing that his control of the centre at Austerlitz was very good chess. To the great man are also attributed some clever skittles.

For Britain, a chess playing general is said to have cost us America. When an English settler sent a small boy with a message that Washington was about to cross the Delaware, General Rahl was so immersed in some Christmas chess that he put the note in his pocket unopened. There it was found when he lay mortally wounded in the subsequent battle.

Nearer home we have been more fortunate: Admiral Drake played bowls. Had that great sailor been involved in a losing game of chess against a junior officer, Sidonia, with his Armada, would have prevailed, and civilization would have suffered disaster. The Ruy Lopez would have become the English Opening.

Part Two

MENTAL PROCESSES
AND ATTITUDES

5 What is hard about chess? (I)

Some years ago I found myself called upon to comfort a rather unsophisticated competitor in a British championship, who complained as follows: that he had played well; in fact he'd followed the book that he had obtained good positions in every one of seven games; that for some reason or other he had lost the lot, whereas I, whom he had seen wallowing in bad, or at least ununderstandable, positions, had managed to secure a respectable number of points. He thought there was something strange about this. But I clarified matters for him. "You," I said, "get good positions. I, on the other hand, make good moves. Games of chess are won by good moves, not by good positions. Moreover, you get your good positions too early. You find yourself burdened with the complex task of keeping them good. I, on the other hand, unprodigal of my treasures, and making my good moves at appropriate times, am never involved in a good position until my opponent resigns."

I cannot add to this story a statement that my interlocutor was comforted. Nor do I say that what I told him is doctrine that can be accepted without a good deal of exegesis. But I will say that it isn't mere paradox. I will say that a good chess player does not think in terms of his position at any one moment. Positions are occasions for moves. If he appears to have, in any position, more scope than his opponent, or more material, with no compensating disadvantage, then he knows that he is in the presence of Fata Morgana, that he must not relax, that he cannot afford second-best moves. In other words, he has to fight against the inertia or acedia which accompanies the appearances of prosperity. The ideal player, who, of course, does not exist, makes the best move every time. May I add that very often the best move does not exist. But every player should always be on the lookout for it. Thinking in terms of position is only legitimate in this way— that along certain perspectives, along certain lines of play, you see the possible crystallisation of a strategic advantage, or you judge that now you are involved in a strategic advantage which you must try not to lose. And, once again, you are faced with the chess player's real problem: what should I do now? what's my move? That means: what move now enables me to cope with as many replies as I can see, as far ahead as I can see?

This is the task that anyone can observe who plays chess at a serious level, or who plays carefully through the games of Masters. Why did Botvinnik do this and not that? Why did Smyslov make one choice and not another? That is the same question as "what should I do now?"

It is often, not always, a hard question. If you are endowed with, or have developed, some vision, then it is interesting rather than hard. The answers will come fairly quickly. Sometimes, if you sit and think, ideas will drift in out of the stratosphere. But staring at the board for a long time is not a good method.

The selectivity of your mind—your mental scanner—will quickly reveal what there is to be thought about; what lines of play must be examined—played through mentally, with the mind's eye wide open for resources available to your opponent and yourself. If the obvious line leads to advantage, look quickly at others, but come back to the first; if it leads to difficulties, look more deliberately at other lines. But whatever time you are spending try to use it in thought. Better to save energy than to endeavour to find more than your capacity is likely to excavate.

On that reasoning do not be impressed or depressed by the great lengths of time that other players consume. A good deal of this time is not occupied on constructive thinking at all, but in repetitions, and in vain regrets. An occasional prodigy like Reshevsky (by nature a very fast player) can "fill the unforgiving minutes with sixty seconds worth of distant thought," and can concentrate with that intensity for more than an hour. But this is perfectionism, which has kept him more than once from the World Championship, and is not typical even of the highest levels. Every player has to think when there is something to think about. (That situation, I concede, is not always obvious.) He also has to make a number of moves without dying of old age or exhaustion. In real psychological fact, chess is much faster than it appears. The model for all of us is Capablanca who never in his life got into time trouble.

Another danger that besets the chess player is the discouragement that can supervene when he contemplates the wealth of learning that surrounds the game. It is as well to bear in mind some truths about this. Bear in mind, first, the fact that most good players were good before they knew of the existence of books of opening variations and general theory. They play melodies before they learn scales; second, good players have to be good when there is no book guidance; third, the stuff that goes into books is the good play of good players. Just as the orator inspires the book of rhetoric, and the great writer the grammarian, so the chess player makes the book, not the book the player.

Certainly, books are not useless. But they must be made subordinate to practical play. At best they help the player to organise and discipline his thought; but they offer no substitute for skill. Anyone who sets out to learn lines of play by heart is setting about chess the wrong way. He is aiming at remembering, instead of seeing and thinking. Certainly it is helpful to be shown something hard to see. But there is very little in the openings (I don't say nothing at all) which absolutely must be learnt. There is very little in the opening—or any part of the game—that is not a soluble problem for the unaided mind. It helps, of course, to be shown a nice analysis in any phase of the game, but only in the way that a poet is helped by reading poetry, or in the way that a good disputant likes to hear a good disputation. It is always helpful "to frequent doctor and saint and hear great argument." But if one merely learns the uttered word by rote, one takes very little out by the door at which one has entered.

If you try to learn chess by heart, at best you'll be repeating what some players saw and did for themselves. You'll get a few good positions, but you'll have my old friend's difficulty in making good moves. If, on the other hand, from your own experience, you get a feeling for what is active and progressive, and what is static or waste of time, you'll be using a better equipment than the memory of lines of play can provide.

Chess does involve memory, but not a "learning" memory. It is not without interest that some (a minority) of good players have had bad memories. That brilliant performer the late Jacques Mieses could not remember his own games. On the other hand, Rubinstein, who had a prodigious "learning" memory, never seemed to use it—and his greatest games are original at all stages, echoing the past only as the poetry of one great poet echoes that of another.

To return to the title. What is hard about chess? I hope I have shown that some of the difficulties believed to exist do not exist. Perhaps I have done this by revealing other difficulties. To anyone who is keen on chess, much of the game is as easy as the expression of his thoughts in his native language. But, as Simonides put it many centuries ago: Χαλεπον εσθλον ἐμμεναι; "It is difficult to become excellent."

6 What is hard about chess? (II)

Good moves win; good positions don't win.

If you ask an experienced player what aspects of chess he finds most thwarting or tantalising he is quite likely to say: the winning of won games. The struggle for a winning position and the fight against strongly placed adverse forces, these conjure up his ideas and stimulate him to exploit the resources of the board. But when his position is so good that victory is highly probable, then his capacity for error comes into play. Paradoxically, even the player to whom chess comes easy often finds the victory that he has fought for elusive. That is because his attention is relaxed. Also, there is a factor of latent fatigue. At the same time the opponent comes to life because his choices are limited and the need for resource invigorating.

In point is a very interesting position from a World Championship match. It occurred in the ninth game of the first match between Botvinnik and Smyslov. The position was as shown in Diagram 6.1:   r4r2, p3pKt1k, 2RpP1pp, 7q, 3Q1PktP, 1P4P1, P7, 4R1K1.

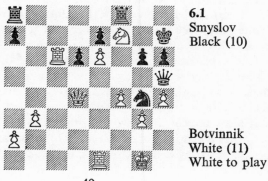

6.1
Smyslov
Black (10)

Botvinnik
White (11)
White to play

White (Botvinnik) has a Pawn to the good and an aggressive formation. It looks like a win, but Black is not dead—and not lying down. White does not play R–B7 (nor the good-looking Kt×QP) because Q–QR4 will be embarrassing. Indeed such is the power of Black's Queen, if mobilised, that at this stage, in order to keep it from QR4, White plays as his twenty-ninth move P–Kt4. For the purpose of capturing the square QB7 and controlling Black's QR4, probably Q–B3 was a better move. White's actual move, though clearly useful, does not prevent the activity of Black's Rooks. Was it nervousness that made Botvinnik refuse to unguard his Q5? The problem is summed up in a saying of that excellent player König: "However good your position is, you can't afford a second best move."

However, White stands well. But Smyslov's hat is still in the ring. 29 . . . , QR–QB1. White has to consider, and reject, the tempting 30   Q×RP, because after 30 . . . , R×R; 31   Q×P, K–Kt1 meets all threats. Also KR–QB1 is difficult because of R×R followed by Q–KB4. Perhaps Q–B3 or B4 was in order for White. Instead Botvinnik went in for what looks a little bit like a gamble. 30   R×R, R×R; 31   Kt×QP. He couldn't play 31   Q×RP because of the reply R–B6 with a mating threat (R×P ch, Kt–R7 etc). Black captures the Knight, 31   . . . , P×Kt. There follows 32   Q×RP ch, K–R1; and now it's not easy, because P–K7 is met by R–K1 followed when necessary by Kt–B3. Best seems, nevertheless, 33   P–K7, R–K1 (not Kt–B3 because of Q–Q4); then Q–Q4 ch followed by Q×P; and with four Pawns for a Knight White should win a fairly hard end-game. Instead Botvinnik seemed to forget what he had seen, and played 33   Q–Q7, and Black, with R–B6, threatened such dangers that White felt driven to perpetual check. That result may well have determined the ultimate result of the match.

One explanation of that game is fatigue. Under fatigue the discriminating, selective, awareness that I have elsewhere referred to, selects and discriminates less clearly, like an electronic scanner that is fading.

It also happens that, owing to the elements of chance on the board, that is to say the emergence of resources that could not be seen, even by excellent players, far enough ahead to be coped with, a player can outplay an opponent and still not be able to win. In point is a position from the eighteenth game of the second Championship match. (Diagram 6.2:   2b5, 1p6, 3P4, 2Pk Pp1p, p4K1P, 16, 2B5.)

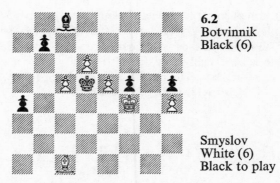

6.2
Botvinnik
Black (6)

Smyslov
White (6)
Black to play

After many skirmishes Botvinnik, who is Black, seems to have arrived at a won end-game, because it looks as if he can eliminate White's centre Pawns and stop the promotion of White's KRP. But the inner truth of the position is not so. Botvinnik did not play K × P; and, for reason, I find a line that is one of the unheard melodies of chess. Try the following:

52	...	K × P
53	K–Kt5	K–Q4
54	K × RP	K × P
55	K–Kt6	K × P
56	B–B4 ch	K–Q4
57	P–R5	P–R6
58	P–R6	P–R7
59	B–K5	and Black's promotion is effectively prevented.

Perhaps this is why, instead of K × P, Botvinnik played 52   B–K3. (A draw was the result.)

It is not often that an end-game study so interesting as this occurs in a critical game of a World Championship. I quote it as another instance of the difficulties that inhibit victory.

In general, sufficient well-placed good moves win; sufficient bad moves lose. The chess task is always to find the best move;

that means to see the consequences of all lines of play that are
reasonably visible and to select the best. Typical of combative
chess is the situation where one player tries a development, and
the other sees (or has already seen) a refutation of it.

Here is an example of this from a game from a very strong
tournament (the Soviet Championship of 1957) in which the
players were White: Keres, a star of great brilliance; Black: Tal.
Tal is one of those new giant stars that keep blazing up on that
horizon. Usually they diminish slightly and decline into ordinary
super-colossi. (Diagram 6.3: 2r3k1, pp1b2pp, 3bp3, kt2q1p2,
3P4, P2BB Kt2, 1P2QPPP, 3R2K1.)

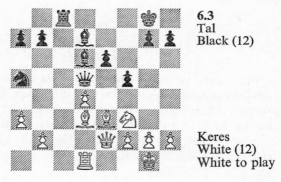

6.3
Tal
Black (12)

Keres
White (12)
White to play

Here Black, having played vigorously, has the more dynamically
placed pieces, but there is no certainty of victory. At this point
Keres feels impelled to start something, and it is clear that for all
his great ability he has not seen all there was to see. (He has seen
more of White's threats than of Black's resources; a very frequent
occurrence even in the highest class.) 20 Kt–K5. If 20 . . . ,
B × Kt; 21   P × B, Q × P; 22   B × RP, Q × Q; 23   B × Q, R–B7;
24   R × B, R × B; 25   P–KKt3, R × KtP; 26   B–Q4 with a
good attack. But Black plays 20   . . . , B–R5, a move showing the
greater board control of Black's pieces, but its real merit consists
in its combination with the next move but one. White plays
21   R–K1 and now 21   . . . , B × Kt; 22   P × B and the surprise
22   . . . , R–Q1. The effect of this, Black's twenty-second move,
is as follows: if the Bishop (no longer double guarded) retreats

23 B–QKt1, Black does not capture the KP (because P–KB4 would give White some attack) but plays some such line as 23..., B–Q8 with considerable control. Therefore Keres decides to try for Bishops of opposite colour. 23 P–QKt4, B–B3, threatening mate; 24 P–B3, Q×B; 25 Q×Q, R×Q; 26 P×Kt, R×P; 27 B×P, R×RP, and Black has emerged from that skirmish with a very important Pawn to the good. It's still a very difficult game to win, because the Bishops are of opposite colour. That makes the Pawn easier to impede. Keres made one more weak move before Tal smartly exchanged Rooks, sacrificed Bishop for a couple of Pawns and won with three Pawns against a Bishop.

I have given this example because it shows how, in practice, advantages are gained or increased by the apprehension of possibilities then and there; and lost by failure to see those possibilities.

A correspondent in *The Times* asked plaintively: "Why do good players lose?" The answer is given in a thought of Tartakover's: "The board is full of mistakes, waiting to be made."

7 Ideas in chess

I remember an occasion when Grandmaster Taimanov, the pianist chess player, having played unprofitable moves for several hours, got up from the board and said to the Kibitzer (who was myself): "I haven't had an idea for the last twenty moves." He had, I may say, played sufficiently well to enable his opponent, very soon after, to go fatally wrong.

Of course, in a sense every chess percept is an idea. But in practice we discriminate between (a) the straightforward processes of developing, attacking and defending pawns and pieces, capturing and recapturing, etc, which are easy to apprehend and of which the logic is easy to state; and (b) those manoeuvres which involve the perception of possibilities that others would miss, either because they are far ahead, or because they depart from ordinary routine, or both.

The varieties of idea are so great that their investigation calls for separate treatment. But the chess use of the word is relatively easy. A player who has ideas is one to whom the geometry and dynamics of the board are more familiar than to those who are confined to a simple logic. Thus in the position in Diagram 7.1 (2r2k2, 8, 1P6, 16, K2p4, 1RP5, 8) the elementary logic and arithmetic of chess suggest a Pawn capture. But if 1 ..., P×P; 2 R×P, Black cannot recapture because after 2 ... R×R; 3 P–Kt7 and the Rook cannot return to the defence. Therefore, Black's best is 1 ..., P–Q7, compelling 2 R–Kt1 (easier than 2 P–Kt7, R–Kt1; 3 R–Kt1, R×P). Now 2 ..., R–Kt1 brings about a draw. To a sophisticated player this point is part of technique. To one below that level it is "an idea."

The ideas need not be very far ahead; but in saying this I must explain that chess moves are not isolates. Every move is taken into consideration with its consequences. And usually, when a

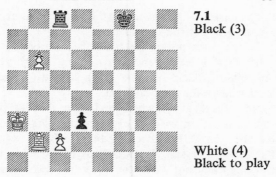

7.1
Black (3)

White (4)
Black to play

move is said to be overlooked, that means (among competent players) that a consequence of some move was overlooked.

I cannot illustrate this better than by quoting a game played, years ago, against an established American Master, by a New York schoolboy of thirteen named Bobby Fischer. The boy exploited his opponent's dilatory play by apprehending and acting upon some ideas. White was Donald Byrne. The opening moves were:

1	Kt–KB3	Kt–KB3
2	P–B4	P–KKt3
3	Kt–B3	B–Kt2
4	P–Q4	0–0
5	B–B4	P–Q4
6	Q–Kt3	P × P
7	Q × P	P–B3
8	P–K4	QKt–Q2
9	R–Q1	Kt–Kt3
10	Q–B5	B–Kt5

And now Byrne wastes a move in pursuit of some notion which is not clear to me. He played 11   B–KKt5, and was taken aback by Fischer's remarkable reply, Kt–R5. This move, putting a piece *en prise*, shows imagination; it could not have been expected by an ordinary opponent. Only a very strong player, whose mind at the time was very active, would see such a possibility in his opponent's field of activity. Dynamic moves are, in the nature of things, easier for the giver than the receiver; easier, as the Americans say, to dish out than to take.

To the great player the board is a unity. But in the practical world there is a difference between the thoughts of White and the thoughts of Black. A move which is hard for the maker to see is harder again for the opponent.

Now this Kt at R5, when you look at the total position evidently cannot be taken without eventual disadvantage. If 12 Kt×Kt, Kt×P; 13 Q–B1, B×Kt; 14 P×B, Q–R4 ch; 15 B–Q2, Kt×B; 16 Q×Kt, Q×Kt. So Byrne, who was well capable of working that out once the idea had been forcibly presented, played 12 Q–R3 entertaining the plan of regaining any Pawn that went lost. There followed 12 ..., Kt×Kt; 13 P×Kt, Kt×P and with 14 B×P White regains the Pawn and appears to win the exchange, but Black has seen much further than this (or else is very lucky). He plays 14 ..., Q–Kt3, letting the Rook go in exchange for the Bishop if White wants it. But White doesn't want it, because if 15 B×R, B×B; 16 Q–Kt3, Kt×QBP gives Black an excellent attack. So White plays 15 B–B4. Comes now Kt×QBP which shows that Black is more than lucky; is really seeing things. If 16 Q×Kt, R–K1. Yet at a second glance it looks as if White with B–B5 is going to be able to win the Knight. But see what happens: 16 B–B5, KR–K1 ch; 17 K–B1, and now comes one of the finest moves that have ever been seen. (That implies that the earlier moves made in contemplation of this were masterly indeed.) 17 ..., B–K3 sacrificing the Queen. White has little option if 18 B×B, Q–Kt4 ch is fatal: there follows a smothered mate (this is an "idea" that has become a part of technique). Therefore, 18 B×Q, B×B ch; 19 K–Kt1, Kt–K7 ch; 20 K–B1, Kt×QP dis ch; 21 K–Kt1, Kt–K7 ch; 22 K–B1, Kt–B6 ch (note that the capture of the QP means that this Knight is now guarded); 23 K–Kt1, P×B; 24 Q–Kt4 (as good as any), R–R5; 25 Q×P, Kt×R and Black has abundant material for his Queen, and a winning attack.

This is the kind of play that is meant when one speaks of the play of ideas. It was right for Fischer to play Kt×QBP only because he saw at least some of the beautiful things he could do afterwards. Much of the best chess is analysable in those terms: X did a move because he saw something. *Y* made a specific move, or failed to make a specific move, because he failed to see something.

It can happen that the game is such that convincing ideas do not present themselves. But I venture to say that in the vast majority of sequences of moves there occur opportunities for a good player to act in the light of imaginative vision and to win because his opponent is not so well endowed.

Sometimes desperation forces inspiration. When one finds a good move under pressure, so to speak, that, too, is an act of vision but we call it by the lesser name of resource. In a hard-fought game it is sometimes hard to say which flow of ideas was controlled by the player and which was thrust upon him.

Here is a piece of play between two of the word's most gifted players, Keres and Reshevsky, played at Zurich in the early 1950s. Keres was White:

1	P–Q4	Kt–KB3
2	P–QB4	P–K3
3	Kt–QB3	B–Kt5
4	P–K3	P–B4
5	B–Q3	0–0
6	P–QR3	B × Kt ch
7	P × B	P–QKt3
8	P–K4	B–Kt2
9	B–Kt5	P–KR3
10	P–KR4	

So far Black has played a Nimzo-Indian in such a way as to give White what looks like dangerous pressure. Now it cannot be believed that White's not very difficult tenth move was not seen by Reshevsky. So I describe his later play as imaginative rather than resourceful. 10 (for Black) P–Q3; 11 P–K5, P × P; 12 P × P and now the good move, B–K5. This is something that White could easily have missed. However, he is ready with a continuation, or a resource, 13 R–R3. There followed B × B; 14 R × B, Q–B2. Now Black can cope (because the Q is centralised) with the attack which White can launch with

B × Kt or P × Kt. (For example, 15   B × Kt, P × B; 16   Q–Kt4 ch,
K–R2; 17   R–Kt3, Q×P ch; 18   Kt–K2, P–B4.) After much
fine play by both, this spectacular game ended in a draw. I
mention these few moves to show how ideas intrude even into
the conventional openings.

In good chess, unless one's position is hopeless, there is always
scope for activity. To the original chess mind (and it isn't a chess
mind unless it's original) ideas keep flowing in. That is what it
seems like. But that apparent passivity is a similar illusion to the
calm of the surface of a waterfall.

8 Is black a bad colour?

I remember puzzling an opponent with whom I had drawn by saying, with an affected petulance: "I've wasted a Black." He replied, in dignified surprise: "You don't expect to win every time you're Black, do you?" He added, modestly, that he preferred White.

Well, his reply embodied the orthodox view—a view that is only too well supported by the fact that, in many tournaments, the majority of undrawn games have been won by the player of the White pieces. Also, in support, there is a famous statement by a player of great brilliance: "When I'm White I win because I'm White, when I'm Black I win because I'm Bogoljubov."

But I feel two things about this: (a) That it is wrong, (b) that if White has a substantial advantage, then there is something wrong with chess. Further, if I may quote, for what it's worth, my own experience, I find that it's terribly easy to go wrong with White, and harder to go wrong with Black. If you have White you are always tempted to mistake your slight initiative for an advantage, and to try to exploit it. The danger with Black is that you may get impatient of restraint. But Black is a discipline, and how very often it happens that the patient player of Black finds when he "equalises" (as they express it) that he has a slight advantage.

Certainly White can start off with a slightly better grip of the centre. If he plays King's or Queen's Gambit he has options not available to his opponent. If he plays Ruy Lopez he can find, against the orthodox defences, that he has a long period of development, relatively unimpeded. But these benefits do not last for ever. In a well-fought Lopez or Queen's Gambit, Black eventually emerges at least as well developed and with his forces as well integrated as White's. Many other "sharp" openings, such

59

as Evans, Möller, and so on, "burn out" against careful defence. In modern chess there should be no feeling of inferiority in Black. Players such as Steinitz, and—more strikingly—Lasker, proved to the world that an attack is nothing to be afraid of; that, on the other hand, an attack, beaten off, leaves the once attacked player very happy. Lasker himself was only too anxious to induce an opponent to attack. Frequently he unbalanced his game, believing that he would outplay his opponent in the skirmishes and the combat. Also, apart from this conceit (a psychologist might say that it was the opposite of confidence) he knew well how to assess the forces against him, and could judge the outcome of the processes to which his opponent's development was leading or could be led.

From a different angle, modern changes in chess fashion have reduced the frequency of central predominance on the part of White. The French Defence alters the form of central controversy. The Sicilian more so. Admittedly, many masters still feel that the best reply to P–K4 is P–K4. They may well be right. But it isn't the only move.

In this century the theorists have realised that the apparently strong centre can be an illusion. The whole of "ultra-modern" chess—that is modern chess—the chess of Nimzovitch, Tarta-kover, Reti and Breyer, made orthodox by Alekhine, is concerned with the eventual undermining of the strong centre. So impressed was Breyer with the possibilities that he declared: "After P–K4, White's game is in the last throes."

One need not go so far as Breyer—who, incidentally, won an immortal game with White. But, on rational lines, is it not clear that Black has great compensations for playing after? He has the power of adapting his play to an opponent who commits himself first—who becomes "engagé" as the existentialists have it. In the cognate game of draughts the second mover is favourite by mathematical demonstration. In chess, is not the last move the winning move? And does not the whole of end-game play illus-trate the frequent importance of playing second?

However, this is theory that may be described as remote from practicality. Granted that there is much to be said for Black, why do more Whites win than Blacks?

The answer, I think, is in psychology, not in pure chess. With White one can take the opening a little more easily—one has more choices. For some time one can preserve a certain degree of apparent safety. One has, in other words, an initiative, that may well last for fifteen moves or more—in some openings rather less.

Black is under strain in the earlier part of the game. So that, between equal players, the psychological factors, and the factors of fatigue and strain, are in White's favour. But objectively there is no disadvantage in Black. If he makes (qualitatively) move for move, losing no tempo, and playing well enough not to suffer a strategic crystallisation of the position to his detriment, he will emerge with an equal middle-game. Indeed, frequently the long initiatives worked out in prepared variations leave Black eventually with a greater control.

What, then, is left of Bogoljubov's dictum. I think he won as Black because he was Bogoljubov—he won as White because his opponents were afraid of Bogoljubov. In World Championship matches Black does not do badly. At lower levels, a number of players of Black lose because they are beaten before they start.

9 Imagination in chess

A series of talks broadcast in 1961, *with a few additions*

I

I should like to describe imagination as a capacity for expecting the unexpected. But I am embarrassed at the outset by a serious criticism emanating from a landscape designer, who, for all the book tells us, did not play chess. The artist in question is Mr Milestone, a character in one of the most brilliant of English satires—*Headlong Hall*, by Thomas Peacock.

They are discussing the aesthetic values to be created in a garden.

"I distinguish," says one of the discutants, "between the picturesque and the beautiful; and I add to them, in the laying out of grounds, a third and distinct character, which I call 'unexpectedness.' "

"Pray Sir," said Mr Milestone, "by what name do you distinguish this character when a person walks round the grounds for the second time?"

The first discutant was chagrined by this; and the chess player sympathises. If the critic is asserting that the beauties—or prettinesses—of life exist independently of the elements of surprise and the difficulty of novel apprehension, I do not know whether I want to agree. Or is he saying that unexpectedness is so evanescent that when Stout Cortez (or Balboa) and his men had seen the Pacific once, then to gaze at each other with wild surmise was an unnecessary incurring of *Zeitnot*? However, if there is a dilemma, I seize both horns of it, and I make reply to the mathematical gardener. In chess at least no one leads himself up the same garden path twice.

That does not mean that there is any lack of garden paths; and there will always, one feels sure, be new ones getting discovered, for chess is, happily, not a tidy garden. Its "god-wottery" is almost infinite. And there will always be a practical, recognisable, difference between those who are apt to find new paths, and those who can only plod along the well-trodden, or else roam at random, discovering nothing, "beating about the bush like a voice crying in the wilderness."

At this point, I think I cannot do better than ask the reader to set up his chessmen and study, with me, the following cautionary tale—a short game played in some not too high class international event:

1	P–Q4	P–Q4
2	P–QB4	P–K3
3	Kt–QB3	Kt–KB3
4	B–Kt5	QKt–Q2
5	P–K3	B–K2
6	Kt–B3	0–0
7	Q–B2	

Move 7, in conjunction with the play that ensues, is of theoretical importance. Normal is 7 R–B1, which is reasonably believed to prevent Black's P–QB4. The usual reply to it is P–QB3. If, however, Black plays P–QB3 in answer to 7 Q–B2, then White, with R–Q1, gains a shade of tempo. In the Lasker–Capablanca match, therefore, 7 Q–B2 was met always by P–QB4; then 8 P × QP, Kt × P, Bishops were exchanged, and all seemed satisfactory for Black. However, this modern player has an idea.

After Black's reply 7 . . ., P–QB4 he plays 8 P × QP and, when Black replies Kt × P, White does not exchange Bishops, but plays 9 Kt × Kt. If Black recaptures the Knight, he has a bad form of Tarrasch Defence. So Black plays 9 . . ., B × B. Now the first feature of surprise: 10 P–KR4. This is an embarrassing move. First of all, Black would like to retain his Bishop if he can. Secondly, if 10 . . ., B–K2, White can exchange Knight for Bishop, or aggress with Kt–Kt5 even before exchanging.

Playable, I think, is 10 ..., B–R3; but 11 Kt–Kt5, P–Kt3; 12 Kt×RP could alarm a nervous player. Black, however, has another plan. Queen's square is also a square—one on which a Bishop can seek sanctuary. Therefore, in answer, to P–KR4, 10 ..., Q–R4 ch is played by Black, expecting that the dislocation of White's King, or the exchange of Queens, or the retreat of the Knight, will be in Black's favour and give time for a Bishop move.

White replies 11 P–QKt4. Probably Black saw this, and thought that P×P would give White no time for aggression. So 11 ..., P×P with a threat. White does not stand on ceremony:

12 Q×P ch   K×Q
13 P×B dis ch   K–Kt3 (or Kt1)
14 Kt–K7 mate

What do you know about that? Well, first, I'm saying that if White saw the whole movement from his seventh move, then, if he isn't an imaginative player, he'll do till a good imaginative player comes along. That kind of perception—or intuition—is comparable to a fine synthesis by a scientist, or a fine aesthetic idea; a figure in the marble that other artists would not see. Even if he saw it by the dim, but concentrated, light of midnight oil, I still award him praise. And if he only saw the Queen sacrifice when it was thrust upon him, he's still a little bit imaginative, because most players would go on thinking about more ordinary processes, retreat of Knight in answer to the check, or even P–QKt4, followed by P×B, which is to be considered (and which Black may have contemplated).

I observe, *en passant*, that at this stage we are realising that imagination can operate over a very short range, as well as over a long one. If White had missed this (Q×P ch), it would have been one of many instances of a quite good player missing a short-range cleverness, because his mind is moving on paths for pedestrians.

Distances are enchanting in the sense of confusing, but we find that the kind of player who can see a clever idea at the beginning of a variation is also likely to see one at the end of a long variation. He might even see the final clever idea before he has clearly

analysed the intervening play—just as a scientist often devises
the experiment in order to test a speculation, or as the artist
carves, or paints, or patterns words or sounds, to an effect
already apprehended.

To return to the game under consideration. Black we can
confidently describe as an unimaginative player, failing to
achieve an idea that was thrust upon him. He, with a few immediate lines of play to worry about, should not have missed the
consequences of Q–R4 ch. As he was playing in an international
event, I expect he went there with plenty of experience of sacrifices at h7. And when one is anxious about h7, differences of
order of approach should be perceptible. Certainly it is more
imaginative to see $Q \times RP$ as an event before $P \times B$ than as a
threat to follow $P \times B$. But is it so much harder?

Good chess players are always struggling to give the lie to
Hegel's dictum that one only learns from experience the fact
that one does not learn from experience. Up to a certain stage
in chess, manoevres become familiar that were once surprising.
I shall return later to this line of thought. Suffice it, at this stage,
to say that that kind of capacity for improvement is a mark of
ability and of a degree or element of imagination.

In this particular case I would say that, by all standards, White
apprehended something hard to expect—he apprehended novelty.
At the closing stages, however, Black should have felt, with the
Latin poet, *Latet anguis in herba*; and he should have found it.
His chess experience, harnessed to mental activity, should have
produced a recognition. What can be said in his defence is this:
until the Queen is away from Q square, the mating threat does
not exist. So he had to conjure up the position with Q at QR4:
not difficult. *But*, not being on the alert for a Queen sacrifice
while his Queen was at Q1, he was not under the mental pressure
that should have been active to make him look very hard at the
position with Q at R4. What I am saying, rather laboriously,
amounts to this, does it not? That you have to be imaginative
to know when to be expectant of the unexpected.

Yet the old landscape artist still has a point. Unfortunately,
neither White nor Black nor any student or spectator will be
able in the future to experience in those same moves the same

creative thrill that White was entitled to feel. The same garden
path will not be trodden twice. But one's horticultural equipment
is enhanced. And such a player as sees, or saw, this idea, will
be finding other pleasant paths that lead to experiences of perfection.

II

When we discuss imagination the difficulty is that this word is
so useful—and so variously applied in practice—that it is almost
useless to attempt a pedantic definition. One must concede that in
most, if not all, mental activity, some creativity, however slight in
degree, is operating. One must also concede that conjuring up,
imagining, a picture may be different from conjuring up the board
three moves hence—may be different, or may be similar—and
that both these activities may be different from the apprehension
of a mathematical short-cut; or the invention of a gadget or
mechanical device; or, again, from the sudden realisation that
an apple falling from a tree is one case of planetary motion;
or from the poetic moulding in words of "thoughts that live—
to perish never."

Suffice it to say that the word imagination covers a multitude
of virtues. To be a solver, need you be a composer? That's one
question among many. So we find, when we talk about chess
imagination, that maybe we do not know what we are talking
about. A not unusual, and not unpleasant, experience. (Nowadays
they call it semantics.)

Let us, therefore, without attempting definitions, endeavour to
describe one or two mental movements, and so illustrate some
chess imagination; for, as that excellent teacher Squeers put it:
"If you want to know about windows, clean them."

In chess a familiar and plausible distinction is between clarity
and cleverness. Before the reader has time to tell himself that
what is clear and easy to one is regarded as hard and clever by
another, I will trouble him to get out his board in order to enable
me to show some examples. (If he can follow without using the
board, he has more imagination than if he can't.)

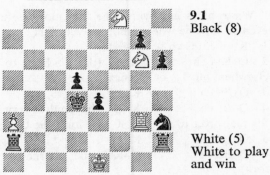

9.1
Black (8)

White (5)
White to play
and win

I start with a position given in one of the old Moorish Manuscripts. (Diagram 9.1: 5Kt2, 6p1, 6Ktp, 3p4, 3kp3, P5Rkt, r6r, 4K3.)

In order to see a win for White one does not require to be an "old Moore."

1 Kt–K6 ch, followed by 2 Kt–K5 ch, followed by 3 R–Kt3 ch, and the Rook, with the aid of the Knights, is mating the Black King. Assuming an ability to give an easy mate in 2 at the proper stage (and I admit that I am begging a question here) I would say that this is an example of play in which the requirement is clarity—and that over a relatively short distance.

Now contrast with this a composition by one of the supreme modern end-game composers, Kubbel. (Diagram 9.2: 8, 4q3, 2p5, 2kt2Q2, p5Kt1, 7k, 8, 1K6.)

Study by Kubbel

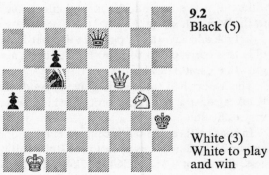

9.2
Black (5)

White (3)
White to play
and win

White plays and wins. The first move is instinctively played even by anyone who cannot see very far:

1 Kt–K3, dis ch   K–Kt6
2 Q–Kt4 ch   K–B7 (there is Mate to be seen if he tries elsewhere on this or the next move)
3 Q–B4 ch   K–K7
4 Q–B1 ch   K–Q7 (it requires very little chess insight for the solver to see that K × Kt loses the Queen)
5 Q–Q1 ch   K–B6
6 Q–B2 ch   K–Kt5 (the alternative K–Q5 allows a fork)
7 Q–Kt2 ch   Kt–Kt6

Forced, because otherwise Mate is effected with Kt and Q in a way not remote from the finish of the Moorish play.

But now Kt–Kt6 by Black seems to put an end to White's ambitions. Well, this is where the unexpected is to be expected:

8 Q–R3 ch   K × Q
9 Kt–B2 mate

That's a surprise that a chess player calls beautiful. Usually, when a chess player says "beautiful" he means "hard to see; unexpected," just as a scientist does when he admires a new formulation. It is quite an imaginative act to see, even on move 8, and told that there was a win, the thing would be easier. But if it arose in play, very many quite fair players would miss it. Coming as it does, as the finish of a nine-move solution, then, by the solver who solves in one act, it has to be seen, if I may repeat the phrase, as a figure in the marble. This is qualitatively different, is it not, from the mental effort, such as it is, involved in the Moorish study?

Let me add, by way of parenthesis, that I am not implying that old chess corresponds to a low level of chess ability and that chess growth recapitulates history.

The Moors had some good players, good enough to win with a Rook against a Knight; a process which, when possible, can be very difficult.

In that culture, the tenth century Persian poet Mansur—better known as Firdausi—gives us a neat study calling for some cleverness. (Diagram 9.3: R2K4, 8, 3k4, 2R5, 24, 7r.)

Study by Firdausi

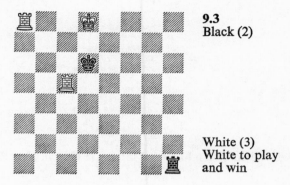

9.3
Black (2)

White (3)
White to play
and win

White to play. It looks as if, threatened with mate as well as loss of the Rook at c5, White cannot prevent Black from drawing. That he can win is due to the availability of 1   R–KR5 threatening mate and the win of a Rook. If ... R×R; 2   R–R6 ch, followed by R–R5 ch and recapture of Rook.

Before retracting from this digression, I would point to some affinity between chess and poetry. The fact that, nearly 1000 years after Firdausi, the French poet Alfred de Musset composed a very neat three-move problem is less well-known to the chess world than that Philidor was a musician and that Buckle combined chess with creative history-writing. (Diagram 9.4:   32, 3Kt4, 5Ktkt1, 4p2R, 1K1k4.)

What is good about modern chess composers is that, after hundreds of years in which the unexpected seems always being made familiar, they continue to create unexpectednesses. Let one example suffice: a study by Zachodjakin. (Diagram 9.5: 3kt4, 8, 4k3, 2p5, 6Kt1, 2K1B3, 4B3, 4kt3.)

This position is sufficiently realistic for even the hardened solver not to speculate about the pawn at c5.

White starts trying to win a Kt, but the process is not so easy as it appears at first glance. 1   B–Q2, Kt–Kt7; 2   B–KB1. now if 2 ... Kt–R5; 3   B–Kt5 forks two Knights, but Black is clever: 2 ..., Kt–B5; 3   B×Kt, K–B4 forking two pieces. Unless you saw this you did not know that there was a problem.

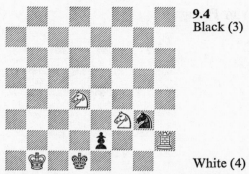

9.4
Black (3)

White (4)

Problem by De Musset. Mate in 3: 1R×P, Kt×R; 2Kt–QKt5.

Study by Zachodjakin

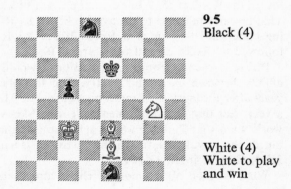

9.5
Black (4)

White (4)
White to play
and win

4   B–B7, desperate to escape, Kt–K3 (two pieces are still attacked);
5   Kt–K3 ch, K–K5. Two pieces are still under attack. 6   Kt–Q5,
(the big surprise) K × Kt; 7   B–Kt2 mate.

And now you see that the Pawn at c5 is not accidentally there.

This, like many of those modern compositions that end in a
mid-board mate, or stalemate, is the more beautiful because the
play, the logical clear play, seems to lead nowhere—unless one
intuits the crowning idea.

Now the need for such intuition holds, not only in the realm of
composition, but in actual play, where—usually without such

aesthetic setting, or such spectacle—a player wins through seeing an idea; and fails to win, or loses, through not seeing it. So we tend to grade chess ability in distinctions between what is hard to see and what is easy to see in each player's task and performance.

As to what is hard and what is easy, that is a question like what is expected and what is unexpected. One man's expectation is another one's surprise—or disappointment. Again, what seems merely clear to one seems clever to another.

Here's a very simple position to illustrate this. The fact that it is the end of a grandmaster's game does not make it any harder. (Diagram 9.6: 16, 2K1k3, 1P1R4, 1r6, 24.)

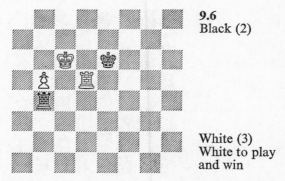

9.6
Black (2)

White (3)
White to play
and win

Some players would now play P–Kt6 for White, and be surprised and, later, distressed, if Black played R × P ch.

Bronstein, for White, played R–QB5 first, and would not describe himself as imaginative for having done so. But to the novice, whose logical moves are simple advances, unsacrificial over even the shortest range, this is "cleverness."

Now suppose the White Pawn were on QR5 and Black pawns stood on Black's QR3 and QKt3, and suppose a player, many moves before, had to realise that, after many captures, checks, and best moves, he would be left unable to win because P × P is met by R × P ch; then he is called upon to have, at least, very clear vision; and if the whole thing were complex enough, and the position of the Black Rook accidental, you could call the total effort an imaginative one.

At a great distance, even the simplest operations can be missed —elementary devices like this exploitation of the King's double function. But chess players can still distinguish between the easy move that is missed because of the distance, because the whole tactical complex was not completely grasped, and the different situation, where something happens at the end of the movement that seems like a clap of thunder out of a clear sky.

I am speaking of the kind of experience that befell that fine player Ossip Bernstein, when his opponent had dictated, but he had been glad to achieve, the following position. (Diagram 9.7: 3r2k1, p4ppp, 1qr5, 3kt4, 8, 1Ktp1P3, P1R 1Q PPP, 2R3K1.)

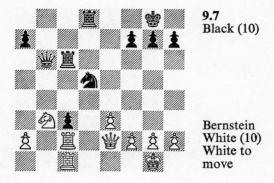

9.7
Black (10)

Bernstein
White (10)
White to
move

Bernstein as White played 26 Kt–Q4, Black: R–B2. I wonder if Bernstein asked himself at that moment why his opponent had not played R–B4 preventing Kt–Kt5. Perhaps he thought Black was trying to avoid a repetition of position, and was relying for victory on chances based on an attack by Kt–Kt5 after White's capture of the QBP. So, in answer to Black's R–B2, White played 27 Kt–Kt5. Answer: R–B4.

Then 28 Kt × P, and now not Kt–Kt5 nor KR–QB1, but simply Kt × Kt; 29 R × Kt, R × R; 30 R × R, and suddenly, out of nowhere, Q–Kt7, revealing, to Bernstein, all that is now implicit in the name Capablanca. The white-headed boy of chess was Black in that position.

I chose that example, not for its historical value, but in order to show something to which nobody can reasonably deny the attributive "unexpected"; and I contrast that with the easy Bronstein position, where to allow R × P ch would be to fail to expect what the vast majority of chess players would expect themselves to expect without difficulty. Indeed they would regard it as elementary sight of the board—as part of ordinary equipment.

Perhaps, then, we should consider what is meant by ordinary equipment; what equipment a chess player has that functions before the great efforts of imagination supervene to surprise us.

III

Let me say, immediately, that I do not agree with those authorities who analyse the logical features of a combination, and then say: had you borne in mind—in looking at that position, present or future—all the features of overloaded defences, double or treble functions, quantities of pressure, deflectability of defences, unreality of guards, and the like, you would have seen what Alekhine could do, or what Rubinstein or Keres or Tal could do.

I have heard at least one "technical" analysis, by a master, of Rubinstein's famous combination against Rotlewi. The impression I got was that the author was pointing to the storm clouds after they had broken. I would say that that is how you describe a combination after it has been played, not how you see it before it has been played. Not all clouds are storm clouds. I permit myself to propound that an imaginative player does not see his combinations developing in logical mathematical process from premises. He sees them, I suggest, as conjured totalities, or movements that flash across his mind.

But this must be conceded to the school of system (it derives from Steinitz and Lasker) that chess players do bring an equipment to a position. Not a series of propositions about the position—heaven forbid!—but a built-in capacity for recognition; a capacity in which experience in the resources latent in pieces is harnessed to the intuitive power of the player. That people learn how to use words, or numbers, or mechanical devices, or chess pieces, and with them do things that nobody thought of doing before, is just the oldest puzzle in the theory of knowledge. Had Socrates played chess, the Meno would have been an even more interesting book. The chess facts are:

1 That players learn quickly, not only the legal moves that the pieces are allowed to make, but also operations that the pieces can carry out, such as forks, knife-thrusts (some say skewers), accumulation of pressure, exploitation of the overloaded defences of pieces or squares, etc.

2 That, having learnt those things, they are always, when seeing their relevance to a position, making a controlled mental effort. The learning is facilitating, in a mysterious way, the effort. But it is not dictating it in a logical "this therefore that" form. The player sees: I cannot capture the Bishop because my Queen has no escape. (Diagram 9.8: r2qkb1r, 1bpp1ppp, p1kt1pkt2, 8, 2BP4, 1QKt1PKt2, PP3PPP, R1B1K2R.)

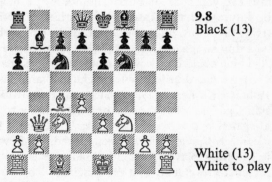

9.8
Black (13)

White (13)
White to play

If 8–Q×B, Kt–R4 wins the Queen.

He does not say: "This is the kind of square on which a Queen being placed will find egress difficult; therefore it is the wrong kind of square for my Queen. It follows that I am unwise to take the Bishop." His mental movement is rather like a flash, which, if described, can only be stated: Q×B, Kt–R4 wins the Queen.

What is the equipment that helps towards such an institution? I shall mention a few items.

1 No piece is static in the chess player's mind: nor is it merely a potential of vague movement.

Thus the player sees his Queen as moving out from its original square to places like QKt3, QR4,KR5, etc. He sees not only this range; but, selectively, the probable squares, not the improbable. She is not yet going up to Q6 to be captured by a Pawn. That hardly needs seeing, though I suppose that, in a sense, it is seen. What is more likely to be thought about is the move Q–Kt3 or KB3, attacking QKt7, KB7, etc. That brings me to a second thought.

2 A chess player sees his piece not only in its immediate motion, but in a series of moves, closely consecutive, or separated. He sees the Queen at QKt3, then at QKt7, then at R6, as it retreats from a Rook attack; back to R5 or R4 or R3, etc, as it gets pursued by a Rook; or, as capturing the RP as well—or something else.

3 He does not see the piece as isolated value, but its value in terms of what it can do now or in the future. The Queen is worthy of protection as any Pawn is, albeit with, usually, better prospects in the future than a Pawn has. But Q × RP ch, giving rise to mate in 2 or 3, is valuing a Queen for what it can do.

4 No good player ever thinks of pieces in isolation. They are operating among opposing pieces and in conjunction with their colleagues. So one does not merely follow the paths of specific pieces. One follows rather a merry-go-round of many pieces— kaleidoscope of movements, in which no piece is irrelevant.

5 No move is an isolated event. Admittedly there are immediate necessities, like getting out of check, guarding a piece or pawn on occasion. But even then, one should be already aware and in control, just as an army retreating remains in touch with the base. A move is part of a series long or short. To see one move ahead is to see more than one—to see many is to see one. To see one good move can be imaginative in high degree.

To illustrate what I have said so far, let me ask you to follow a few moves from the original position.

1   P–Q4   P–QKt4

The Polish Defence. I ominously lost a game with it in August 1939; but it really isn't bad. (The following moves are from a game that I won.)

2 Kt–KB3   B–Kt2
3 P–K3   P–QR3
4 P–B4   P×P
5 B×P   P–K3
6 Kt–B3   Kt–KB3

And now suppose White is thinking of processes such as 7 Q–Kt3 in order to dislocate that Bishop and push P–Q5, etc. It's not the best line of thought, but it's dynamic, and shows that White has enough equipment to enable him to see processes rather than isolated moves and stationary figures.

So he tries 7 Q–Kt3 and is surprised when Black plays Kt–QB3, (giving the position on Diagram 9.8). Because now if 8 Q×B, Kt–R4 wins the Queen.

This is the kind of situation in which I diagnose lack of imagination—lack of not very spectacular, not remarkably creative, imagination; lack of the useful. Whether to call Black imaginative or not is a more difficult question.

But go a little bit further back. On move 6 he could have played Kt–QB3 immediately instead of Kt–KB3. That stops Q–Kt3 (because of Kt–R4) but it allows P–K4, and there is much to be analysed. To be happy about Kt–KB3, he has to see the answer to Q–Kt3. For White's part, had a Black Knight stood at its QB3, he couldn't have dreamed of Q–Kt3. What he wasn't imagining, as the moves actually went, was the emergence of the Queen's Knight after the Queen had gone to QKt3. This example shows us:

1   Chess players thinking dynamically.
2   One of them failing to see a point of play, because there is something in it of, to him, the unexpected.

Why unexpected? Either because the player has little capacity (he has not acquired the ability to look at the game in the way I have described) or he has not mobilised his powers—perhaps is bad at mobilising them. Quite good players miss points of play because their awareness—a keen light when concentrated—is diffused elsewhere. To revert to the horticultural metaphor, they follow one path, and miss the blossoms along other paths of thought.

Here is a position in which minor grandmaster Bilek failed to follow the ideas of major grandmaster Korchnoi. (Diagram 9.9: r4r1k, 1bpkt1ppp, pp1pp3, 2kt5, q1PKtPP1P, P1PP2P1, R3Q1B1, 2B1R1K1.)

Black has wandered into a thicket where a man should not venture without a guidedog. His last move was P–QR3 and the move before that KKt–Q2. With great vigour on the Queen's side he's threatening nothing.

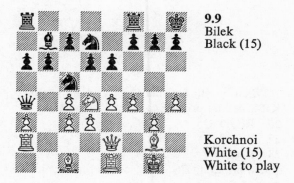

9.9
Bilek
Black (15)

Korchnoi
White (15)
White to play

Korchnoi plays the quite easy to see move 18 R–Kt2. Now Bilek would not be playing Korchnoi unless he was capable of anticipating that. But, of course, he was seeing much more. He was seeing what he thought to be Korchnoi's probable play—his best line. Bilek played 18 ..., Q×RP, expecting 19 R×P, Q×P; 20 B–Kt2, Q×QP and that's very good for Black.

The moves following are easy to see for a long way. But Korchnoi disobliged with 19 Q–Q2, and Bilek, having carefully arranged not to be able to move his Knight conveniently from c5, is *in angustis rebus*. If Kt–R5, White plays R–R2. Black has been pushed into a path that he didn't explore. He's been ambushed. Anyway, he's lost.

Apart from confusion of paths, there is such an error as failing to see far enough along one path; and there is a failure to observe the queer features of the terrain—to say nothing of dangers from beyond. Thus how did Capablanca come into the following position? 4rtk1, r2kt1p2, 1p1R2pp, pP5q, 4b3, P3KtKtP1, 1Q3PBP, 3R2K1. (Diagram 9.10.)

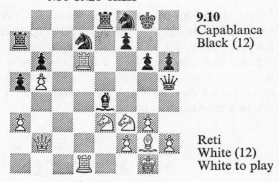

9.10
Capablanca
Black (12)

Reti
White (12)
White to play

When he allowed his Queen on move 25 to go from QB4 to
KR4, he had probably satisfied himself about:

26 R(Q1)–Q5   B × R
27 P–Kt4   B × Kt
28 P × Q   B × P

But what about 26 Kt–Q4? Did he intend:

26 ...   B × B
27 K × B   R × Kt
28 P × R   Q × R?

He was off form in that game (against Reti in New York in 1924).
Because when 26 Kt–Q4 was played, he realised too late that
after

26 ...   B × B
27 K × B   R × Kt
28 P × R   Q × R
29 Kt–B5

—attacking the Queen and threatening mate is a move with all
the terrors of the unanswerable.

Features of the board such as this bring me to the sixth item
in the chess player's catechism.

6 No square and no piece (the word includes Pawn) is irrelevant:
and no piece or square is an island.

An example that impresses me (whom it shouldn't) is the following position: r1bq2k1, pp1kt2pp, 3bpr1kt, 3p1p2, 3P4, 1P1BPKt2,
PB1Kt1PPP, R2Q1RK1. (Diagram 9.11.)

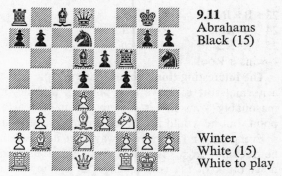

9.11
Abrahams
Black (15)

Winter
White (15)
White to play

From a game played in 1934 between the late William Winter, who was White, and myself. I draw attention to White's Knight at Q2, and I offer the observation that so fine a positional judge as Winter did not regard it as an "unprotected island." The play (in answer to my R–B3):

11	Kt–K5	Kt–KKt5
12	Kt × KKt	P × Kt
13	Q × P	P–K4
14	Q–R4	P–K5
15	B–K2	

My opponent, who spent a long time on his eleventh and twelfth moves, had seen all this and realised that I could not now play R–R3, because the Rook is pinned. But I have a *Zwischenzug* that, earlier on, he had not seen:

| 15 | ... | Q–R4 |

—attacking the loose Knight on his Q2: and that makes all the difference. There followed:

| 16 | P–QKt4 | Q × P |
| 17 | Kt–Kt3 | Kt–B1 |

—and Black is aggressing with favourable omens.

White, defending ingeniously, missed a further point: but I think he was lost in any event. The play continued:

18	P–KB4	P × P ep
19	B × P	R–R3
20	B × P ch	B–K3
21	Q–K4	B × P ch
22	K–B2	Q–Q3

23	B × B ch	R × B
24	Q–Kt4	R–B3 ch
25	K–K2	Q–R3 ch

—wins a Rook.

The interesting thing about that example is that Winter played a normal sort of move in a position that he thought—perhaps reasonably—was in his favour. He missed a far away tactical point, but he would not have seen it by a mere use of logic.

Every player knows in a way that no piece is an island, but he does not say: "This Knight at Q2 is insularly situated, so I must think of the consequences of leaving it unguarded." One has to *see* the relevance of the maxim before one applies the maxim—and by then it's already applied.

In addition to those general concepts, and framed in them, giving them meaning, are all the little tricks of the trade, all the little devices: the Greek Gift at h7, the dangers at QKt7, the sacrifice of a Kt at K5 followed by a fork—and hundreds of other methods of play, including innumerable end-game processes, which all good players have at their finger-tips, and which, for want of a better word, I call technique.

Many little devices in the promotion of Pawns—sacrifices for the opposition, etc—are called surprises by novices; are unexpected by them, but are so normal to good players that to overlook such things would be condemned as blunder, gross oversight, *finger fehler*.

Now all these techniques and all these principles are in a player's equipment; but he isn't always mobilising them all. So, if I call a player imaginative, one of my meanings may well be that the player concerned has mobilised thoughts and technique that others would not mobilise in that position or at that stage.

Another way of putting it is that some player's awareness is richer, wider, subtler than that of others. The need for the high degrees of ability, of which Imagination with a capital I is a constituent, is only illustratable in rare pieces of play, and in studies.

Let me introduce a simple study by saying that everybody knows about captures and forks to follow. (Diagram 9.12: 4R3, 16, k3kt3, 8, Kt7, 6K1, 4q3.)

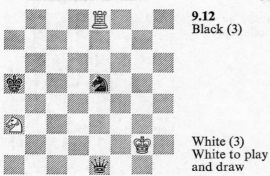

9.12
Black (3)

White (3)
White to play
and draw

Very easy is R × Kt ch, Q × R, Kt–B4 forking King and Queen.
I can make this more complicated. The Black King is at c5,
the White Knight is at a5, White Rook as before at e8, Black
Queen as before at e1, Black Knight at e5. Add White Pawn at
d3. This is not hard. (Diagram 9.13: 4R3, 16, Kt1k1kt3, 8,
3P4, 6K1, 4q3.)

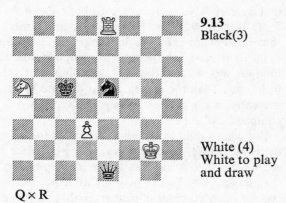

9.13
Black(3)

White (4)
White to play
and draw

1	R × Kt ch	Q × R
2	P–Q4 ch	
	If K × P	
3	Kt–B6 ch	
	If Q × P	
3	Kt–Kt3 ch	

In the light of that examine the following position: 7R, 7p,
1K3pp1, 3p1k1Kt, P7, 8, 3pP3, 8. White wins. (Diagram 9.14.)

Study by
Berkquist

9.14
Black (6)

White (5)
White to play
and win

Are you well enough equipped now to see the relevance of that
Rook to the promoting Pawn?

1   R–Q8   P–Q8 = Q
2   R × P ch   Q × R
3   P–K4 ch   With Knight fork to follow.

One subtracts marks for imagination in this solution, for the fact
that solvers have learned a lot about Pawn forks, and Knight
forks to follow, from Henri Rinck and others very expert in
showing how the great are delivered into the hands of the weak.

But it needed imagination to compose this. Less to solve it,
because the presentation of the thing as a problem conjures
technique. Then the person who is assisted by acquired technique
evidently has a greater solving ability than one less technically
equipped and experienced.

But what would be imaginative is this: for a player to work out
the capture of a piece or pawn, seeing a danger which is hard to
see, and seeing such a neat way remaining to him for coping with
that danger. It's in the play before a position of the Berkquist
type or other complex of cleverness that players act imaginatively
at a high level.

From actual play in an Amsterdam Tournament of the 1950s
here is an effort by minor grandmaster Pilnik (one is forced to
these classifications) in play against major grandmaster Keres.
The position after Black's 26th is as follows: r2r3k, 5p1p, 2ppb1pq,
1pkt1p3, 4P3, 1PP1Kt1RP, P3QPP1, 1B2R1K1. (Diagram
9.15.)

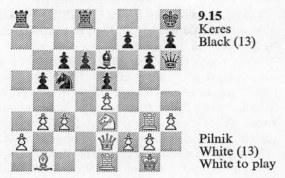

9.15
Keres
Black (13)

Pilnik
White (13)
White to play

Now at move 27, why did White, Pilnik, play Kt–B2? Could be a bad move? He had already made one or two obscure ones, though not like that. Or is there something there? Watch the sequel:

27 Kt–B2   P–B4
28 P × P   P × P
29 Kt–Q4

In the ancient phrase, a "bobby dazzler," because this apparent sacrifice really achieves something.

29 ...   P × Kt (this seems the best)
30 P × P

And now you may say: "Well, let him put the Knight into K5 and White doesn't recapture." But consider the effect of:

31 B × Kt   P × B
32 P–Q5

—with that mating threat on the diagonal. So it is understandable that Keres continued not with 30 ..., Kt–K5 but with 30 ..., P–B5. There followed:

31 R–QB3   B–Q4
32 P × Kt   Q–Kt2

And it looks as if White's play has not been so good. Threat of mate and attack on the Rook. But R–KB3 is not forced.

White's 33 is Q–Kt4! If you look at the prospects of White's King's Rook if it gets to K7, you will see that Keres was right not to play Q × R. Instead he played R–KKt1 and the game was thereafter reduced to a draw.

The comment on this is that Pilnik's Kt–B2 was a fine imaginative act. I should not be surprised to learn that it was unexpected by his excellent opponent.

What I wish to observe about this kind of play is that there's something very voluntary about it. Nobody forced that idea into Pilnik's mind, and it did not follow by any process of deduction from the many things that that man knows about chess. What he knows about chess was, however, brilliantly co-ordinated into a pattern, as an artist co-ordinates his abilities and his raw materials.

This kind of chess is recognisably different, is it not? from the seeing of a long series of straightforward captures, recaptures checks, Pawn races and play after promotion. The distinction is between *clarity* and *imagination*.

Allowing that you cannot achieve great clarity without an imaginative power, and that you cannot be really imaginative without a general clarity, and allowing that, in the very greatest, the whole vision is so integrated as to be unanalysable into functions, yet we can recognise the differences of play and style that give a real meaning (however indefinable) to the word imaginative. We know what it means, even though we cannot exactly articulate it. Need one define an elephant?

For an example to show the difficulty of separating the functions of clarity and cleverness, I go again to Amsterdam, to a game between Bronstein and Geller. The position is: 2r2rk1, 3bqp2, p1pb3p, 1p1p2p1, P2PktKt2, 1B1KtPQ1P, 1PR2PP1, R5K1. (Diagram 9.16.)

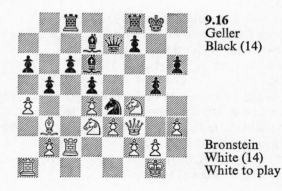

9.16
Geller
Black (14)

Bronstein
White (14)
White to play

Bronstein (White) played 27 Kt–R5. One asks oneself why not:

27	B × P	P × B
28	R × R	R × R
29	Kt × P	Q–K3
30	Q × Kt	Q × Q
31	Kt–B6 ch?	

Couldn't Bronstein see that? He could. But he could also see a rather fine departure. After 27 B × P, P × B; 28 R × R Black does not recapture the Rook but plays P × Kt. There follows:

29	R × R ch	Q × R
30	Kt × P	B × Kt
31	Q × B	

And, though he has winning chances, he isn't convinced.

There is also some nice speculation arising from 27 P × P. Suffice it to say that Bronstein showed what some imaginative players lack. He showed restraint, showed the ability to apprehend one of the unheard melodies of chess, and to refrain from making it audible.

The best imaginative players do not strive after effects. They see the beauties as variations in games that they are constructing—blossoms that cannot be forced. Indeed it is often impossible to say how far ahead the player of the brilliant combination saw the dénouement. Occasionally one can say: "Had he not seen this he would have played differently." That is the right comment on Bronstein's play in the position we have considered. Compendiously, the imaginative perception is just a feature of the great player's total apprehension of the board.

Strikingly, the thing is clear in imperfection. Pilnik, who is, of course, exceedingly strong, is also, may it be respectfully said, not the best of the best, and his chess in that tournament was not, before that quoted piece of play, marked by any intellectual richness on his part.

I mention this in a restatement of the thought that imagination is not present in all good players in equal degree, and that it is possible for a player to be more imaginative—not merely fanciful, or wildly speculative—than are other players who excel him in clarity, and in general mastery of the resources of the board.

It follows, also, from this reasoning that imaginative chess need

not be the best possible play. There is an historic case—of very
great chess—which has been much debated. Every schoolboy
(I hope!) knows Anderssen's Evergreen game against Dufresne.
(Diagram 9.17: 1r2k1r1, pbppktp1p, 1bkt2p2, 7q, Q7, B1PB1Kt2,
P4PPP, R3R1K1.)

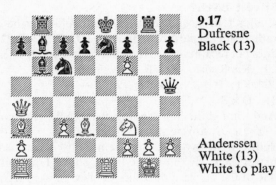

9.17
Dufresne
Black (13)

Anderssen
White (13)
White to play

There follows:

19	QR–Q1	Q × Kt
20	R × Kt ch	Kt × R
21	Q × P ch	K × Q
22	B–B5 dbl ch	K–K1
23	B–Q7 ch	with mate next move

At move 19 of that game Anderssen played QR–Q1, which is
made in the contemplation of one of the most spectacular sacrificial sequences ever seen. He has allowed a Knight to be captured,
then throws in the exchange and follows with a Queen sacrifice.

Dufresne was not very bright to accept the second sacrifice
(the Rook). He could have refused it, and refused a repetition of
it—after which Anderssen could still win, but only with hard
play. Thus:

19	QR–Q1	Q × Kt
20	R × Kt ch	K–Q1 (K–B1 loses the Queen)
21	R × P ch	K–B1
22	R–Q8 ch	K × R
23	B–K2 dis ch	Kt–Q5
24	B × Q	B × B
25	P–Kt3	B × R
26	Q × B	

And a glorious world ends here "not with a bang but a whimper."

Lamentably a Russian school of thought is now suggesting that perhaps 19 QR–Q1 was a bad, or second-best, move. To which I can only reply that I hope that all my future second-best moves are no worse than Anderssen's R–Q1.

But the moral of the story is: that some acts of that constructive imagination which makes great chess possible are, as it were, specialised into what is distinguishable as strange, unusual, unexpected; and that a flair for this kind of construction is a feature of the play of some players in greater degree than is manifest in the play of others; but that the unexpected manoeuvres are not always the most effective chess. The complete player, need it be added, should have this flair, but as a feature of his total intellectual power.

Minds, however, are idiosyncratic. Some powerful minds are less imaginative than are some less-powerful minds. Within the realms of the unexpected, also, it may be said that different minds produce different kinds of surprise. In appearance an Alekhine combination is different from a combination by Morphy, Capablanca, Rubinstein or Fischer, and that a combination by Tal is more suggestive of Alekhine's style—albeit, perhaps, without the same tremendous power, or that sense of the overwhelming.

Examples could be multiplied. A common denominator in all of those that we have seen is that on some occasion some player has expected what others do not expect. Let us consider, further, whether examples can show us what imagination is not.

IV

First, do not think that imagination is always part of a hard effort. When you are concentrating normally, ideas occur—seep into the mind, out of the everywhere into the here. Often they are short clear ideas that make the task much lighter, positive laboursavers. Look at this position: 24, 5bk1, 8, 3kt1B2, r4PPP, 5RK1. (Diagram 9.18.)

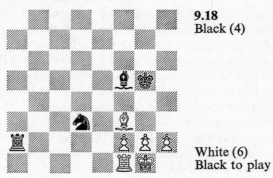

9.18
Black (4)

White (6)
Black to play

Black, to move, offers White a draw. White replies, politely:
I think my 3 Pawns are better than your Knight. (Arithmetically
he's right). All right, says Black, let's get rid of one:

1 ...   Kt × P
2 R × Kt   R–R8 ch
3 R–B1   R × R ch
4 K × R   B–R6

White is left with a Bishop and two Pawns to the good—and a
stone-cold draw. How very much easier than the laborious working out of lines of play with King, Rook, Bishop and three Pawns
against King, Rook, Bishop and Knight.

Second, don't confuse imaginative chess with sacrifices. As a
matter of brute fact, players start life less equipped to see sacrifices
in the distance than to see ordinary moves, because their technique includes valuations which make them take for granted that
Queens are not giving themselves up for guarded pawns—and in
consequence their minds are treating as irrelevant aspects of the
board that may be really important.

But many typical sacrifices are so well built-in to a good equipment that they are part of technique. In the process of promoting
a Pawn, one deflects a Rook, or other piece, by checking in
between that piece and the King, drawing it from the file rank or
diagonal, as the case may be; or one pins it with a piece that can
be captured. To some players this would seem clever play; to
others a normal end-game method.

At earlier stages of the game there are sacrifices, at points like h7, f7, etc, which, being done, cannot always be called imaginative except in the very lowest degree. Often they are severely technical.

Moreover, there are players who are so technically equipped that they can see sacrificial captures, where they miss sacrifices on empty squares. Sacrifices on empty squares can be more beautiful. Zukertort's Q–Kt4 against Blackburn is a famous example.

In turn there are players who can see sacrifices by capture, and on empty squares, but miss really powerful moves that do not sacrifice, do not capture, do not check, do not even threaten anything immediate, yet lead to devastating lines of play if they are not anticipated or adequately met.

Indeed, in distinguishing between clarity and imagination, we must not forget that clarity can on occasion be so difficult to achieve that it involves imagination of a high order, unassisted by the apprehension of forcing processes, whether those be initiated by sacrificial capture or sacrifice on empty squares.

For a relatively easy example, the followers of modern games may remember that Tal, in a Candidates' Tournament, snatched a draw against Keres by sacrificing a Rook at KKt8, and getting a perpetual check with Q operating from KKt5 to Q8. In contrast, in a tournament in 1961, Bobby Fischer, having outplayed Tal, had two Rooks on the seventh against Tal's Queen. Fischer refused a pawn capture because it gave Tal a series of checks, difficult to follow. Now it may be that Fischer relied on judgement, which is an economy of effort, but I find it easier to believe that he worked the thing out; and I would say that that process was harder, and involved more imagination, than Tal's apprehension of the draw against Keres.

The diagram position (from earlier in the game referred to) shows Fischer in a superior position: but superior positions require winning. (Diagram 9.19: 2b1k1r1, 1pqp1pPp, 4pQ2, 1p6, r4P2, 6P1, PPP1B2P, R3K2R.)

His first decision is a fine example of insight, clear and imaginative, both. 19 0–0–0! (The safer seeming 0–0 does not lose a Pawn, because if 19 ..., Q×P 20 R–QB1 is fatal. But 19 ..., Q–B4 ch followed by Q–B4 relieves, as it were, some inflammation.) 19 ..., R×RP; 20 K–Kt1 (and White has

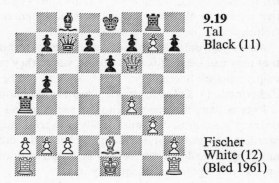

Fischer
White (12)
(Bled 1961)

seen that 20 ..., Q–R4; 21 P–Kt3 leaves Black even less mobilised than at present.) 20 ..., R–R3 a slight counter attack; 21 B×P, R–Kt3; 22 B–Q3, P–K4; 23 P×P. Hardly a Queen "sacrifice." White must be clear, however, that he wins two Rooks without losing his Bishop. 23 ..., R×Q; 24 P×R, Q–B4. (Black cannot get at the White pawns quickly. If 24 ..., Q–K4; 25 R–K1. If 24 ..., Q–B3 25 KR–B1 and h5 is unreachable.)

25	B×P	Q–KKt4
26	B×R	Q×BP
27	KR–B1	Q×KKtP
28	B×P ch	K–Q1
29	B–K6	Q–R3
30	B×P	B×B
31	R–B7	Q×P
32	R(1)×B ch	K–K1
33	R(Q)–K7 ch	K–Q1
34	R–Q7 ch	K–B1
35	R–B7 ch	K–Q1

And now not 36. R×P because he sees a series of Queen checks (h1, d5, a5, e5, etc) and, not seeing their termination, plays 36 KR–Q7 ch and 37 R–Q1, winning fairly easily.

The apprehension of powerful, but otherwise quiet, moves, to follow at the end of a line of play, is the mark of the play of Capablanca (whom Fischer resembles), communicating to us how clearly that great player saw the movement that was to begin after the Allegro, Adagio and/or Scherzo had ended. To that intuition of the beyond no one can deny the description "imaginative." Clarity, unless it be understood in a very sophisticated way, does not give the proper description.

Only rarely can we demonstrate "must have seen." A good case, I think, is that of Zukertort against Blackburne. In the position in Diagram 9.20 (not usually presented), White is playing a bad move unless he saw that five moves later he could counter Black's strong attack with a glorious Queen offer. (2r3k1, pbr1q2p, 1p2pktp1, 3p4,3P1P2, 1P1BR3, PB1Q2PP, 5RK1.)

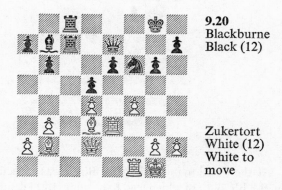

9.20
Blackburne
Black (12)

Zukertort
White (12)
White to
move

23	P–B5!	Kt–K5
24	B×Kt	P×Kt
25	P×KtP	R–B7
26	P×P ch	K–R1
27	P–Q5 ch	P–K4
28	Q–Kt4!	QR–B4 because, if Black captures the Queen,

B×P ch initiates a mating process.

In contrast, let me point out that imagination is not always characterised by the distance ahead of what is apprehended. Some fine imaginative moves are present in an occasional foreground. Marshall's Queen sacrifice against Levitski is, in a sense, one move deep—that is to say, the consequences are immediate. (Marshall probably saw it much earlier, Levitski not until it arrived.) And, if I may say so, I have to my credit one Queen sacrifice on an empty square, which, though I did see it ahead, yet has failed to be seen by some very good players to whom it has been shown as a problem. I give it here, not out of vanity—in which nobody is lacking—but because it so forcibly illustrates the point. The position (Diagram 9.21) is: r1b1rk2, pp3ppQ, 1ktp5, 4q3, 2B4Kt, 4P3, PP3PP1, 2R2K1R.

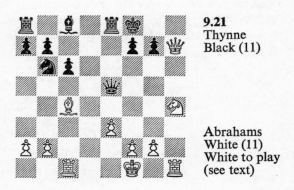

9.21
Thynne
Black (11)

Abrahams
White (11)
White to play
(see text)

At the position in the diagram Black was expecting Kt–Kt6 ch, or B × BP, both of which lead to nothing. But I disobliged him with 20 Q–Kt8 ch. If he takes the Queen, Kt–Kt6 leads to mate. There followed:

20	...	K–K2
21	Q × BP ch	K–Q1
22	R–Q1 ch	B–Q2
23	Kt–Kt6	
24	Q × R ch	resigns (because after K × Q, R–R8 mates).

And now let me add a weak but amusing echo of this. (Diagram 9.22: 8, 4Rppk, 5kt1p, 8, 4p3, 1B5P, Pr1r1PP1, 5RK1.)

In a game played in Jerusalem, 1964, my Bishop's Pawn seemed doomed, but was saved by 43 ..., Kt–R4. If either Pawn be captured: 44 ..., Kt–Kt6 with a fine attack. Forced, then, is 44 K–R2 and 44 ..., P–B4 achieves advantage. I learnt from my own ideas. I offer it as an argument for a good subconscious,

9.22
Abrahams
Black (8)

Blumenfeld
White (8)
Black to play
and save a
pawn

Of course, distance adds a value. When Dr Euwe, defending against Geller, who had his Queen up at KR7, and was threatening murder, decoyed the Queen with R–R1, and won cleverly thereafter, he probably saw it a long way ahead (Diagram 9.23: 2r1ktr2, pb1p1kpQ, 4qp1B, 1p6, 3P3R, P5Kt1, 6PP, R5K1) before he encouraged a King's side attack which he could have inhibited. If he didn't, it's still a very fine move. Certainly Geller didn't see it ahead, so that, as something which that imaginative "middle grandmaster" failed to anticipate, it ranks as a fine imaginative idea.

Zurich 1953

9.23
Euwe
Black (11)

Geller
White (10)
Black to move

22	...	KR–R1
23	Q×R	R–B7
24	R–QB1(P–Q5 has been suggested, but seems inadequate)
24	...	R×P ch
35	K–B1	Q–Kt6
26	K–K1	Q–KB6
27	Resigns (R–KB4 allows Q–K6 ch)

In chess it is misleading to talk of distance. Many "long" variations are simple—and logically short—because they include numerous King and Pawn moves, quite easy to follow and count.

More difficult can be "the movement after next." An idea is seen, but there remains a position after that idea has been turned into reality; and an idea is latent in that position.

In point is the position in Diagram 9.24: r4rk1, pp2p1bp, 2ktp2p1, 8, 1PPktBq2, 3QKt3, P4PPP, 1RB2RK1. Black saw that he could offer a Knight, winning a Queen if it were captured. What he did not see was that, thereafter, his own Queen would be in a net.

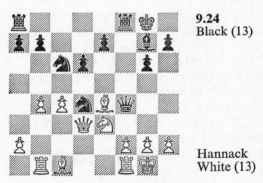

9.24
Black (13)

Hannack
White (13)

1st movement 1 ...   Kt–K4
            2   Q×Kt   Kt–B6 ch
            3   P×Kt!   B×Q
2nd movement 4   Kt–Kt4 and the Queen has no escape–Now that there is no Bishop on g7, Q–B2 fails to Kt–R6 ch.

How far White saw when he played up to the Diagram position is anybody's guess. All we are sure of is what Black failed to see.

It is obvious that a good game can include series of "movements" involving many moves and many changes of shape. To apprehend them is fine chess. To grasp one of the ideas when the position is desperate is also imaginative; but we denigrate this process as *ingenuity*.

To recapitulate, given an imaginative player, it can happen that he sees the distant idea or series of ideas as easily as he sees the immediately effective one. Either one sees figures in the marble or one doesn't. A fine training in sculpture enables many to see good uses to which pieces of marble can be put. But not theirs the Phidias of Praxiteles, or the Laocoon. Let it be added that there are men who see figures in marble, but are not good enough sculptors to make them step out and walk.

V

Finally, a word on the dangers of imagination. The need for control we have already seen, but there is more to it than that. Too fertile an imagination can make a player lazy. He is full of quick and clever intuitions that make life easy, and he economises his effort, until effort becomes irksome. That was a danger besetting such great ones as Lasker and Capablanca, though not the disciplined athlete that was Alekhine.

Can this be the explanation of the meteor which is Tal? There are minds that mature quickly and are characterised by speed. Flohr, in his youth, was such a one, and so Reshevsky. Their minds raced (and, I think still do race) through variations, at speeds from which the speed of light might be subtracted. When such a player is at his best, the ideas, and all the variations that include them, are grasped in so rapid an intuition as to be all present immediately—and nothing is absent within the wide range of that player's capacity. Efforts will be made when called for; yet, on the whole, the game is easy.

But let such a player go stale, let him not be at his best, then he is incapable of the tremendous efforts of willpower and patience that are the strength of Botvinnik (who described Tal as a "positional genius") and we have the story of hare and tortoise recapitulated.

Perhaps that explains why, when Tal beat Botvinnik, Botvinnik was not annihilated; but when Botvinnik beat Tal, there were games played in which Tal seemed hopelessly out-classed. So imagination, when it wavers, falls far short of a less spectacular clarity. "Vaulting ambition overleaps itself and falls."

Genius (it has been said) does what it must, talent what it can.

But an inventive genius has told us that genius is also an infinite capacity for taking pains.

In the above essay I have dealt mainly with the practical player. Special mention should, however, be made of composers. Problem composers, setting mates in two, three, four, etc, vary in their quality as players. Their constructions are of effects which need not amount to difficult chess.

Of end-game composers, one feels that the great architects of ideas, the Troitzkys, Rincks, Kubbels, must have been capable of fine chess, because, for the most part, their work is realistic. What they add is the "unusual" theme or possibility in the real game. In point is a study by one of the greatest, Wotawa, in which an idea is presented that, clearly, can occur, albeit rarely. Being grasped, it becomes an addition to chess equipment. (Diagram 9.25: 7R,8, 3RP3, 16, 1K6, 4p1P1, 1k1r4.)

Study by Wotawa

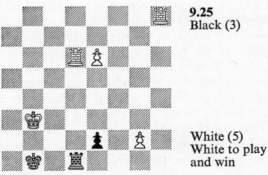

9.25
Black (3)

White (5)
White to play
and win

1	R–Q2	(threatening mate)
1	...	R × R
2	R–R1 ch	R–Q8
3	R–K1	(a beautiful echo of the keymove)
3	...	R × R
4	P–K7	R moves
5	P–K8(=Q)	P–K8(=Q)
6	Q–Kt6 ch, forcing mate.	

9.26
Black (1)

White (4)
White to play
mates at KB7

Since the above was written there has appeared a very good example of a problem idea, apprehended as the conclusion of a fine piece of play.

The problem idea simply stated is Diagram 9.26: 16, 4k1P1, 8, 5Q2, 8, 7B, K7. Now see the relevance of that idea to the finish of a game by Minic (Black) against Forintos. (Diagram 9.27: r1kt2k1r, 1p3p2, p2p4, 2pPq1p1, P2b2p1, 2P3P1, 4BPK1, R2Q1R2.) Black's twenty-third move was Q–K5 ch; 24 P–B3. There followed 24 ..., R–R7 ch and White resigned because after 25 K × R, Q–R2 ch; 26 K–Kt2, Q–R6 mate.

Pula 1972

9.27
Minic
Black (12)

Forintos
White (11)
Black to play

Finally, to be imaginatively active you have to be "in form." Here is a position where a fine player (Spassky) showed lack of imagination. By placing his Queen on B3 he allowed a counter-movement by Fischer, made possible by the "half-pin." In extenuation, let it be added that, when one is involved in plans for an attack, the counter-play can only be conjured by brilliant intuition. (Diagram 9.28: r1q1r1k1, 1pp1ppb1, 1kt4pp, 2KtbP3, p2Kt1PPB, 2Q4P, 1PP5, 3RR1K1.)

Reykavik 1972 (13th game)

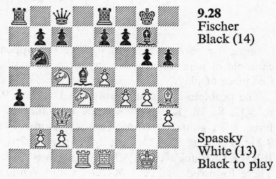

9.28
Fischer
Black (14)

Spassky
White (13)
Black to play

White has played 25–Q–B3 (into a half-pin). There followed:

25	. . .	P–K3
26	K–R2	Kt–Q2
27	Kt–Q3	P–QB4
28	Kt–Kt5	Q–B3
29	Kt–Q6	Q × Kt (exploiting the pin)
30	P × Q	B × Q
31	P × B and Black is left with a much superior position.

10 Memory in chess

I recall a vague picture of a position I saw reached in a strong Premier Reserves Tournament at Hastings in the late 1930s. At about the twentieth move of a Petroff each player (one of them, I think, was that excellent performer König) had most of his pieces well inside his opponent's half of the board. Indeed one could only be sure of which player was White and which Black by the position of the Kings. It seemed to me that each master was threatening desperately to lose, and that his opponent could only stop him from doing so by losing first. I made some comment to this effect to a Lithuanian expert, who was also kibitzing that game. He replied: *"Das ist eine bekannte russiche Analyse"* ("This is a familiar Russian analysis.") Later in the same tournament, when I found myself highly compromised through having improvised somewhat against a Meran Defence, I was told by the same expert that I had failed to adopt a Russian finding that would have saved me. To round off this narrative, let me add that, for all his knowledge of East European researches, that man lost some games; and when, some weeks later, he turned up mysteriously with a Midlands team to play against Manchester, his opponent had no difficulty with him.

Of that tournament, and many other occasions where I have seen prepared lines played—even up to the thirtieth move and beyond—I was reminded by a remark attributed to that fine player Jonathan Penrose. After his excellent win over Tal at Leipzig, Penrose is quoted as having said that, against Tal's Benoni defence, he had adopted a strategy used by the Finnish player Ojanen in a game against Keres. Those who have played through the Penrose–Tal game will agree with me that this is a very modest assessment of an excellent piece of chess. But the remark is most interesting. Coming as it does from a player who

is capable of seeing clearly through complexities for a long way
ahead, it conjures the question: to what extent do good players
employ their memories when they play? Knowing as we do that
the normal chess act is an endeavour to see ahead, can we accept
the possibility that learning is available to reduce this effort to a
minimum? If that is the case, then what are all those Grandmasters doing when, in the first twenty moves (including conventional openings), they think themselves into hopeless time
trouble? Are they straining the eyesight of the mind's eye, or are
they racking their brains for memories of what other players,
or they themselves, have done before? Are they intuiting time
future or intuiting the past?

The reader may suggest that perhaps a slight clue is afforded by
Penrose's exact words: "... a strategy adopted by Ojanen."
He remembered a method, rather than a specific series of moves.
But this leads to no solution, for we are aware of specific lines
of play that players do become acquainted with by rote. Thus that
line in the Lopez, played long ago by Tarrasch against Marco,
and misnamed "the Tarrasch trap," is a series of moves that can
be seen by the naked eye of a very good player; but I concede that
it is a sequence hard to work through. When chess is being played
with clocks it is obviously very helpful to know that, in that
specific position, Black should not castle before exchanging
pawns.

There are plenty of long variations in openings (I have in mind
the Lopez, the Sicilian, Hanham's Defence, the Vienna, the
Scotch, the Moller, the Max Lange, various King's Gambits,
the Meran, etc.) where, not general method, but exact series of
moves, have been found to lead to clear advantage or clear
disadvantage. The common denominator of the variations referred to is that they start with, or include, compromising moves
that do a little violence to positional judgement. Contemplating
the initiation of the complexities, one can make a mighty effort
and think it through; or one can avoid it, or one may find oneself
lucky enough to know it sufficiently to be able to execute the
proper plan.

I confess I feel a little sorry for a player of the Max Lange
who, after many moves, finds Black sacrificing a Rook at him.

MAX LANGE

1	P–K4	P–K4
2	Kt–KB3	Kt–QB3
3	P–Q4	P × P
4	B–B4	B–B4
5	0–0	Kt–B3
6	P–K5	P–Q4
7	P × Kt	P × B
8	R–K1 ch	B–K3
9	Kt–Kt5	Q–Q4
10	Kt–QB3	Q–B4
11	QKt–K4	0–0–0
12	P–KKt4	Q–K4
13	Kt–KB3	Q–Q4
14	P × P	B × P
15	P × R (= Q)	R × Q

And Black, having given a Rook for two pawns, is left with a strong attack. There followed

16	Kt–B6	Q × Kt
17	Q × Q	B × Q
18	R–K8 ch	R × R
19	Kt × R	Kt–Kt5
20	P–B3	Kt–Q6
21	P × P	B × P

White resigns. The Knight is lost. (Played by Dr Holmes, 1910.)

I would not say to the unhappy one: "Leave the Max Lange alone." In this, and in other variations, the danger should be visible to the tolerably good player at a stage when White still has control. So a good player should not fall for it. But I do not like the thought that a certain game was won by the player with the better equipped memory rather than by the player of greater vision.

In further support of the proposition that learning helps, may I, with whatever modesty I can muster, refer to the fact that in 1925, in a game at Liverpool, I found a line of play that has came to be known as Abrahams' Defence. (Really it is a counter attack). This has proved useful to many players, including me. Although, in the first instance, I saw it while playing, I do not blame anyone who learns it. And the value of learning I can attest with a story of which I am not the hero. At a late stage of this opening, as Black, I always used to play a Knight to K5, and was always unhappy about the possibility of a certain interposed check. I thought I could cope with it, though I never exhausted a research. However when, thirty years from origin, I found Gligoric allowing me to play the counter-attack, the thought occurred that he might try the check. Rashly I decided: "Here is a good chance to test it." The result was an unhappy one. But Gligoric told me afterwards that he had found the line in a Slav magazine. I believe that I am the architect of this, my own misfortune, for I had shown the danger to a Swedish Master some years before, and I know that he played it—not that it's so hard to see.

If I may add another experience of my own. I played in 1960 at Leicester against a good player, with vision enough, I think, for him to be able to dispense with some of his learning. He played Grünfeld's Defence, and I, quite without ulterior motive, tried something different from my usual (and original) treatment of that opening. After the game my opponent asked me why I had not played lines that I had used against Flohr, Gereben and others; and made it clear that he had looked up the annals of my past. Fortunately my chess past is so chequered that no opponent can learn from it anything that grounds any prediction of the particular error, or other surprise, that I shall present to him.

To return to my question: do good players use much memory? Do they really come to the board with an equipment that they hope will operate as a built-in handicap in their favour?

An indication that there is some substance in this suggestion is afforded by the fact that tournaments seem to follow fashion, and create fashion. Thus I found, in the tournament referred to, a good deal of Benoni Defence. At the previous tournament I had attended I had found a lot of Queen's Gambit Accepted (more acceptable at Leicester). At a high level, at most of the Grandmaster events, the Interzonal Tournaments, for example, one usually finds that a particular variation—good or bad or indifferent—is popular.

The inference is that this line, whatever it may be, is being currently much analysed. Perhaps a stimulating annotation in *Schachmat* has triggered-off professional interest. When players adopt these lines, with the stains of midnight oil on their fingers, they are saving themselves a certain amount of energy, and they are applying their minds along paths where they have made the going easier. At least an effort is saved at an early stage. So it is, also, in matches. The Alekhine–Capablanca match is patterned with orthodox Queen's Gambit of the Rubinstein form. Before that, the Lasker–Capablanca Match was distinguished by the working out, in many games, of another QGD variation (7   Q–B2 instead of R–B1). Later, Alekhine and Bogolubov produced quantities of Gambit Acceptances. At least one Botvinnik match is a long study in Caro-Kann; and comparable patterns will be found in most World Championship chess ever since.

What, then, are these players doing? Trying to come to the board with ready-made winning devices? I think not. Rather, though their clocks do not suggest this, they are labour-saving. That they use plenty of time while following prepared variations, indicates—does it not?—that they are thinking through even what they know by heart. Perhaps they are not relying on memory except to this degree, that they rely on the belief gained, in the trials, or in a study of the efforts of other players, that a certain position is not a bad one, a certain move not a losing one.

It may well be that the distinction between seeing and remembering is in danger of being overstressed. If one reflects on how one remembers, one realises that sometimes one is repeating by habit, sometimes one is actually seeing something as it happened, looking at the past as it were, sometimes one is logically reconstructing. A good student, sitting for an examination in history, literature, languages, law, or one of the natural sciences, may find himself doing all these processes, namely psittacine repetition, or conjuring something quite specific (possibly a passage of text) as a presentation, or reconstructing the thing by reasoning and imagination from a rather vague or sketchy schema.

The last type of remembering is analogous to learning from experience and applying the lessons of experience in one's thought. This is much done in chess when one "judges." But the problem that we are discussing relates rather to the other, parrot and photographic, types of recollection, retention or recall. In considering the slavish reproduction of what has happened before, let me mention that, occasionally, games of chess are exactly duplicated without any such intention on the part of the players. Smyslov once arrived at a position achieved by Tchigorin, and failed to see the winning move that his spiritual ancestor had seen. The move is very easy to see. In order to miss it Smyslov did not need to be forgetful. He had to be asleep. (Diagram 10.1: 2r2q1k, 3R2rp, p3pQ1Kt, 1p3p2, 8, 2P2P2, 4P2P, 7K.) Tchigorin against Rubinstein (Lodz 1906) won with R–KB7. Smyslov, against Lundin (Gröningen 1946—colours reversed) could only find Kt–B7 ch and a draw.

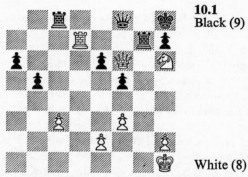

10.1
Black (9)

White (8)

Tchigorin–Rubinstein, Smyslov–Lundin (with colours reversed).

When, in a Hastings tournament, the English Master Tylor defeated Koltanowski very cleverly in a Philidor, I do not know whether he actually knew the play between Holzhausen and Tarrasch that he was reproducing. The good moves (sacrifices at f7 and e6) were visible to a good player, without being remembered. Certainly Koltanowski, of prodigious memory, did not remember them. (Perhaps he had not seen the precedent.)

The mention of Koltanowski conjures, by association of ideas, Blindfold Chess, which is something rather special. In this field there have flourished men of prodigious memory, including Alekhine, who could remember everything that had ever happened to him on a chessboard, seen or unseen, for the whole of his life.

But blindfold players do not seem at all precise on how they remember during the blindfold exhibitions. And their accounts vary. If I may speak from my own experience—and in my youth I tried up to twelve boards—it is a tremendously fatiguing effort (Lasker and Capablanca both deplored it) in which one uses, fortuitously, both a photographic element (not necessarily a picture of the entire board) and a power of reconstruction with the aid of reasoning. Thus if one is not sure whether, at board 7, the King's Rook's Pawn has moved, one either calls up a picture (quite difficult this) or one plays through the mental score with the aid of a conception of one's plans, purposes, hopes and disappointments on that particular board.

I believe that the marathon blindfold players use all manner of mnemonic devices (association of ideas), but I gather from talks with Koltanowski and Najdorf that the bulk of their performance is mental photography. They do not, I think, carry any complete board in their memory cells, but enough of it to enable them to summon up the whole on demand.

That blindfold methods are individual was established by the great psychologist Binet, who took statements from Tarrasch and others. Tarrasch gave an account rather as I have described. Binet's results, in this and other intellectual fields, he summed up as follows: "*La pensée en acte ne se décrit pas, ne se perçoit pas: à moins d'employer des métaphores on ne peut rien dire de ce qu'elle est.*" But that is a too modest summary of his findings.

Incidentally, most good players can conduct at least one game *sans voir*. Their power to hold changing positions in their mind is related to what they do when they analyse ahead for any long distance.

From the standpoint of retention, blindfold play takes place over a comparatively short period. The question under discussion is whether players use, in ordinary chess, recollections, from more or less remote time, of lines of play that they have seen, of analyses that they have worked through. I believe that not so much of this is done as those persons think who apply themselves to learning.

The simple fact is that what was seen once can be seen again. To good players the seeing comes easier than the remembering. Among good players one finds that there is more pride in the act of vision than in the act of remembering. I recall my sneering at an expert who, when I did not make the mistake of 4 P–K3 in the Albin Counter-Gambit, told me that I had avoided a book-trap. It is one move deep. Most things that the "book player" remembers were at one time seen over the board, in actual play, by somebody else. There are, perhaps, variations, arrived at by trial and error, when the midnight oil was burning low—"I prepared this variation for Tarrasch or Schlechter or Tchigorin or Golombek," as the case may be. This has been said. But did it win? Not necessarily. The preparer got a good position. But good positions do not win games. Games are won by good moves, by many good moves, in conjunction with the opponent's bad moves.[1] Looking up variations, remembering long lines of play; looking up previous performances of one's prospective opponents, these are practices that are valuable to the extent that they keep the toiler from drink and the temptations that develop in idleness. But they can be overdone.

I am apt to burst into happy laughter when I remember the Radio Match of 1946 with Russia. I was told after the match that my unfortunate opponent had spent long hours studying my methods. I was at once flattered, and conscious of guilt, because I appear to have spoilt his chess.

If you think about what you are doing when you are playing chess, you will probably find that, at each move, you are looking ahead—sometimes far, sometimes foreground. Now I add words that I would heavily underscore. Even if you are contemplating moves that you have made before, you are still thinking through them; you are still looking ahead; you are not really completely relying on memory.

If you are playing by rote you are ceasing to be a good player; you are playing mechanically, and badly; and there will come a stage in the game when you have to start to think, and you are not

---

[1] A fine example of this truth is afforded by a recent event. In the first game of the World Championship semi-final match between Bobby Fischer and Petrosian the latter produced, at move 11 of the Sicilian, an interesting and novel sacrifice, which seemed to give some advantage to Black. Fischer, after twenty minutes of thought, accepted the sacrifice, and thereafter outplayed his opponent in a game where his opponent continued to play fine chess.

able to. You are not "run-in," not "tuned-up." Your synchro-
meshes are slack. That is why many good players improvise a
little in the opening, or vary their openings. They want to be at
work from the beginning, so that when effort is required they
will not be lazy. Unfortunately, they may then be tired or they
may have unnecessarily bad positions. But that is another story.

The point I am endeavouring to make is that the essential
chess act, strength in the performance of which makes the good
player good, is the act of seeing all the possibilities and all the
impossibilities that lie ahead. Ahead, not in the past. It hardly
needs saying that at no position in a game of chess does one not
require to remember the moves that have gone before (apart
from those relevant to the rule about castling, and the record for
time-keeping purposes). Very often players cannot quite recon-
struct their games because they forget the exact order of some
moves. (Sometimes the logic of the game facilitates perfect reproduction.) I can speak of two masters that I knew well—the late
Jacques Mieses and the late Geza Maroczy. Maroczy had a
prodigious memory of a photographic type. When he played
through a tournament he could remember, at the end, not only
every move he had made, but almost every move of significance
made by most other players in the tournament. His chess, be it
quickly added, was frequently characterised by originality and
novelty. Mieses at his best was perhaps a little more creative than
Maroczy; but his memory was deplorable. He could not remember
his own best games—many of which were of the most ravishing.

But we must not oversimplify the diagnosis. A player like
Mieses, master of middle-game combination and of end-game
subtlety, may not have had a memory that retained many games,
many long prepared analyses, etc: but surely memory was still
relevant to his intellectual equipment. From seeing beauties
and subtleties, including those achieved by himself, he had equipped
himself with a facility in these creative movements comparable
to that of the poet who, in reading poetry, is inspired to write
different, but equally meritorious, poetry.

The truth of the matter is that the word memory covers a
multitude—the Freudian would say of sins, I would say: of
seeings.

Capacity for actual retention of events that have happened, this the chess player, *par excellence*, does not (in the last analysis) require. He has it as a part of his general intelligence, but need not use it in chess. He can forget every move that has been made before it became his turn to move. Let him only be sure that his opponent has or has not disqualified himself from castling, and that the opponent has not surreptitiously altered the position of a piece.

In this independence of the past the chess player is different from the bridge player. I make no apology for referring to this popular card game, because it has been well said that every good chess player needs at least one other major vice. In many cases that I know, the other vice is bridge. Now in bridge one must remember what has been played in the course of the particular hand—also what has been said in the course of the auction. This is not very difficult. It is rather a question of attention than of remembering. If one is concentrating, the cards that are played are registered in what the psychologists may call one's "specious present"—the short interval that characterises even the most rapid mental act—and are retained in the pattern of thinking that is in process.

In chess this kind of process is not integral to the game. But there is a type of memory—I am not sure that I am right in calling it memory, but I know of no better word—that is involved when one is thinking ahead. Thus, running through a long series of future moves, one seems to *remember* that, as these mental moves are made, pieces change their places, or disappear; squares that were occupied become vacant, vacant squares become occupied; open lines are closed, closed lines are opened. So, if I am seeing a position at, say, the sixth move ahead, I am remembering —or should be—that a Knight with which I started out has gone from the board, that a guard has been removed from a certain piece, that another piece has become pinned. Is this memory? Am I remembering when I retain, or recall, what will have happened, rather than what has happened? Or am I visualising clearly a whole that I have constructed? Am I imagining? Am I just "seeing"?

I do, in describing this act, use the word memory, because I see

in it something of the process that goes on in blindfold play. That
holding in the mind which makes analysis possible is precisely
what makes blindfold play possible.

However, if memory is involved in what chess players call
analysis (they really mean synthesis), it is a different function or
aspect of memory from Winston Churchill's activity when he
was able to recite a page of Gibbon or Macaulay, or from
Maroczy's action when he played through, in the presence of an
interested audience of which I was a member, a game he had seen
played between Vera Menchik and Capablanca a fortnight
previously.

Memory of the photographic type cannot, I would say, be
valueless, cannot be anything but a good servant. What is under
discussion is whether many players are in danger of adopting it
as a bad master.

That memory is relevant to chess I am obviously not trying to
deny. Even if the perception or projection of "what will have
happened" is not properly called memory, there are other functions that operate. They may be compared to the stages in the
acquisition of language and literacy. There are levels of learning,
levels that are revealed in the pathological state which is amnesia.
A man forgets his identity and his recent history, but he retains
his power of speech, his command of words, his ability to think.
This fact tells us that there are levels of memory. And this is
relevant to chess. Thus at the very outset, one's mastering of the
moves of the pieces—as one learns the alphabet—is mnemonic.
Later, when one acquires what is called a technique—an efficiency
in the doing of processes, such as winning with Rook and Pawn
against Rook—one is being assisted, at the conscious level or
below it, by the recollection of having done it before, of having
solved a study, of having attentively followed an exploitation
by somebody else. (Here we have a fusion of the levels or varieties
of memory.) There are even endings, such as King and two
Knights against King and Pawn, when a player who has time in
hand is tempted to slip out and steal a copy of Troitsky and con
it in a convenient place.

That would be a case of learning in chess. The advantages of
learning (I mean learning by rote or "photography") whether of

openings or end-games, are obvious. The disadvantage of reliance
on it is less obvious, but is real. Unless what you have learnt
by heart is reasonably decisive, you have only reached a position,
and you now have to find your own move. From this moment on
it isn't Alekhine or Rubinstein or Troitsky or Tal that is playing,
but you yourself. And unless one of these celebrities has carried
you far enough to make the win automatic, you can still lose on
your own resources.

That is why I am of the opinion that even the midnight oil
users among the masters do not rely overmuch on their memories.
Their concentration is always operating to change the remembered
into the actually seen. There memories are signposts for their
attention and not leading strings or guide dogs.

On the other hand, I am not advising any player to under-
estimate the value of memory. People laugh at the young man
(well known in chess and journalism, a very good player withal)
whose interleaved copy of *Modern Chess Openings* is so crammed
with added pages of learning that he has to pay for the extra
weight when he travels by air. On the other hand, I am quite
certain that any one of the most original of players owes much to
memories—even to temporarily forgotten memories. Through
having seen ideas exhibited, he is the more capable of recognising
promising situations, more capable, even, of achieving novelty.
Association of ideas is too well known to require stressing. But
ideas are even more stimulating than in the triggering of the
forgotten. They can, I believe, stimulate to the apprehension of
the new. They are the exercises that strengthen, rather than
instructions that are pedantically obeyed.

If this view of a function of creativity in memory is correct,
then it follows that the virtue is not in the retention of specific
lines of play. I have tried to suggest that that operation is calculated to make the player stale, uncreative, even lacking in
confidence. I have seen very learned toilers seething in anxiety-
neuroses, because they think they have forgotten the best reply
to P–K4.

If the memory is taken for granted as part of mental equipment,
then let it be used for the absorption of experience, personal and
vicarious, for an enrichment of the mind, but only occasionally

as a machine of sorts, calculated to save the efforts of vision and imagination that are the essence of chess. If further support is required for my proposition, let me mention that the electronic brain is not a good chess player.

11 What the computer teaches us about chess

To adapt a phrase from Isaac Barrow, the computer arithmetises almost eternally. All problems soluble by formal modes of calculation can be solved by this calculator, even if the variables approach infinity in their variety. Also it remembers for as near eternity as it can endure; and at any moment of time can initiate the recall of all that it has experienced.

So wonderfully equipped, why is it bad at chess? The fault, dear programmer, is not in your stars but in our game, because it is not arithmetic. Chess is not mathematical, not even inferential, and not mnemonic. Scientific, yes, but an inexact science, like practical engineering or clinical medicine. Accuracy and exactitude characterise the intuitions of the good player, but these accuracies resemble the precision of a drilling process rather than the execution of a mathematical exercise.

In chess, we are engaged in apprehending the consequences of our moves; we are looking ahead along lines of play, through few, or many, moves, and along branch lines, which usually increase in number with the distance of the perspective. We achieve this with vision. Included in this faculty is the power of selecting the relevant, and so facilitating the task. Now the machine has no faculty of vision, and no selective powers. If we cannot equip it with a formula to operate, whether an inferential process, or a matrix, then what is left for it to do? It has a memory, but what can its memory achieve? Theoretically, we can teach it the moves, laboriously transcribing them in binary notation. These are regulative categories. They permit and they exclude, but they do not guide. Within the rules the player has arbitrary choice. To the immanent problem (what is the best move?) the rules offer no way of arriving at a solution. Consequently, the machine must try every possible move, every possible answer to each, every possible answer to each of these possible answers, and so forward.

The immensity of this task is evident in the very first chess effort on the part of a computer known to me. In about 1949, Dr Prinz programmed a Ferranti digital machine to solve the following two-move problem: 5Kbk, 6pp, 6P1, 32, 7R (Diagram 11.1).

The first computer effort

11.1
Black (4)

White (3)

Mate in 2: 1 R–R6.

The solution, which should take any player above the beginner's standard less than a minute, took the machine (using valves, not transistors) fifteen minutes. It had to consider nineteen possible moves by White (I am excluding impossible moves, such as the Rook going over the edge of the board). There are nine possible Black answers to each of the White moves. White now has some nineteen replies. One of these will be mate. Now Black has a possibility of sixteen moves (if the bishop is in the centre) in order to test whether he has a legal move left. This is a rough description, to be modified in the light of the programmer's skill in using memory, acquired on the first half-move, in order to reduce the later task. Further, one should think, not in terms of moves, but in terms of operations. There may be several per move; at an intelligent guess, therefore, the machine needed close to 50 000 operations and the machines work was complicated by its need to refer to its built-in rule book.

What the chess player sees is that the mating move will be

By the brothers Wharton

11.2
Black (9)

White (8)

Mate in 3: 1 Q–Q1 (see text).

R × P, when the bishop has moved. He sees that he can be thwarted by P–R3. Having seen this he sees R–R6; and that is the solution. The player is guided by his perceptions. The logical necessities become clear after the perception has been experienced.

In order to show that one has to see before one can deduce, I invite the reader to consider the following problem (mate in three) by the brothers Wharton: 3K4, Rp2B3, PP5p, 4pPlk, 3pKtlktP, 7b, 4Q3, 7kt (Diagram 11.2). As you study the position, you will see that a rapid mating process seems to be made impossible by the fact that the White Knight's check takes place on a square where it interferes with the protection of the Rook's Pawn. Now look for a method of combining a process of guarding that pawn with that check. If he is quite a good player he may try R × P (in order to make possible B–Kt5, to be followed by Kt–B6 mate). One point of the Rook move is that if the Bishop be captured, R–R7 gives mate. But nothing as easy as that would solve a Wharton. A further meditation will show him that Black can reply to R × P with P–Q6. Then if B–Kt5, P × Q leaves the Black Knight on g4 unpinned.

Much finer vision is required for the solution. One must visualise a totally new method of guarding the pawn on h4. One must intuit that if the Queen is on a4, and the pawn has moved from d4, and the Knight from g4, then the pawn at h4 is guarded by the Queen.

The key is 1   Q–Q1. If 1   ..., P–Q6, 2   Q–R4. Now mate is threatened at e8. In order to prevent this Black must move the Knight from g4. Then Kt–B6 gives mate. The solver must also see that if 1   ..., B–Kt7; 2   Kt–B6 ch, K × P; 3   Q × Kt, mate.

The point of this illustration is that the solver conjures a redistribution of the pieces and a creation of fresh lines of action. Calculate, if you have time, how many trials over six half-moves the computer must make in order to be sure of a mate in 3. Let it be added that in the average middle-game there are more pieces on the board and more possible first moves than in the Wharton problem.

The player uses selective powers and judgement in aid of the concentration of the light waves of his mind along the important paths.

The computer, however, has no judgement, except the arithmetical. They say of the computer that if it has to choose between two clocks, it prefers the one that has stopped to the one that loses a second a day, because the former is accurate twice a day and the other is only accurate after many days. In this the computer resembles an unlamented *Times* correspondent who reviewed the position at the adjournment in a Hastings Congress. On each of five boards he predicted victory for the player with the Pawn to the good. In every case that player lost.

Theoretically a computer could be set to play from a limited number of selected first moves, exhausting all the possibilities over, let us say, six moves, and it could file all the results in its memory, having assessed all the positions to the best of the programmer's ingenuity. Even with that limited horizon, the undertaking would be time-consuming beyond the lifetime of even long-lived programmers.

Different, be it observed, is the case of draughts. In draughts the moves are few, and for the most part irreversible. Consequently, Shannon was able to program a computer practically to exhaust draughts. The computer memory, aided by the mathematical "rule of the move" constituted a champion draughts player. In chess there is nothing analogous to the rule of the move i.e. no mathematics.

Compendiously, chess is not mathematical in the accepted sense of mathematics—that is to say, the application of formulas to variables.

Let us consider the mathematical aspect. Obviously if chess presented a group of formulas to cope with variables, no complexity would prevent the computer from the solution of any problem, encountered by any player, at any stage of the game. But this possibility—or rather impossibility—has only to be stated for the truth to be manifest that chess is just not mathematical, and that all those who speak of the mathematical mind of the chess player are using false analogies.

Admittedly there are levels of mathematics at which the creative mathematician intuits a pattern, as when Archimedes saw a method of counting the sand, and, in that act of vision, created logarithms. (It may be of interest that the late W R Thomas, a chess player, and father of a chess player, wrote an essay embodying the suggestion that Napier was indebted to Archimedes' Sand-Reckoner.)

But what the mathematician intuits is different from what the chess player sees in degree and in direction. The mathematician sees how detail is to be classified, and how each class inheres in a wider class. So he moves to the more and more abstract. The chess player, on the other hand, has to see, in great detail, fine differences and class concepts help him little. His mind in action moves in narrowing channels. There are many of these, and they take the mind far. *Ex hypothesi*, this concentration on the very specific cannot be assisted by formula. It follows that Edgar Allan Poe is wrong when he dismisses chess as a process of calculation. That interesting man would have learnt much from a course of programming.

An important difference between chess and mathematics can be compendiously stated. The rules of chess are regulative only; the rules of mathematics are constitutive. Therefore the immanent problems of mathematics can be formally solved, by the application of formula to variable; the immanent problems of chess are not susceptible to formal treatment. Where mathematical skill is intuitive, in the apprehension of new classes, there chess ability would be useful to the mathematician; but the skill of the mathematician would be of little utility to the chess player.

It may be suggested that, at that relatively empirical level of mathematics which is inference among words and specific symbols, chess reasoning offers some analogy. Inference, as done by a computer, is memory plus calculation. Inference as done by a human being is memory of meanings, with an apprehension of relations made possible by the meanings, and controlled by the rules of logic. It adds to knowledge, because words are lively oracles. It adds to knowledge, as when a Law Lord says that income tax is a tax on income. The computer's inference is less lively, being done in symbols, which have no meaning, and no livelier for being the arithmetic of the immense (as when it works out all possible paths for a projectile).

Sometimes an illusion of logicality is presented in chess analysis (which I prefer to call synthesis). I had a choice of A, B, C. A was refuted by X; B was refuted by Y. Therefore I chose C. But that was not how the mind worked. The chess act saw the effect of A, saw the effect of B, saw the effect of C. This was not logical deduction. The deductive form frames itself for the annotator after the possibilities have been apprehended. Some memory, as of the specious present, is relevant. I had to remember when I chose C, that I had excluded A and B. But that is a minor feature of the chess act.

Suffice it, then, to say that all that the inferential forms can contribute is later clarification—explanation of what could or could not be done, whether by reason of the rules, or because a perceptible brute fact rejected a possibility. But clarification is different from operating by classification.

Botvinnik has constructed an Algorithm, which describes elements in sets of moves as something like causal processes. But when he applies this to his famous combination against Capablanca (Avro 1938) he achieves nothing more than a geometric description. Yet no laws of geometry determined Botvinnik's vision. He saw what others, with equal mathematical equipment, but less good at chess, would fail to see.

Nor is it likely that, in that game, he was consciously influenced by a combination that Capablanca had achieved against Corzo, a lifetime previously.

To resume, a computer equipped with calculus can guide a rocket to the Moon, but there is no calculus for chess. The computer answers the astronaut's question: "What is my next move?" but not the chess player's, except to say, if it says anything: "Don't expose your King to check," or "Don't castle, you've moved your King."

To be useful in chess, it appears that the computer relies mainly on its memory. It records series of variations, stores them, and is programmed to select from them. It has been suggested that some day it will be so equipped with variations that it will force its opponents to play well. That would be a triumph for memory.

At the present stage the computer shows us how good players do not play, and what kind of chess can be produced by memory alone.

In the human being the modes of memory are a technique of forgetting and recalling. In the computer memory is the main "mental" operation, and all its memory is always in being. At every moment of its action the computer is remembering everything with which it is programmed. It is at all times actively remembering the moves of the various pieces; and not only the moves but their limits on the board.

It is as if a child, learning to use words, were scanning its entire vocabulary, and all its control of voice, in every situation where it is called upon to be articulate. The computer is, in this way, recapitulating stages in the evolution of the equipment of its programmers, which they themselves do not remember. As it plays it remembers that the Rook moves along files and ranks, and that it stops at the edge of the board. It remembers all the rules and facts relevant to the rules—as that the King has, or has not, moved; that it is White's turn to play, or Black's, as the case may be.

Keeping it primed with all this information, men of genius, and/or men with an infinite capacity for taking pains, devise methods of instructing the computer—not without clever "short cuts" such as mini-max assessment—to find the effect of any move of any White piece when it is White's turn to move. It does this by trying every possible move of every Black piece in reply, every possible White reply in answer to all of those possible Black moves, and so on till every possible four-move line of play (if that is the practical maximum) has been explored and the result assessed by remembered criteria. During this work new memories are being created, stored and referred to in a way suggestive of the human player's memory of the passing phases of the future, when he looks further and further ahead.

Every process is the direct, or indirect, result of specific instructions. There is no "intuition." That is to say, there is no direct apprehension of meaning, or of the future, and the memories are mechanical memories, not an intuition of the past.

According to some scientists, we are being shown, by the programmers of computers, something of the way in which the myriad cell combinations of the human brain operate when we think. These scientists think in terms of "circuits"—electrical connections when we are remembering the specious, or presented, present (as when we use a dictated telephone number in order to dial) and chemical-electrical circuits for the deeper-seated memories.

But, so far, no computer process simulates what Sherrington called "the integrative action of the nervous system." It follows that no computer is yet able to achieve "awareness." Its perpetually recurring task is mechanical reference to precedent and rules.

Certainly the human brain includes a great deal of "machinery." We see this in the operation of "association of ideas." But from association of ideas there is no mechanical generation of ideas.

Mechanical processes may describe some of the mechanism of memory, but not the creativity of memory. Let a computer be programmed to solve a study by Troitsky. That education will not result, as human education seems to do, in a facility in apprehending other ideas in other studies by Troitsky.

The important concept is "the idea." This the computer lacks. What the computer illustrates is the defect of the mnemonic human player. What that person fails to produce is the idea, which, being apprehended, makes possible the good, or, at least, the original move. And the original move is the hallmark of real chess.

12 Mental processes in chess and bridge

I have already quoted the dictum that every good chess player has at least one other major vice. That may well be understatement. Bridge players, on the other hand, get so much bridge that they haven't time to do justice to other vices. Yet it happens that several very fine bridge players started life as chess players. Gardner, for example, is believed to have been very strong in Berlin Café chess. The late Leslie Dodds and one of the Tarlos played chess for their counties; the late Harold Saunders was formidable in both fields. So too Professor Wheatcroft (a good blindfold chess player). Of a younger generation, Truscott was a high-class chess player who eventually concentrated his energies on high-class bridge.

I would base on these facts a suggestion that real chess players who apply themselves to bridge can achieve very good bridge. I am not aware of any bridge player who (later) took up chess and became really good at it. The reason for this may be that the language of chess must be mastered early in life—like languages generally. Bridge (or the part of it that is not arithmetic) can be learnt later in life successfully. This is not to say that bridge is easy. My old friend, the late Victor Wahltuch, brilliant chess player and clever bridge player, said that some bridge situations can be as hard as chess problems. But, in general, bridge lies in a smaller compass. Much of the work in it is simple counting; bridge insight is nearer to common sense than is chess insight. I would add that all "applied" common sense is, *ipso facto*, uncommon sense.

What deserves investigation is, surely, this question. How do the workings of the mind in bridge and chess resemble each other and differ from each other?

First I would lay it down that the seeing, in advance, of later events and possibilities, which is the essence of chess, takes place also in bridge—to some degree. I would suggest that the scope for this vision is limited in bridge, yet considerable. A limited field can be a very rich one. On the other hand, there are operations peculiar to bridge, which are not manifest in chess. I have in mind inference and arithmetical calculation. Chess, we know, is not arithmetical on any scale. In bridge, arithmetic has to be applied quickly and exactly. Because it is arithmetic, it is, *ex hypothesi*, easier than a process of apprehension, such as chess, which is little aided by arithmetical technique.

Here is an example, that I saw in play, which shows some resemblance between chess and bridge:

```
        S   A Q 4 3
        H   K 9
        D   7 3
        C   A Q 10 5 2
                    N
        W                   E
                    S
        S   10 5 2
        H   A Q J 10 6 4
        D   A 5
        C   9 6
```

The contract is 4H by South. East has bid 2D.

W led D 2 on which E played the K. South captured.

Now a chess player could not have done that. A chess player, or a good bridge player (who, to that extent is playing chess), sees quite easily that when any finesse fails (and the finesses will fail here) it will not be good if E can put his partner in. So hold off the Ace. Will the next Diamond be ruffed? Here the pure bridge player answers. From E's K I infer that his partner has the Q. If E had the Q he would play it instead of the K so as to tell his partner that Declarer hadn't got the Q. Also the arithmetical bridge brain reports that, for the hold-off to be dangerous, E must hold eight Diamonds, and it doesn't look as if he holds so many. Evidently W has led his lowest from Qxxx or Qxx.

To revert to chess. Here is a sort of board with moves to be made on it. I doubt whether there is a mathematician subtle enough to make a fifty-two-square board and state for it rules of piece-play as if the game were a type of draughts or chess. Nevertheless, at times one feels that one is making moves on a board. Particularly is this true in an end-play, when the throw of the lead puts the cards into a required "position."

In this example before us the chess player wants to execute the following manoeuvre. He wants to get rid of E's CJ with his 9, then to get rid of E's CK with the 10. Then, using SA as an entry, he'll discard his losing Spades on CAQ.

What happened to the man I'm talking about? Taking the first D he finessed C9. E captured with J and returned a D to W. W played S8. (Experienced bridge players attack through the shorter suits: but there is vision in this as well, namely the possibility of the long suit becoming established by ruffing while there is a re-entry.) Now Declarer proved that he was not only not a chess player; he was not even a bridge player. He put the Ace on, drew trumps, and finessed CQ. When this failed and SK was cashed, he said: "The cards were stacked partner." The latter obligingly replied: "Bad luck partner," and both of them hate that Kibitzer who does not like to hear the word "luck" misused.

On the fourth move, of course, a bridge player would still get home. He would let the spade run, E would capture with J and return trump. Now there's a squeeze with Vienna Coup, HK, SA and all the remaining Hearts). Declarer's S10 is a happy accident. Is this chess or pure bridge? Well, there is an element of vision in the squeeze. In the position, there seems to be a set of numbers to be seen. Much depends on the purely arithmetical fact that when I hold two cards I cannot hold 3. Declarer, playing two hands, can hold three important cards between two sets of two. (In South S10 and Cx; in Dummy CAQ.) For chess players coming to bridge, squeeze-play requires more learning than, say, elimination play and the throw of a lead. And he requires practice before he throws in one opponent to make his winners, so squeezing the other defender. Counting is involved. Yet these processes of play are percepts.

The arts of bridge that are just not chess are not manoeuvres of the above sort. Real bridge includes "the count." When a chess player trying his hand at bridge gets an Ace ruffed, he begins to think rapidly as to how he can recover the lost trick. Will he now have to finesse? He then gets driven to working out the holdings; but finds this difficult. On the other hand, the real bridge player's first reaction is, I think, on these lines: "Now I know that X started with five Diamonds, and as he has bid Spades I know at least ten of his cards. What are his three others? Now Y has . . . etc."

In point is the play of Ghestem, the French master:

```
        S   A Q 10 xx
        H   A xx
        D   xxx
    •   C   K x
            N
    W               E
            S
        S   K J xxx
        H   K xx
        D   A xx
        C   A x
```

He is playing 4S, and CQ is led. Absently putting on the King, he is horrified to see it ruffed by E. But the resources of Science are not easily exhausted. "Nine Clubs in one hand," says he, "we have an end-game." So he throws the A on the King! He then captures the returned D, draws trumps, eliminates H A K and throws W in with a Club. W now plays another Club, on which N plays a D and S a Heart. On the next Club N throws a D and S ruffs. Having started with Ax Kx of Clubs he has lost three tricks in Clubs. But that's all. Now this is vision framed in a rather special bridge technique—bridge not without chess. I may say that when I saw the hand—*as a problem*—I solved it very quickly. But if it happened in play, would a chess player think immediately in the purely numerical terms?

I remember watching the late Mr Kosky thinking very hard, and watching a lot of discards very keenly, in order to ascertain what to do with: S   A J xx in North and S   1 0 xxx in South.

That honours were divided he assumed. But if Kx or Qx were in W, then the proper play was Sx to the J. If W held Kxx or Qxx, the proper play was 10 through, or X to the 10 from the table, He arrived at a correct decision, because the character on the left behaved as if he held a guard in diamonds, and the rest was arithmetic.

This I would say is pure bridge, not chess. There is no chess in the inferential side of bridge, because *in chess there is no inference*. (I apprehend that inference can be regarded as a sort of perception—of the relations between things, or between words —and/or symbols. But the perception is in a relatively closed circle. So a practical distinction between perception (or vision) and inference is valid.) You can lay out a set of variations saying: this fails because . . . , and that fails because . . . , therefore the other is necessary. But you did not think it out like that. The apprehension was vision along three perspectives, and the selection of the move that initiated the play along the best perspective. The logical form is only in the subsequent exposition, demonstrating the rebuttal of alternative defences.

But in bridge Ghestem founded the manoeuvre I described above on arithmetical inference. Indeed, in every hand of bridge one infers; one looks at the table and sees A Q and one projects a K into partner's hand, but you check this by working out the holding of Declarer from the bidding, or noticing that he's playing like a man who has the missing King, etc.

In actual play one leads the lowest from Kxxx and partner's J is taken by Declarer's A. So partner holds the Queen! I am waiting patiently for the following opportunity—which I may not recognise when it comes. Holding bare A Q but desperately anxious for opponent not to switch, I shall capture East's J with A, get into Dummy, finesse into W and expect him to return a small card to my Q I may be thwarted by the fact that E was finessing against his partner.

There will be an element of chess in this, but it introduces another factor: psychology. Whatever they say to the contrary, there's practically no psychology, in the conventional sense, in chess. The chess player plays the board—and only in desperation relies on an opponent's aptitude for error. He plays, normally, as if his opponent, however weak, will make the best possible reply. In other words, the chess player is his own opponent.

Now in bridge, in good circles, one also assumes that the opponents will play well. But one can deceive them. (In other words, a bridge player plays opponents, one, two, three—even four.) Suppose you hold C K 4 2: the table C J 10 9 8 7 3. Your partner has called Clubs, and East has doubled your 4S in order to get a Club lead; C 5 is led. A from E. Not too quickly, and not too slowly, you drop the K. He won't play the Q now. Incidentally, that's a "sacrifice," but it's very different from a chess sacrifice. If you sacrifice at chess your opponent accepts or rejects your sacrifice on its visible merits. There's nothing concealed from him. Your superiority consists in this—that you saw it in advance, saw that it was sound, and he didn't see the latent resources early enough. But this sacrifice in bridge is a bluff. A bluff so good that it will work against anybody except, possibly, the Terence Reeses of the game. I mention Reese, because he it was who found himself with H A J xx in Dummy and Q 9 in hand. To his 7S H 10 is led. Nothing can be done about the losing Heart, and the finesse is doomed. So Reese nonchalantly plays A, dropping Q from hand and returns a small H. Naturally E holds off the King. Reese, I may add, is something of a chess player. He saw ahead here, but in a context of behaviour.

I am not aware whether the French Master Théron is a chess player, but he plays like a man seeing ahead: constructs a possible situation (in chess, one sees a possible situation) and acts on the assumption that his construction is right.

In the hand in question he held, as East, Q 9 2 of Spades (Trumps). Dummy (N) holds K 8 4. A Club has been led, which seemed to be a singleton. When Declarer captures and plays a small S from hand to Dummy's K Théron discards Q. This is the only way to induce Declarer let him in—that is to return to hand and play a small trump towards W's J (because he will think W held J xxx). So it fell out, E was allowed in, and a Club was ruffed.

Again, Albarron, with A K J 10 in hand and xxx on the table, sees in Dummy K xx K xx and he does not want E to have a chance of signalling which of those suits he wants. So instead of A K, etc, he plays S 10 first. It may even steal a trick. W puts in the Q, but has no information, and leads the right card—for Declarer.

These coups are possibly "chessy," but are bridge essentially by reason of the fact that the bridge board is part concealed. (That's one of the reasons why my mathematician would not find it easy to construct a board expressive of bridge.)

Bridge offers scope to constructive imaginative. But it differs from chess in this way. In chess one works a long way along lines of thought which are series of moves; in bridge one has to construct a possible position (of cards and persons) a very little way ahead. Figures in the marble both—but different marble.

I shall mention two situations in which I have found myself, not knowing whether I was playing chess or bridge.

On my left, 2 C, on my right 3 C. I hold S xxx H A xxxxx D——C xxx. I anticipate a declaration of 6C with my partner to lead. So I bid 3 D. Doubled and taken out, and I double 6 C to confirm that I have been telling the truth. My partner, the late Harold Saunders, was not a believer in the "Lightner" nonsense: leads a D which I ruff, and I make my H A. "Moves ahead," in a bridge context.

I am a little proud of the following—which nobody believes. I held, as South:

S   K Q J 10 9 8
H   xxx
D   xxx
C   x

On my left Dummy holds

S   A xxx
H   10 9 x
D   K Q J 10 9 8
C   ——

Bidding: E 2C W 3D E 4C W 4D E 4NT W 5D E 6C W 6 N T All pass. I led KS and Declarer refused it. And I "saw" something. Saw, in a limited context, the curious fact that my K had been refused. Once you know there's a problem, the solution is not hard to find. If I played a second Spade Declarer might discard his bare D A on it. So I switched to D, to confirm my belief, and so it was. Declarer held: Sx, H A K Q J, D A, C A K Q 10 9xx. (My partner held a defence in Clubs.)

Truer to bridge proper is the art of trading on the opponent's ignorance. In the nature of things, Bridge is played partly in the dark, unlike chess which is completely open.

Here is an example of bridge. Table holds S K xxxx. You (Declarer) hold S J x and you think W holds A and you hope E has Q. So you play x from the table. Q does not go in. Nor does W put in his A, because he thinks you have the Q. When having drawn enough trumps to allay his suspicions (but not to allow any revealing discard) you now play x to the K, E still holds off. Then x back and A and Q fall together to your small trump, and E and W come to blows. I did this coup over forty years ago, and reflected that the imaginative construction was Chessic; but it is bridge because it's a use of opponent's mentalities, rather than of their pieces.

Bridge does, to an extent, fill the gap that is left by ignorance of the position of the cards with the technique by which players use the cards. I refer, for example, to Rule of 11, to a rule for deciding whether to finesse a King with ten cards, elementary signals, playing of "true" informative cards, McKinney signals, etc. But there are large gaps left to fill. Omitting a desirable excursus on the nature of imagination, let me say compendiously that bridge contains a factor of ignorance, where chess only contains a factor of stupidity. I may win at chess because my opponent failed to see or understand something. I may win at bridge because my opponent did not know something. Similarly, I may lose at chess through failing to see something. I may lose at bridge for that reason; but I can also lose at bridge because I do not know something. Maybe I had no reason at all to guess it or infer it. Has my partner A of Hearts or A of Spades. He has had no way of signalling. I guess wrong! This type of ignorance doesn't manifest itself in chess.

Now I am not emphasising the element of chance, or element of luck (which is different), but pointing out that bridge players use the opponent's ignorance. One plays from Axx, suspecting that

Declarer holds KJ and one's partner Qxx. Declarer may guess wrong.

And always the bridge player is using arithmetic in order to infer the closed hand. A bridge player thinks as follows (I must say that this is a guess on my part): "X may hold one of a few possible holdings. Have I a defence adequate to all the combinations? [At this point he sees lines of play—like a chess player.] If I have no defence to all possible holdings, I'll construct his hand as follows . . . [Here enters some inference.] and play as follows . . . ."

The further difficulty then arises. Will partner be able to participate? Will he make the right return, or co-operate in the deception? And every bridge player knows that there's a partner born every minute.

I could develop this, but would be open to the criticism that I had gone to the zoo and not seen the elephant. The elephant never forgets—the bridge player always remembers. *The chess player is not called upon to remember.* Let me amplify that. As we have seen, a chess player working through a long line of play has to remember that early in the variation a pawn disappeared from square X, a piece that was on Y has moved to Z, etc. But while he plays he is not called upon to remember moves already made—except that he's moved his King or Rook and can't castle. He can be very good indeed without knowing any learning, without knowing the many variations—after all, they are only aggregates of good moves that somebody had to see. He can be very good and play very well, and fail to remember the game very soon after it's finished. Most good players have, in fact, good memories. On the other hand, some very good players cannot even remember their own masterpieces.

But the bridge player remembers the cards that have gone. This is not as difficult as it seems, but it needs practice. The essential is that he *observes* the cards that go. The player who claims to have a bad card memory usually means that he hasn't the capacity for concentration that would enable him to *notice* the cards that go. If he noticed them they wouldn't be hard to remember. If a chess player comes to bridge and finds it difficult, one reason will probably be that he fails to achieve the knack of seeing the fall of the cards. If he is not a moron (and few chess players are morons) he will acquire this knack. But it will not be as easy to all chess players as it is to all real bridge players.

There is also some talk about "card sense." The late Emanuel Rose (brother of the late international Willy Rose) seemed to be an uncanny judge of whether the suit would break or the finesse succeed. Perhaps he was psychologically "aware." I think that there is a lot in atmosphere. An opponent is exuding tension, or is nonchalantly looking like a man whose K of trumps is not bare. Strain is evident in the way the cards come out. Also one gets to know opponents' mannerisms. On odd occasions, when I've played a lot of bridge, I feel a certain flair. It doesn't last for ever. I may add that chess players sometimes sense that a good-looking move is not as good as it looks, and they think again and discover an opponent's resource. I can only add to this that I believe in extra sensory perception. But what is sometimes meant by "flair" is the fact that good bridge players seem to judge well when to take a risk. To lead Kx, or not to lead it? To play in the assumption that partner holds a Q or not? This is probably a skill that comes with experience. Chess players starting bridge late in life do not achieve this light-heartedness in decision, this flexibility.

Perhaps that is why Emanuel Lasker, whose brain was second to none, mastered every move of bridge without being a successful performer. I never saw him play bridge, but hearsay tells of his rigidity. I saw Capablanca play bridge. He played very well indeed, but woodenly. He whose chess was so fluid. These two great chess players failed to develop a "flair" for cards.

Finally, would one say that bridge is comparable to chess for general difficulty? Assuming that a man has, on the one hand, a grasp of chess techniques and, on the other hand, a grasp of bridge technique, I think that he will find much greater depth in chess, much greater scope for imaginative creation. He can, after all, find himself working out very long lines of play, and looking all the time for clever deviation. The thoughts of the bridge player, are not such "long thoughts." But that does not imply that bridge is to be regarded by the chess player as easy. Every chess player knows that one move ahead can be hard to see, that a

two-move problem can perplex, a three-move can really puzzle.
The shortness of the bridge range does not guarantee easiness.
A bridge player can find himself with a really difficult analysis of
the possibilities latent in five or six cards. Speaking for myself, I
enjoy a bridge problem nearly as much as I enjoy a chess problem.
If I enjoy chess problems more, prehaps that is because their
solutions come more easily to me, or perhaps because there is
much greater variety in the materials from which the problem
is constructed.

One more, and very important, difference. In chess every game
is a unit, indeed every move is a unit. In bridge every hand is a
member of a class. Thus, as South with A 10xx and Q 9xx in
North (Dummy) I want to give myself the best chance. So I
play A and a small one to the Queen. So I'm wrong, because
E has K Jx (that can't be helped); or because E has Kx and
W Jxx. Yet I haven't played badly, because *in a majority of cases*
this play is right. In the long run my methods will pay (I hope!).
But in chess I do not play any move merely because it will be good
in a majority of games. I play the move because it's the best I
can find in this game, and for no other reason. What I am saying
amounts, perhaps, to this: a game of pure skill allows an exactitude not to be achieved in a game that contains elements of
chance.

I will now essay a further point: that the majority of bridge
hands are uninteresting; the minority interesting. My experience
is that one must not assume that any hand is pointless. I have in
mind a strong player who, playing against a Slam and holding
S J 10 xxx to Dummy's A K Q x, permitted himself to discard
the fifth Spade. That discard allowed Declarer to throw him in
with the fourth Spade—to squeeze his partner. Had he a fifth
Spade he could have downed the Contract. This gave me, his
partner, one of the pleasures of bridge, an opportunity for sar-
casm at the expense of a somewhat arrogant "expert."

There are, I may add, some better, and greater, pleasures in
bridge. When, once in ten years, one executes a double-squeeze,
or, once in twenty-five years, a smother-play, one feels that one
has done something nearly as good as convincingly winning a
game of chess.

Since the above was written I have been fortunate enough to find myself in a position where I was able to create a problem for an opponent and to illustrate that in bridge one can be entirely dependent on an opponent's failure to solve a problem. If one is dependent on an opponent in chess that is only because one has failed to control all his possible manoeuvres. In the following deal I was South:

```
                    S   9 6 2
                    H   A J 9 2
                    D   4 3
                    C   K Q 9 6

                         N
S   5                                      S   7
H   6 3            W              E         H   K 10 7 4
D   Q J 8 7 6 2                             D   A K 10 5
C   10 5 4 3                                C   A J 8 7
                         S

                    S   A K Q J 10 8 4 3
                    H   Q 8 5
                    D   4
                    C   2
           Bidding: E   1D
                    S   4S
                    W   5D
                    N   5S
                    E   Double
```

West led D Q and followed with a D which was ruffed by South. S A was played.

At this point it looks as if I must lose a Club and a Heart, and so be one down. Accordingly I played some "chess." Small Club to Dummy's six captured by East's 7. Now East has a problem. He is afraid of a diamond return giving a ruff discard (which puts me home); he is afraid of A of Clubs (which also puts me home). Accordingly he said to himself; if my partner hasn't got the Q of Hearts, it's hopeless. So he led a heart and put me home.

Yet he could have defeated the contract had he combined the analysis which is bridge with the foresight which is chess.

What does he know? Well, he should know that I have all the remaining Spades, that I only had one Diamond, that my Club is a singleton. So I have three hearts, and am trying to get rid of two of them. But he has a play that only enables me to get rid of one of them. He should play the eight of Clubs. His partner's ten extracts the Queen. One heart only is discarded, and now East is sitting over dummy, unsqueezable, because he discards after dummy, and at the end he must make his King of Hearts. Let me add, in my opponent's defence, that some better players than he have failed to see this solution.

Part Three
CHESS PERSONALITIES

13 World champions
   I have known

One Saturday afternoon in the autumn of 1923, in the old and strong Liverpool Chess Club, there appeared a young, tall, blond, athletic-looking man, with the erect carriage and the frozen blue eyes of the Russian, or Prussian, officer. This was Alexander Alekhine, ex-cadet of Tsar Nicholas, and a chess genius more spectacular than any that the world has since produced. Against sixty opponents (including myself, in the shape of a young boy) he started play at 2 p.m. At 9 p.m. he was still in play, having won, and won, and won, and his opponents were now reduced to four, including myself, who retained a surprisingly sound position.

Now the strict rule in simultaneous play is that each player makes his move immediately on the arrival of the performer at his board. This is only fair, and in every simultaneous exhibition should be enforced. There is, however, one generally admitted exception. If the player is left with very few opponents, so that there is practically no time gap between his appearances—instead of arriving once every ten minutes or more he arrives in seconds—then it is conceded that the challenger is allowed a moment or so in which to think. The extreme case is when one opponent is left. This eventually happened to me. Three boards placed near to mine quickly succumbed to the moves of the long arms. And there was Alekhine, standing over the board, insisting on instantaneous replies. He thought, then made his move, rapped sharply on the table and made impatient sounds in Russian.

The position was hard. Pawns wedged with pawns, and my King Bishop and Knight, endeavouring to be on guard at all moments against his King, and two fantastically wheeling Knights.

135

After twelve lightning moves under these conditions, the boy went wrong, found a pawn indefensible, and resigned. The grandmaster swept the pieces aside brusquely, and stalked away. He was, let me emphasise, entirely within his rights.

To this story, there is a contrast and sequel. The contrast takes place in the later 1920s. Capablanca, the Cuban virtuoso, is playing, in London, a very strong set of some sixty opponents, including me. After some hours, I am hanging on, rather desperately and ingeniously, to a compromised, but just tenable, position. (It included a Rook on R2 guarding a Pawn next to it.) Capablanca appeared: "My friend, you've been making some good moves." "They'll be exhausted soon," I murmured. "Well," said he, "would you like a draw?" And he gave me a draw when I stood worse than I had stood against Alekhine. In later years, when Alekhine, having defeated Capablanca (this was a surprise to many, not to me), stood on his strict rights and permanently evaded Capablanca's claims to a return match, I know where my sympathies were engaged. (According to Znosko-Borovsky, his friend, Alekhine wanted to avoid risk.) In the 1930s when Alekhine himself—admittedly through taking liberties, and through alcoholic excess—lost the championship to Euwe, whom he overconfidently played in preference to Capablanca, that sporting Dutchman gave him a quick return match, which the Russian won. There is a moral in that, somewhere, but I don't know what it is.

My sequel to the Liverpool incident took place in 1936 at Nottingham. The third Mrs Alekhine, a delightful American lady, required the signature of an English professional man, on some application for visa renewal. Alekhine asked me to oblige, and I gladly did so. He said: "If I can ever do anything for you, please ask me." I replied: "You can do something for me." He raised an interrogative eyebrow. I said: "Be more considerate to small boys." The frozen blue eyes stared at me for some seconds. "Yes," he said, "I remember, Liverpool 1923. You had pawns, bishop and knight, against my pawns and two knights. You should have drawn that game." (I may add that in 1929 Alekhine had published, from memory, another of the games played on that occasion—a most interesting game against Spencer—[See: *Auf dem Wege zur Weltmeisterschaft.*])

At that same tournament (Nottingham 1936), where I was playing in the Premier Reserves, I was asked, at the last moment, to cover the Premier Tournament for Tass. I was to write reports in English and put them on a train to London. There they were translated and relayed to the USSR. Tass later offered me the job of interviewing the leading players. Accordingly, I dealt with Lasker and Capablanca and Euwe in English, with Flohr, Tartakover and Bogoljubov in German, French and German respectively; with Reshevsky and Fine in American. But what about Botvinnik?

Botvinnik, joint winner of that tournament with Capablanca, was then showing the hitherto undisclosed extent of his tremendous powers. But he was very much the "Russian representative." (The State had given him a car.) He would not admit to any knowledge of English, French, German or Yiddish— some of which I suspected he knew. But with him, apart from his beautiful wife, a Ballerina from the Bolshoi (I saw her dancing there in 1950) there was also a character called Missouri, whom we dubbed "the GPU man," and who attended the master day and night. Missouri I cornered. Pointing to myself fiercely, I said: "Tass." That made an impression. It then transpired that Missouri spoke French, whereupon we came to an arrangement. I, in Missouri's presence, was to ask Botvinnik questions. Missouri would write down the replies, copy them for me, and I would send the Russian scripts to London.

It went smoothly. I took Missouri to Botvinnik, indicated Tass, and Missouri furnished a Russian explanation. Botvinnik indicated willingness to talk. Knowing, at that time, no Russian, I simply put names to him, in a tone that invited comment. "Capablanca?" Botvinnik talked; Missouri wrote. "Lasker?" Botvinnik talked; Missouri wrote. And so, through Alekhine, Euwe, Reshevsky and all the rest, culminating in "Botvinnik?" To that, a smile and a smooth-sounding torrent.

Missouri got it all down, made what I trusted to be a true copy, and I put his manuscript on the train. The resultant script was a great success. Tass paid me double for that interview. They informed me that my interview had been published throughout the Soviet Union "from Minsk to Vladivostok, from the frozen wastes of Murmansk to the golden sands of Samarkand." But to this day I don't know what I sent them. I claim that at that point I achieved the acme of journalism. This story, too, has a small sequel. When, at the end of 1949, I went to Moscow, to cover some chess for the *Manchester Guardian*, I very soon met Botvinnik; seeing me, he shouted "Tass!" Some chess players never forget.

After the death of Alekhine, who, after some disgusting literary collaboration with the Nazis, finally choked himself on a piece of Spanish bull, the way was almost clear for Botvinnik, who, in 1948, won a special World Championship Tournament, defeating, among others, the only player I thought to be better, Sammy Reshevsky of America—a child prodigy of 1920, who has remained prodigious. Since then, sets of tournaments have provided Botvinnik with challengers: Bronstein, who drew the challenge match, leaving the title where it stood; then Smyslov, also drawing the challenge match; then Smyslov again, winning; then Smyslov losing the return—and so on, via Tal, Petrosian, Spassky, into contemporary history.

When I visited Moscow, in 1949, I found that Botvinnik was treated, to all intents and purposes, as if he were a Commissar. He was among the panel of speakers when high officials of the Sports Committee (a subcommittee of the Soviet Praesidium) made their pronouncements. I had the satisfaction of hearing him quote (unacknowledged) my published description of Moscow as "the Capital of Chess." I found him to be quite fluent in English, French and German (one can learn a lot in fourteen years); also polite and tolerably friendly; but with a high diplomatic disinclination to commit himself to any clear statement on anything—very *parteigenossen*. Smyslov, on the other hand, is geniality itself, to say nothing of genius. He has studied languages (his English is good) and physics (perhaps because Botvinnik is a successful engineer) and opera singing. The Russians say that he is a good opera singer for a chess player. But let me add that one can be a very good singer without qualifying to sing inside (or even outside) the Bolshoi.

It may be of interest to observe that the great chess players usually have something else. Lasker, whom I only met when he was very old, but who preserved great strength to the end, said that an educated mind was necessary if one were to preserve one's powers. Capablanca was educated at Columbia and was a fair writer. The Cuban Government subsidised him by appointing him "Ambassador Extraordinary and Plenipotentiary General of the Republic of Cuba to the World at Large." He had a better conceit of himself than had Alekhine, but was a much nicer and much better-liked man. Alekhine was qualified as a lawyer and had a powerful intellect. He was the only man I ever met who was arrogant without being conceited. What do I mean by arrogant? He treated inferiors as if they were inferiors—but he very rarely made Capablanca's mistake of taking his own powers for granted.

All three men, Lasker (who showed great promise in mathematical philosophy, in which he lectured at one time in Manchester), Capablanca the diplomat, and Alekhine (non-practising lawyer) made chess pay and made a living from it. Only World Champions could do this in their period. But Botvinnik and his East European challengers have lived under different conditions. They live in a system where there is no need for official professionalism, because the State and the trade unions co-operate to give to every potential champion, in any field, from the ice-hockey rink to the chessboard, every possible facility (all desirable leave for training as well as play) for fulfilment of their powers. Even in that system, however, there are, and always will be, tremendous psychological differences between champions. Smyslov bade fair to be the most popular title-holder since Capablanca. Unfortunately he did not retain the title long. Nor did the brilliant Tal (described by Botvinnik as a "positional genius") retain his health and powers sufficiently to enable his bright personality to illumine the chess throne. Of Botvinnik's successors, Petrosian and Spassky, let it be said only that they differ as Armenian from Muscovite—neither lacking in virtues; and neither colossal, bestriding the world, as did the members of the great group that I have described.

After all these—Fischer. But that is another story.

14 Assessment of Alekhine

Alekhine was the chess player's chess player, in the same way that Shelley was the poet's poet. More important than the question of his strength relative to his great predecessors is the degree to which he enriched the art and the science in which he achieved immortality. Nobody can judge whether Alekhine at his best was more or less greatly endowed with chess genius than were, at the height of their powers, Morphy, Zukertort, Steinitz, Lasker or Capablanca. Certainly there is nothing in the recorded chess of 150 years profounder than the depths of insight achieved by Alekhine in such a game as the thirty-fourth of his famous match with a Capablanca, who, though then not at his best, was still among the very greatest. To compare that performance with the great games of others is made difficult by differences of style. But what is certain is that Alekhine enriched the game more than his predecessors. That fact may be due precisely to those differences of style, may be due in some degree to a fault, as Romanticism may be due to a lack of the flair for perfection which is classical.

In Lasker, at times, and more definitely in Capablanca, there was a subtlety that made the game seem easy, an art that concealed art. Alekhine, on the other hand, seemed to play as if he were desperate to force his own ideas into the game. He seemed never to trust his opponent with equality. Therefore he crowded the board with genius. "Crowded" is the right word, for the additional reason that Alekhine aimed always at complexity, not at the exquisite simplifications for which Capablanca is famous. Both of these great players achieved, almost invariably, victory over masters as outstanding as Rubinstein, Nimzovitch and Bogoljubov. Capablanca seemed to win effortlessly. But the games which Alekhine won against these masters contain ideas so novel, so complex, and so ingenious as to amount to a creative contribution. In point are such ingenious Knight manoeuvres as are seen in the game against Grünfeld in 1923, echoed ten years later in one of the games of the first match with Bogoljubov. Very much in contrast is the kind of victory that Capablanca won over Bernstein at San Sebastian, or the Bishop manoeuvres that gave Capablanca his victory over Lasker.

Further, Alekhine was a greater contributor to modern chess theory than were his rivals, in the degree that he was more experimental. He seemed to take over neo-Romanticism and make it part of a perfect equipment. He could play all kinds of chess. Did Nimzovitch aim at *Zugzwang*? Then Alekhine, at Bled, showed him how it should be done, in a game that is not lacking in humour.

For the rest, what went with Alekhine's style was an enormous capacity for work. Mentally and physically he was equipped for extraordinary concentration. Even after years of excesses that power did not desert him, though there were lapses when he lost to men less well-endowed. At his best he was always working, even when the game was completely won. And that same capacity for work makes Alekhine's books and annotations much more valuable to any student of chess than the more fluent and polished writings of his predecessors. Most players improve by studying Capablanca; masters learn from Alekhine.

Critics have suggested that Alekhine's profound notes include much that he did not see at the table. I think I am a witness to the contrary. At Margate in 1938 I had the pleasure of watching his beautiful game against Böök. Immediately after the game, he demonstrated to his opponent, at a remarkable speed, a large number of possible lines of play, one of which included a very pretty Queen-sacrifice. That incident (when he was not at his best) makes me think that he had no need to invent lines of play for his annotations.

Perhaps we old players are *laudatores temporis acti*. Certainly, my good and experienced friend, Harry Golombek (who has been a judge at all recent World Championships) agrees with me that so far (unless Fischer achieves his full potential) there are no Capablancas, no Alekhines, no Laskers. It may be said in criticism of this view that world chess is now so strong—there are so many putative grandmasters—that it is impossible for any one man to bestride the chess world as did the old colossi. But this, I think, is a mistake due to the confusion between quality and quantity. Quantity (as Marx said) makes possible quality— but there are degrees of quality. Certainly at this moment there are (because of intense Russian productivity) more men within striking distance of the World Championship than there have ever been before. They cannot be contained in a tournament of twenty, or even forty, players. But when Alekhine, Capablanca and Lasker were in their prime, they won tournaments which included only the best, and all the best, players in the world; and those players (such as Rubinstein, Nimzovitch, Bogoljubov, Réti, Spielmann, Tartakover, Maroczy, Vidmar, to name pre-1950 celebrities) were, at their best, so strong, that any one of them could hold his own in the very strongest contemporary company.

Let it be conceded that the average, at the top level, is nowadays more even, and that consequently, to be outstanding is a status calling for great genius rather than abundant talent. Then it remains true that Capablanca and Alekhine were stars of the greatest light and that the skies of the pre-Fischer modern chess world have only revealed an immense galaxy of confusing degrees of brightness.

Does the modern organisation of chess make achievement more difficult? Before 1948, World Championships were claimed by and defended against individual aspirants with financial backing. The modern machinery, grinding out a challenger, from zonals, interzonals and candidate's tournament, may well constitute a greater strain on stamina than did the chess lives of the old champions. They were, in reality, professionals then, and the present grandmasters are in reality, all "vocationals" now. But the lives of the Iron Curtain professionals are far less anxious than were the lives of their predecessors. The present "tournament men" (being supported by trade unions and sports committees) come to their tournaments with no anxiety about wages, with no unhappy feeling that unless they win prizes they will starve;

indeed, with awareness that, given adequacy, they will have many future chances. But, owing to the sheer weakness of the flesh, it is more chancy to try nominate the challengers these days because the process of production is too long. That long process of production also guarantees (is this good?) that a top-line chess player must be physically in fine condition. The synthesis of *mens suprema in corpore supremo* is hard to achieve. Alekhine approached this synthesis.

The above note was written long before the advent of Fischer. One is tempted to speculate that, of all the Champions of the past, perhaps only Alekhine could command the powers that would challenge the young American.

NOTE ON RELATIVE MERITS

Was Alekhine better than Capablanca or vice versa? An impossible question, but I have asked it of experts.

That most objective of players, Sämisch, said: "*Capablanca war stärker, ohne Zweifel, denn Alekhine konnte nur durch Combinationen gewinnen.*" But that difference seems to be one of style. Surely the control implicit in the play of Capablanca, or Rubinstein, or Fischer, implies an apprehension of profound combinational changes; and surely the great combinations of Alekhine reveal as complete a grasp of the board as anyone has ever achieved.

Very interesting is Russian opinion. Keres, with hard experience of both opponents, told me: "It was impossible to win against Capablanca; against Alekhine it was impossible to play."

Botvinnik, whom I have had the privilege of interviewing for the press twice (at intervals of thirty-five years) is objective enough to be wary of assessments. His own record against an admittedly ageing Capablanca is impressive. But I think he never showed his promise so strikingly as when at Nottingham in 1936 he faced a fierce Alekhine attack, and, with no aid from midnight oil, found the best defence and forced a spectacular draw.

When I asked him about relative merits, he told me that Alekhine had described Capablanca as the greatest player who had ever lived. But that praise must be discounted by classification. I mean that it coheres with an ageing Capablanca's praise of Lasker, and Lasker's insistence on the supremacy of Steinitz.

Botvinnik, himself, is too scientific to attempt classifications of merit. He praised, without making comparisons. For example, he described Tal as "a positional genius"—a thought to compare with Sämisch's judgement on Alekhine.

When I asked Botvinnik how he thought a young Capablanca or a young Alekhine would have fared against the players of today, he made the interesting suggestion that a properly programmed computer would some day answer that. Botvinnik, let me add, believes in computers because he believes chess to be mathematical. I wonder how long it would take a computer, even with the aid of Botvinnik's ingenious algorithms, to assess Botvinnik, or reproduce any of his own fine chess performances.

To return to the original question, one point is to be remembered. The spectacle is more effective when the public sees and is dazzled—Alekhine's performances are wonderfully visible; Capablanca's are concealed art.

15 Assessment of Lasker

(Review of *Emanuel Lasker*, by J Hannak)

This is a book which will be of value to all chess players, and of particular interest to Jewish readers. From a somewhat sentimental presentation—garnished with painfully collected irrelevancies—there emerges a chiaroscuro of a fascinating German Jew. Some aspects of Lasker's life, foreshadowed by his early experiences in Berlin, bring to my mind the autobiography of *Wunderkind* Solomon Maimon. He went to study—and remained to play. Not for pleasure, be it added, and not without regret. Lasker carried through life, what the Polish *Wunderkind* possessed in measure, a Jewish combination of indolence, ambition and great intellectual sharpness; also that readiness, given incentive and stimulus, to plunge into profundities, problems and intellectual struggles. All Lasker's German and European culture never succeeded in concealing from one of his admirers that this was an Ilui manqué.

The book under review contains a collection of more than 100 of the great Master's games, with brief, too brief, annotations, quoted from reliable persons. Unfortunately, the author, and his excellent translator (Assiac of the *New Statesman*, good player and good writer), have allowed themselves to be misled by Reti's superficial pronouncement that "Lasker played the man rather than the board." If this pronouncement tells us anything, it tells us that Reti as a thinker is not even an "echo" of Reti as a player.

Reti foisted on the world the belief that Lasker "played the man." This is an extravagance based on a misunderstanding. Anyone who cares to play through that famous second game against Tarrasch (cited by Reti), with the Kt–Kt5 resource, will realise that Lasker was not trying to trap Tarrasch. He was making a foray for freedom, and would have felt compelled to do so against any opponent. Reti's psychological notes on the play amount, therefore, to journalism, which I have described elsewhere as the study of the irrelevant.

The truth of the matter may emerge from the following:

1 Lasker was terribly lazy. The authors of the book do not say this, but it is written clearly between the lines. (With more energy he would have been a great mathematician.) I have it from Amos Burn and Gunsberg and Mieses that, in his early tournaments, Lasker was in the habit of driving up to the hall in a barouche or droshky, in order to find himself with twenty moves to make in as little as five minutes. I have it from Levenfisch that he showed the same inertia when they gave him opportunities for mathematical research at Moscow. He was content to "throw out ideas."

2 He needed the incentive of difficulty. Then would be manifest his Jewish enthusiasm for an intellectual problem. In situations of difficulty he had a quite wonderful capacity for seeing long and rich lines of play beyond the immediate skirmish. I doubt whether any player has ever seen further along the perspectives of the board than Lasker did.

3 From this it follows that he thought in moves, and in combative processes, rather than in "positions" (as Tarrasch did). This explains his tendency to invite skirmishing and attacks against him. He could usually see the compensations latent in his own position and available after his opponent's pressure had achieved some local success. If he had a style (and this is doubtful in one so versatile) it is revealed in a desire for an unbalanced game; a different type of imbalance from that sought by Alekhine, and possibly a greater strain on playing power. To this must be added the fact that he was begrudging of preparatory moves that might lose tempo. This stylistic impatience caused rash moves, product of haste and laziness; whereafter he had to fight very hard.

For the rest, he frequently declared that chess was a struggle. (He wrote a book called *Kampf*.) In the battles that he fought he was conscious of the truth that there need not be "a best move."

The consequence is that Lasker played a type of chess that is difficult to describe. His vision was very great; Morphy Capablanca and Alekhine stand comparison. But no one ever saw further. Consequently he was always dissatisfied (as Alekhine often, but Capablanca never was) and frequently sought to unbalance the game because of the possibilities that he saw—the battle after the skirmish, the course of the war beyond the battle. I have mentioned that he was more interested in lines of play than in the assessments of position. That partly describes his difference from Tarrasch (the other element of difference being the margin between genius and great talent).

Further, being slow to effort, and in need of strong stimulus, Lasker often played superficially in the early game (he did not overvalue openings), and sometimes he begrudged a preparatory move that might lose tempo. So he frequently found himself fighting hard. Then his enormous combative powers would bring him victory, and some spectator might think that he had purposely lulled an opponent into a false sense of security. That theory has been condemned above. Chess players play against themselves, not against their opponents. Yet the legend has absurdly survived.

Of comparison with other players, it is hard to venture into any assessment against present-day masters. But it is worth mentioning that nothing of ultra-modernism is unLaskerean—or is, indeed, ultra-modern! When Lasker went to Moscow between the wars, he was getting old; but he more than held his own. He attributed to his general culture the fact that his chess powers did not completely abate. But there was in the nature of things, no possibility of the pre 1914–18 war Lasker meeting the post second war Botvinnik. Lasker, being a student of relativism (and Einstein writes a kindly foreword to this book), might have commented on this particular problem in simultaneity. My own view, for what it is worth, is that the best Botvinnik "could not have lived with" the best Lasker. From a human point of view it is still too early to compare their careers as unhappy Jews.

16 Quo vadis, piscator? (*c* 1962)

There are professors of physics who will spend time in convincing you that electrons move as waves. When you are thoroughly persuaded, they will then demonstrate equally clearly that you were really right when you thought of electrons as corpuscles. For a few minutes I am going to behave like one of those professors, moving from the first into the second phase. Having always preached that chess mastery, to be great, must be supported by considerable culture, I now take time off in order to ask myself whether, perhaps, Bobby Fischer is right in setting a course for the World Championship along the lines of chess, and nothing but chess, with deviations only into the pursuit of physical fitness and parlour games.

Among the grandmasters, and others, whose views were capably canvassed by Leonard Barden when the question arose, there seems to have been unanimity. "That boy," they said "would benefit from the education that he evidently lacks. Other World Champions have all been men of considerable culture. Without culture, Bobby is handicapped." When I listened to these utterances, I thought of what Emanuel Lasker had pronounced. "Culture," he used to say, "enables one to *preserve* one's chess powers." Can that, perhaps, be interpreted to mean this: when you are World Champion, or grandmaster, and are getting old, or in danger of getting stale, your intellectual reserves support you. True—and how Botvinnik would agree. But in the first fine careless rapture, in the strong movement that leads to the summit, may not those reserves be irrelevant? May not the accumulation of those reserves be a dissipation of functional energy? The question is cognate, perhaps, to the old one about good losing. It may be true (and I think it is) that the

148

greatest players are not bad losers; that Dr Burger (the American chess coach) is wrong in asking for ferocity in his pupils. But the form of consolation of the good loser may be wrong. If the player says to himself: "I must preserve my game against that kind of fault. So I have learnt something"—well and good. But suppose he says to himself: "After all, I can always stay at home in the evenings and write a good book. I can always put in an effort to becoming Attorney-General, or professor of mathematics, or invent a new kind of rocket, or go to the Moon." If he says something on those lines, he is clearly departing from the strict standards of specialisation that have developed in the modern world. The serious questions then arise: is this escapism? is he weakening?

The present Bobby Fischer view—chess and chess only—is one that I heard expressed and saw practised in the years 1929–34. I am referring to the case of that strange but excellent British champion, Sultan Khan (see the note at the end of this chapter). He was, in those days, a totally ignorant man, who, even when he learnt some English, never seemed to acquire any general ideas. He was a sort of vassal in the retinue of the late Sir Umar Hayat Khan Tiwana, a Nawab from the Punjab, who was aide-de-camp to King George V. Sir Umar brought Sultan to England in order to have him play chess; and he made him play chess, and do nothing else except play chess. Sir Umar (who had achieved excellence in pig-sticking and diplomacy) said, more than once, in my hearing: "A runner becomes a better runner by running. A hunter becomes a better hunter by hunting. A chess player becomes a better chess player by playing chess."

Without comment on the analogies, let me say only that in Sultan's case the procedure was profitable. Having won the British Championship by accident in 1929, he held it in subsequent years by sheer merit. By the time he left England—I think it was in 1934—he was very much stronger than he had been on arrival. Let me add that his age, when he arrived, seemed to be the early twenties. He never learnt anything while here—except the basic rudiments of vocabulary, with the names of opponents and chess friends. I do not call him a moron, but I never observed any intelligence in him above the most elementary common sense. I think that Stefan Zweig was probably describing him—and doing so tolerably well—in his picture of the Balkan chess prodigy, in that brilliant story *The Royal Game*.

Do not let us, then, dogmatise about the need for culture. Highly specialised prodigies have survived in other fields and continued prodigious. Admittedly not many. But I can think of one brilliant mathematician who has never at any time had any important thought outside mathematics. At Cambridge, he "sported his oak" against the world, and remained involved in his particular geometries, which might, or might not, be relevant to reality.

In chess, instances are hard to isolate. The great prodigy Reshevsky, and several Russian youths of promise, were all, at some time, given a good general education, and enjoyed it, and thereafter maintained interest in other topics. It is significant that Reshevsky, playing very little chess in his teens and twenties, remained strong enough to extend all the great Russians, and quite recently, to hold our hero, Bobby Fischer. I have also met uneducated chess masters, who were regretful of their lack of education. Most of them did something about it. Nor, in those days, can Fischer supply what the scientists call a "pure case." He lives, after all, in a world of newspapers and interviews and wireless and television, and cannot, therefore, go uninformed. He absorbs, *malgré lui*. But, so far as it is possible within that framework, he lives at the moment for chess only. What will be the effect, on his chess, of that isolated dedication?

Fischer, If I may inoffensively say so, did not sound to me (when I heard him) to be moronic. His views on men and things seemed immature and poor, contrasting wonderfully with the heavy maturity of his chess analysis. But he was sharp. A young Jew from Brooklyn, he has the vigour and liveliness of his group; and, if I may use a technical term, *chutzpah*. I would observe that I saw several young Jews from the Central Europe of between the wars, who were chess masters before they had any education, and who, now, are men of considerable culture. (The great Salo Flohr will not mind my saying he was one of these.) In some cases they suffered staleness at times through excessive chess. Would other interests have helped or hindered them? I don't know. But a conclusion cannot be drawn from their vicissitudes, because the history of the 1930s, and the supervening war, made those chess careers harder to judge than are the careers of the players of today.

There are other points, I think, that may be overlooked and that deserve mention. The chess player who reads chess, and talks chess, and mixes with chess masters, is *per accidens*, acquiring a measure of education. Among other things one learns languages. But, more specifically, one cannot analyse a game in the company of a Keres, a Gligoric, a Szabo or a Flohr, or any of a thousand others, without acquiring a certain mental discipline, operating beyond the specific chess context. In the same way, a musician cannot live among musicians without learning more than music.

Chess, at the highest level, is spoken of, and written about, in the discursive terms of an educated vocabulary. Chess, therefore, can teach a person more than chess.

Secondly, when Fischer said to Barden that you can be intelligent without getting a university education, he was right, and he was showing intelligence. Certainly Fischer did not at that moment appreciate the value of the broadening, the enrichment, of the mind that almost inevitably accompanies a few years of study among the students and teachers of the academic. But he will teach himself a good deal in his travels and in his reactions to experience. The "university of life" will not be for him—as it has been for many—something of an industrial school, or a borstal institution.

If I am right in thinking that chess is usually a manifestation of a general factor of intelligence, then he has it in him to educate himself, or to show himself the need for other learning. Among adolescents, I remember the late Gordon Crown emerging from chess into intellect. He, too, had a phenomenal memory, developed by his intense interest in the game. But he grew beyond it. His chess genius was not that of Fischer, but the comparison is useful. Fischer has a prodigious memory, and it is to be conjectured that if, and when, anything in life or letters, or the world of science, intrigues him, the task of absorbing knowledge will be easy, and his capacity for imaginative construction may harness that knowledge to great effect.

If I may mention another name, highly respected by European players, the Canadian, Yanofsky, was at one time totally immersed in chess; he later emerged to take high Honours in Law at Oxford University. Nor did academic success weaken his great chess powers.

Of the immature Fischer who has been said to regard Emanuel Lasker, with benevolent contempt, as a weak player, will he not, in the atmosphere of the chess world, acquire thoughts that will, at least, connect him with Lasker's wider thinking about chess and life? As his chess wisdom increases, unfolding the conceptions of science and art that are latent in the self-conscious thought of chess players, he may or may not decide that Lasker was a good player; but he must inevitably learn, I think, some appreciation of the achievements and values beyond chess that men like Lasker expounded in their lives. His future is then a fascinating object-lesson in education. On the chess side, will a player of his strength, at a level where improvements are so slight and so hard to achieve, be helped or hindered in his progress, by the lack of cultural maturity? At Bled, and subsequently, it has appeared that his strength has waxed, not waned. Adolescence did not wither him, nor staleness mar his variety. At Bled it will be remembered, Alekhine showed increase of strength. That was an older, educated, mind. Whether Fischer will achieve such maturity, we can only speculate; and wait. If he goes for some years, devoting himself to chess only, will his improvement—if it takes place—be limited to chess. Certainly his well-wishers, who are many, will not only be interested in the success of his method as a way to world-mastery. They will also watch, with fascination, the possible emergence, here, unforced, of those mature thinking powers, and that general grasp of ideas and of values, which, however acquired, are the permanent hallmarks of true culture.

NOTE ON SULTAN KHAN

When I say that Sultan won the British Championship by accident, I have in mind some strange occurrences. Having lost in the first round to Reverend Hammond, a brilliant militant, he proceeded to gain compensating gifts from providence. *Inter alia,* players as strong as R P Michell and J A J Drewitt left pieces *en prise* to him. Winter allowed him to snatch a stalemate. Others, including myself, were handicapped by not knowing how to ask for a draw in Urdu. (The interpreter understood no European language—not even if one shouted.)

The theory was mooted that the man exuded some strange oriental power of an hypnotic type. This thought was supported by no less than Communist Winter, who said: "It is remarkable that the only person to beat him was a clergyman of the Established Church."

When I reported this to Hammond, that monumental man roared with laughter and shouted: "Yes, there's a lot to be said for God and the Angels." He laughed even more heartily when I observed that they had helped Hammond in his (accidental, of course) win against me.

Let it only be added that in subsequent British Championships the forces of Islam seem to have taken over, because Sultan was all but impregnable. He played a non-committal, evidently subtle, kind of chess, resembling the play with which the Armenian Petrosian was to win the World Championship. *Ex oriente lux.*

17 Quo vadis, piscator? (1972)

(from the *Daily Telegraph*, 5 August 1972)

FISCHER AND THE UNHAPPINESSES OF CHESS

They speak of the loneliness of the long-distance runner. His deprivation is surely less than that of the protagonist in the drama of self-conquest which is a chess career.

An athlete who thinks about his defeats will be unhappy But no athletic performance can possess, can totally occupy, the mind in the way that a lost game of chess does; as the loser follows paths, through the dimensions of time, of all the variations that might have been.

The dedicated chess player is constantly deafened by the intolerable noise of unheard melodies. Yet he need not allow himself to manifest melancholy or hysteria. The dedicated player need not be a bad loser, a hater of successful opponents. Indeed, the finest players tend to generosity over the board and in the analysis room. A generous objectivity pervades, for example, Bobby Fischer's book of his memorable games.

But the chess careerist is condemned to a struggle; against unhappinesses in defeat, and against all the anxieties of effort. These emotions of the intellect are impossible to share. Therefore it behoves him to have other mental resources, even if their enjoyment consumes time that could be devoted to chess study. Also he must try to achieve the kind of escape into life which is available to those who are fortunate in their families and their friends.

Chess is a good mistress but a bad master. When Fischer decided, some fifteen years ago, to postpone all formal education until he had won the world championship, he caused much speculation among his admirers. Had not the great Lasker said that culture enables one to preserve one's chess powers? Does that imply that culture is useful in the process of development of those powers? Fischer thought not.

"You can be intelligent," he pronounced, "without getting a university education." That was a percept. Yet Bobby was failing to see, on "the chequer board of nights and days," as many moves ahead as he can see in the course of the game.

He was failing to anticipate the unhappinesses of chess. He was failing, also, to see the pattern of life that chess success would develop in the context of his personality—his vulnerable personality. A life of hotel rooms and lonely journeys; a life embittered by the trivial hostilities of the trivial; the life of a dragon in a pool, a prey to newts.

I think that the boy who won that immortal game against Donald Byrne so long ago could not have anticipated his future self: displaying at Curaçao, at Sousse, and elsewhere that excessive reaction to the annoying or the unfair which superficial diagnosticians label persecution mania.

The Fischer syndrome is not pathological. Much is explicable by the fact that there *are* newts who do annoy dragons. Much is explicable as showmanship by way of compensation for unsatisfied emotions. Given better environment, given the background of relaxed living enjoyed by the Soviet giants, he would cease to feel the need for permanent defensive aggression. As it is now, his life is much less confident than his chess.

What, then, has he gained by his dedication? Has he become, by way of reward, the greatest player in the history of the game? That claim would be difficult to substantiate.

Nominations are unnecessary. Let me suggest that, just as on the board there can at some moment be more than one best move, so, in the history of chess, there is more than one best player. Great players are incommensurable.

To mention the colossi who bestrode the chess world between the wars, who could say that the classical chess, the always well-balanced chess, of Capablanca or Rubinstein was superior to, or inferior to, the disciplined imbalance of Alekhine, as that ferocious intellect crowded the board with ideas?

In style, Fischer is with Capablanca and Rubinstein. The journalist chess master Reti said of Capablanca (I paraphrase) that he brought an American efficiency and economy into the game. That economy, that efficiency, and the Capablanca clarity, make the hallmark of Fischer. But he does not crowd the board with ideas, as Alekhine did, or as Bronstein and, more effectively, Mikhael Tal have sought to do.

If time machines were available, would Fischer beat the best Morphy, the best Capablanca, the best Lasker or Alekhine? Would Mohammed Ali, one may ask, have defeated Jack Dempsey?

Relative assessments are made more difficult by the fact that, although the quantity of master chess has increased immeasurably, the standard at the highest level does not seem to have risen. In playing through the games of the victors of the modern tournaments, one does not sense an impressive dominance. It is significant that world champions do not nowadays win tournaments.

In match chess, since Lasker and Capablanca totally destroyed strong opponents like Marshall and Janowsky, no one has presented such an appearance of invincibility until Fischer played Taimanov and Larsen. But the cognoscenti did not find those matches convincing. Then Petrosian demonstrated that Fischer can be made to fight. Perhaps it was then that Fischer put himself into the class of the great.

Fischer combines three attributes—the massive memory of Rubinstein, which, as in Rubinstein's case, enhances judgement but does not inhibit originality: the clarity and easy style of Capablanca; and Alekhine's prodigious capacity for work, over the board and away from it.

Is Fischer better than Spassky? Spassky's previous record against Fischer is good but was achieved a long time ago. Spassky is a great fighter, but I think that he lacks Fischer's comprehensive equipment. I shall probably regard Fischer as better than Spassky, even if Fischer fails to win the world title. The circumstances are such that nowadays one cannot be sure that the better man will win.

And if he wins? Will he have wasted his life? The mediaevals disapproved of chess because it did not lead, in their opinions, to the betterment of the world. We, who value science for its own sake, irrespectively of utility, value chess as well. On the chessboard Bobby Fischer has already satisfied the demand of the King of Brobdingnag by making two blades of grass grow where only one grew before.

And if some day he gives up chess, and undertakes some other activity, will he be able to harness his enormous memory, his extraordinary powers of concentration, to that other task?

I permit myself to suggest that psychology does not work so easily as to enable a positive answer. Taking a line through Lasker, the mathematician, and through Botvinnik, the high-class engineer, one feels that no great chess player will ever quite achieve outside chess his excellence over the board. But let Fischer try. In any event, the chess world (and this includes the Russian chess world) will wish him well on his journey.

18 What Achilles saw
among women

The recent emergence from spectacular Georgia of a spectacular female player conjures to my mind many speculations and many memories, some of which go back to the days when I would have had to call this excursus "Chess among Ladies."

Let me speak first of Britain, which, remarkably, is pioneer. When I first discovered the British Chess Federation, in 1924, lady chess players in a ladies' championship were not new. Indeed most of them were very old, and had competed before 1914. They belonged to a world in which blue-stockings were not flesh-coloured. The youngest among them were, I think, the first Mrs Stevenson and Mrs R P Michell, kindly women both. Miss Price, the strongest of them, was long past her first youth. She, in her sixties and very formidable in appearance, was not among the senior members. She was to retain the championship even in her seventies. Their clothing was for the most part Victorian, and the overall appearance suggestive of Mme Tussaud's. I hasten to add that all were nice ladies. It was their chess that belonged to the Chamber of Horrors. But they took it very seriously. Many years later one of them confided to me that it was the accepted thing to weep a little on the board at the moment of resignation. Without dogmatism I will add that I doubt whether this happens today, but I deeply sympathise.

As I have now arrived at "anecdotage" let me recall one incident before I dismiss these gentle shades into the limbo. There was one Miss Abraham of Herne Bay, a little Dresden China dove with an appealing wispiness as to the hair, and her chess was wispier. But no one saw her really flutter until a day at Ramsgate in 1929. In the first round of the British Championship (my first game in British Championship chess) I was first to finish with quite a nice win over the favourite, Willy Winter. This was too much for a Kibitzer, who ran round to Miss Abraham, at that moment two pieces down, and shouted in her ear: "Your son has just won a wonderful game." I describe it as sheer coincidence that she never spoke to me after that.

But by 1929 there was a harbinger. The lamented, refined and charming Vera Menchik, later Mrs Stevenson, constituted the cloud somewhat bigger than a man's hand. Settling in England, this talented player found splendid teachers at Hastings, in the late J A J Drewitt (a retired philosophy don) and Geza Maroczy, and profited much from their teaching.

Vera's chess was, up to a point, masterly. She was, however, deficient in imagination. I mention this because I have observed this defect in many women chess players, and in many women engaged in the arts and sciences. In contradiction of the conventional platitude, I have found women to be logical, good arithmeticians at the bridge table, sound scholars in many fields of scholarship, but almost completely lacking in creative imagination, and in that grade of it which they call intuition. Intuition I have found among males. Vera, however, had clarity, and played so well that I'll venture this proposition: unless this Georgian girl (whose play against the great is yet to be seen) produces something to rebut me, then Vera was, by a long way, the strongest woman chess player the world has seen. At the first post-war Women's Championship at Moscow, in 1949, Salo Flohr and Levenfisch agreed cordially with this appraisal.

Of Vera s niceness I am witness. At Canterbury in 1930 she was doing very well—beating Yates and Winter and Seitz and drawing with Sir George Thomas. About the fifth round she had White against me and (as Yates had predicted) lost quickly to my Black counter-attack. She rushed away from the board, with a suggestion of tears, and upset, but she quickly returned, apologised to me for what she called her rudeness, and carefully analysed the game with me. For that I never ceased to admire her as a magnanimous woman. I add for the record that her limitations were further exposed the next day when she met my Liverpool comrade-in-arms, Spencer. He played 1 P–K4 and in answer to 1 ..., P–K3 essayed 2 B–Kt5.

He explained to me that whatever square she drove it to would be a better one. That's strategy. Vera lost three-quarters of an hour on her clock (we were playing twenty an hour) and the game in less than twenty moves.

Vera, not being British, never played in the British Ladies' Championship. But youth was at last appearing. First, an Indian woman, Fatima, from the entourage of Sir Umar Hayat Khan's wives. (He was the patron of Sultan Khan, champion in 1929, 1930, and 1933.) Fatima, in one of those years—I think 1933—ate up the ladies. How good she was I don't know. Her chess meat was not very tough.

In the mid-1930s came two charming schoolgirls, happily still with us, Elaine Saunders, now Mrs Pritchard, and Rowena Dew, now Mrs Bruce. They were receiving odds of half a century from the field. More spectacular at that time, in the visual sense, was a Premier Reserves German woman, a young, slim, huskily-spoken specimen of the Marlene Dietrich type, named Sonja Graf. Her play was wild, but interesting. Her height of achievement was a win at Nottingham, against the redoubtable Ernst Klein. Even allowing for the nemesis that follows chess contempt (as in the case of Tarrasch–Yates at Hamburg) I still find it very difficult to believe that the event actually happened. The lady subsequently married an American, and died lamentably young.

To revert to the British Ladies, they were joined in the late 1930s by a very able pupil of Miss Menchik, the Yorkshire clarinettist Eileen Tranmer; a woman whose chess I have seen to express some admirable qualities of mind and character. I had the privilege of watching her in Moscow in 1949–50, when, handicapped by influenza of a particularly virulent kind—what the Russians call "grippe"—she won some five or six consecutive games, to finish in the prize list of the new official Women's World Championship. There had been two championships before, which Vera had won easily. Since Vera had unhappily perished in the Blitz, they looked at Moscow for her successor. Suffice it to say that they found a winner (Rudenko) but not in Vera's class. That tournament was screamingly funny. Particularly funny was the spectacle of Russians queuing up in forty degrees of frost in order to pay money to be spectators of bad chess.

And how they spectated! They taught me the Russian word for spectator—*bolelchik* (a sufferer)—and they suffered.

As for me, I have told elsewhere how, sitting in the front row, I fell asleep once and dreamt that I was an Eastern potentate on holiday at Monte Carlo, distracted by the knowledge that the harem had escaped to the gaming tables. When I woke up I found that they *were* playing roulette. Later I escaped from the hall, from time to time, and, wandering through the immense building where the women played, I discovered, in another wing, the Championship of the Red Army in progress. That was a healthy sight. Not so the women.

Even before the influenza epidemic started the whole tournament, with the exception of Yorkshire's Tranmer, was in a state of hysterical neurasthenia; including an aged Polish doctor, and an Italian nurse, and the Russian women whom one would have thought too plain for hypersensitivity. (The lady umpires, I suggested to a photographer, would have made a more satisfactory contingent; he cordially agreed.) At an early stage, war was narrowly averted when the American Gisella Gresser, in an opening round, defeated Rudenko. As Gisella went on to lose a lot of games the incident was forgotten. But high diplomacy was very nearly involved later when, after Gresser and polyglot May Karff, had made poor scores, a character named Kotov wrote in the Moscow Bolshevik that this illustrated the *degradazia* of American chess. *Degradazia* (Latin *de-gradu*) means decline; it does not mean degradation. But the Russian censors, as ignorant a gang as could be assembled, insisted on Degradation going through as the translation. That was the only time I ever saw that great journalist Henry Shapero rattled.

For my part, I did a little experiment in the possibilities of exacerbation. Having spent half an hour in a chemist's shop, laboriously discovering that the Russian word for glycerine is *glitzyerin* and that they had none, I suggested later to an interpreter that evidently the Russians were using all their glycerine for bomb-making. I rather enjoyed the reaction: but I was too kind-hearted not to reveal to her my later discovery that the Russians were selling glycerine, not in chemists, but in cosmetic shops. But that's how wars are made.

F

Of the Russian attitude to the women chess players, let me tell another anecdote. I wrote a Russian article, with the aid of my interpreter, on Moscow chess. I called it "The Capital of Chess" (Botvinnik borrowed this phrase). I started by saying that chess players approach Moscow as Mohammedan pilgrims approach Mecca. I described the merits of their organisation; and I added a paragraph on women. My theme song was "logic without imagination." (Intuition is done by men.) Women, I said, were ballerinas, not choreographers, actresses not dramatists, sitters not painters, characters in novels rather than creative novelists—and, as for chess, not even Queens on the Russian chessboard, where the corresponding piece is the *Vizier*. (*Firze*, early English *Fers*, before the first Elizabeth, or other female monarch, inspired the word Queen.)

Henry Shapero told me that they'd leave out the pilgrim, that's religion, and they'd leave out the women, that's against the Marxist, Leninist, Stalinist egalitarian line. He was only half right. They left in the pilgrim, but they left out the women. I went, with a show of fury, to the editor, Alatortzeff, a charming man, who could run a school for diplomats. He gave me 248 roubles for the article, and apologised for the omission of my words by saying that he had to make room for my photograph.

Since 1949 there have been several women's tournaments. Russian women have been borrowing the title from each other at the end of bouts of moderate chess. And now Goprandashvili is dominant. Rumour has it that the Georgian girl is someone for the men to play with—at chess I mean.

In Britain, three women—Mrs Bruce, Mrs Pritchard and Miss Tranmer—now represent chess at a respectable level; but, as they would all admit, below the upper half of the British Championship proper. This list has been strengthened lately by the advent of Mrs Hartston, from Czechoslovakia, married to a strong British player. Results are yet to be seen from the growing practice among good players of marrying lady novices and training them for the women's event. One thing is certain, in Britain, at least, women's chess has become much more "spectatable," and I'm not only speaking of the chess.

By way of appendix, let me add some good chess by Vera Menchik against some of the strongest tournament players of the period.

R P Michell   V Menchik
        (played 1931)

1	P–Q4	Kt–KB3
2	P–QB4	P–K3
3	Kt–QB3	P–Q4
4	B–Kt5	QKt–Q2
5	P–K3	P–B3
6	Kt–B3	Q–R4 (Cambridge Springs)
7	Kt–Q2	B–Kt5
8	Q–B2	0–0
9	B–K2	P–K4 (introducing a good idea)
10	P×KP	Kt–K5!
11	KKt×Kt	P×Kt
12	B–B4	Kt×P
13	R–QB1	Kt–Q6 ch
14	B×Kt	P×B
15	Q×P	B–KB4
16	Q–Q1 (P–K4 is met by B×P)	
16	...,	Q×P
17	0–0	Q×BP

Black, playing accurately, won the game through her Q side pawns.

In Diagram 18.1 (2rr2k1, 5ppp, 16, p2pR2P, 1b1B1P2, 1P4P1, 1K5R.) she is seen finishing, very efficiently, a well-played game against Sultan Khan.

The next position (8, 4RK1k, r4P2, 40) is one of theoretical importance, which Miss Menchik lost. But its reproduction here is no slur on her memory. For few have come so close to drawing with Capablanca.

18.1
V Menchik
Black (9)

Sultan Khan
White (8)

31	...	R–Kt1
32	K–R1	R–Kt5
33	KR–K1	B–K3
34	R–K5	P–R6
35	P–QKt3	(If P×P, 35 ... R–R1)
		(If R–R5, 35 ... R×P)
35	...	R×P
36	B–B4	R–Kt7
37	B×B	P×B
38	R–QR5	P–Q6
39	R×RP	P–Q7
40	R–Q1	R–B7
41	resigns	

18.2
Miss Menchik
(1930)
Black (2)

Capablanca
White (3)

56	R–Q7?	R–R1
57	R–K7	R–R3?

(At this point 57 R–QKt1 draws)

58	K–B8 ch	K–Kt3
59	P–B7	R–R1 ch
60	R–K8	R–R2

61	R–K6 ch	K–R2
62	R–K1	R–R1 ch
63	K–K7	R–R2 ch
64	K–B6	resigns

For a final postscript, here is Goprandashvili, conducting a heavy attack continuously and ineluctably.

GOPRANDASHVILI—KINNMARK (GOTEBURG 1971)

WHITE		BLACK
1	P–K4	P–QB4
2	Kt–KB3	P–K3
3	P–Q4	P × P
4	Kt × P	P–QR3
5	B–Q3	Kt–QB3
6	Kt × Kt	KtP × Kt
7	0–0	P–Q4
8	P–QB4	

A move played later by Bobby Fischer.

8	...	Kt–B3
9	Kt–B3	B–K2
10	BP × P	BP × P
11	P × P	P × P
12	B–K3	

Fischer played 12 Q–R4 ch, Q–Q2; 13 R–K1. But the text is quite good.

12	...	0–0
13	B–Q4	P–KR3
14	R–B1	R–Kt1
15	P–QR3	P–QR4
16	R–K1	B–Q3
17	P–R3	B–K3
18	Q–B3	Kt–K1

Better seems 18 ... R–K1. 18 ... R × P is met by Kt–Kt5 winning the exchange. White has a much freer game at this stage.

| 19 | Kt–Kt5 | |

Initiating vigorous and interesting play.

| 19 | ... | B–K2 |
| 20 | Kt–R7 | R–Kt2 |

Perhaps R–R1 is better, but the White attack is promising even without the gain of a pawn.

| 21 | Kt–B6 | Q–Q2 |

He wishes to protect the Bishop at e6.

22	Kt × P	R–B2
23	Kt–Kt3	Q–R5
24	R × R	Kt × R
25	R–QB1	

Good: although I like B × P.

25	...	B–Q3
26	B–QB5	B × B
27	R × B	Kt–R1
28	B–B2	Kt–Kt3
29	Q–Q3	P–Kt3
30	Kt–Q4	Q–Q2
31	R–B6	R–Kt1
32	Q–Kt5	Q–Q1
33	Kt × B	P × Kt
34	R × P	Kt–B5
35	R × P ch	K–B2
36	Q–B5	R × P
37	Q–R7 ch	Resigns

The play from move 28 is impressive. This, if I may say so, is a man's game.

Part Four
TECHNIQUE AND BEYOND

19 Habits of mind and technique

Once one has learnt the moves and the rules, chess is (theoretically) all vision. The essential task is to see possibilities and consequences —as in argument; replies, and replies to replies, for a long way ahead, and over a wide range of possibility, along direct lines and branch lines and subordinate lines; and to select, in the light of that, the best move—if there is one—or a choice of evils.

But, in fact, that task is too hard. A very great number of positions are opaque rather than translucent. Whether the board is packed or empty is not the criterion. Some positions just cannot be exhaustively analysed. Then the experienced player copes with these positions by thought, as in strategy, when he considers the shape of the position that he is aiming at or hoping to preserve; the eventual control of space, the probable end-game position. In a word, strategy guides him as to what to do when he has nothing to do, or cannot see what to do.

At a different level, there develop certain habits of mind which economise mental effort—for example, in his valuation of the pieces—so that the ordinary player does not entertain seriously the possibility of giving a Queen for a smaller piece, or putting a piece *en prise*, etc. Of course, good players see through the values of their pieces to their functions—and the game is full of sacrifices, the giving of pieces for the sake of an attacking line or an attacking position, etc. Nevertheless, the primary values, while constituting a guide and an economy, do so condition the minds of even the best players, that they miss, in consequence, quite immediate things. They can miss, even at short range, any possibility of a slightly unusual form—an idea however uncomplex. Thus here is a position from a game between Keres, that hero of the Soviet chess world, and Boleslavsky, an adequate specimen

169

of grandmaster. (Diagram 19.1:   2r2k2, 1r2ktpp1, pp1Rp2p, 4P3, PPPKt4, 1K4P1, 7P, 3R4.)

19.1
Boleslavsky
Black (10)

Keres
White (10)

White stands better, is, indeed, dominant. But if Boleslavsky had played K–K1, Keres' task of exploitation would have been very difficult indeed. In fact the position is typical of an attack which forces the resources of the defence up to adequacy. However, Boleslavsky obligingly played 1   ... R (from Kt2) to B2, completely overlooking White s KtKt5; overlooking, that is, the fact that this threatens mate. May I add that a player who has had a long hard defence to play finds it easy to relax and make mistakes when he has beaten off a lot of serious threats. I cite this position to illustrate habits of mind; in this case a valuation which at a critical moment prevented the player from realising that there was any imminent crisis.

But habits of mind have their advantages as well. In a sense the whole of chess is a habit of mind rather than a hobby. One learns chess best in youth—as one learns languages and musical instruments. One gets familiar with the ways of the board. There are many features of chess geometry which, being acquired, like grammar, save mental effort: e.g. the fact (and its demonstration) that two Knights with a King cannot force mate; methods of forcing mate with King, Bishop and Knight; the difficulty of winning with a Pawn advantage when one's Bishop is on squares of a different colour from one's opponent's Bishop; the nature of "opposition" by King and King; the subtler theory of "related squares." These methods and these difficulties are elementary examples of the chess equipment which one can call technique.

Such processes can be described as functions of the pieces. Some functions are so simple that, unless you know them, you cannot claim to know the basic powers of the pieces. Thus a player who cannot force mate with King and Rook can hardly claim that he knows the Rook move or the King move.

Less elementary (if the phrase be permitted) are the following diagrams.

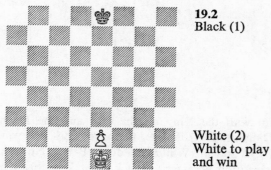

19.2
Black (1)

White (2)
White to play
and win

Technique of promotion

1	K–Q2	K–K2
2	K–K3	K–K3
3	K–K4	K–K2

(if 3 . . . K–Q3, 4 K–B5)

4	K–K5	K–K1
5	K–K6	K–Q1
6	P–K4	K–K1
8	P–K5	K–Q1
7	K–B7 wins	

How to queen pawns. Relatively easy is the ordinary "opposition play" and the method of achieving stalemate with King in front of opposing Pawn. More difficult is the technique of avoiding stalemate by preparatory King moves. Thus you have a King at K1, Pawn at K2 and the opponent's King at his K1. (Diagram 19.2: 4k3, 40, 4P3, 4K3.) Now the technician does not touch the Pawn for a long time. He rushes with his K via Q2 and K3 as far up the board as he can get. Then he moves the Pawn in order to make the other King give ground. This is one special instance of the wider principle of *Zugzwang*—winning by forcing the other player to move to his detriment (I have translated the expression "in *Zugzwang*" as "movebound.")

The matter is not to be oversimplified.

With King on the sixth rank the win is certain (Diagram 19.3).

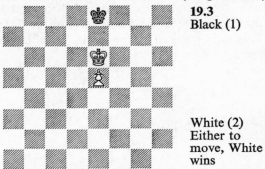

19.3
Black (1)

White (2)
Either to
move, White
wins

But with the King on the fifth and the Pawn on the fourth (Diagram 19.4), White, to move, does not win. Thus 1 K–Q5, K–Q2 and all White can do is P–K5. Now there is only one precaution necessary—Black must keep his King, at a critical moment, on the line of the Pawn. So after:

2	P–K5	K–K2
3	P–K6	the only move is K–K1, so that after
4	K–Q6	K–Q1
5	P–K7 ch	K–K1
6	K–K6	brings about stalemate

This is important learning.

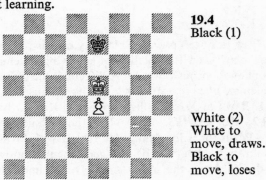

19.4
Black (1)

White (2)
White to
move, draws.
Black to
move, loses

But technical devices are not confined to the end-game position. At all stages there are features of the board which are syntactical. (The word "accidental" is dangerous.)

You have Pawns at QR2 and QKt2. The opponent has a Pawn at his QR4. You want to get your Knight's Pawn to QKt4. Simple vision can show you the difficulty; but the technician does not have to use his vision at all to play P–QKt3 before P–QR3. If one plays P–QR3 first then one is sabotaged by the opponent's P–QR5.

Again, the well-known danger of a Bishop sacrifice at KR7 against the castled King, followed by attack with Knight and Queen is technique, not brilliance. The method of gaining a move by exchange of Pawns (for what it is worth) is technique. In the middle game, placing of Bishops behind blocked Pawns is done by the technician, because experience teaches that it will come to life. In point, also, are the breaking up of Pawn chains; the sacrifice of Pawns so as to hold a square like K5 (Nimzovitch's great contribution to the theory of the French Defence). I would also mention the overprotection of Pawns when one has nothing else to do; and the old slogan: Put your Rook on line of Queen, no matter how many pieces intervene.

Again the order of moves in development is technique; the avoidance of pins, dangers of fork, etc. But technique is at its most learnable in the end-game. Here are some examples:

1 Your opponent has a Pawn on his QR7 and his Rook on his QR8. Your Rook is behind the Pawn at your QR8. Now he is threatening to move his Rook with check, queening thereafter. Where do you want your King to be? Well you'd like it to be at QKt2 or QB2. But it is not there. The alternative is very surprising at first sight. KKt2, or KR2, a long way away. It has to be on the second rank, so as to be able to capture the Rook if it checks. But it must not be on Q2, K2 or KB2, because the Rook would play across to its KR8. Then if R × P, R–R7 ch wins the Rook. That's a point worth knowing.

2 Another important point is the advantage of relatively un-committed Pawns. If your Pawns are unmoved, and your opponent's Pawns are committed, then, when it comes to King

manoeuvring you have a tempo in hand. Here is a position (set up some years ago by the Manchester expert Mr Joseph) to illustrate this: k7, 1kt3ppp, 8, p7, P7, 5B1P, 5PP1, 3K4.

Study by Joseph

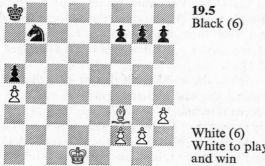

19.5
Black (6)

White (6)
White to play
and win

How does White gain a winning end-game? First B–K4, disturbing the KRP or KKtP. That being done, B–Q5 disturbing the KBP. Then K–K2 and when Black moves his King, B × Kt and a further King move. If now the Pawns were undisturbed it would be a draw. Because they are disturbed, White should win by careful opposition play. That is fine technique. But two things require to be said by way of warning.

First, technique is not enough—you cannot play the whole game without compromising your Pawns. If you are outplayed in the middle game, and you find your opponent's King at his K4 blockading your Pawn, his Pawn at Q5 blocked only by your King, and his wing Pawns able to lose a move, so as to put your *Zugzwang*, then don't put it down to technique. You've got what you should have avoided—a bad position.

Second, rules are impossible to state reliably. Thus two joined Pawns are better than two split Pawns; but there is one class of end-game position where this is not true. Let your Pawns be at KR6 and KKt7 inhibited by his King at his KB2; his Pawns are at his QR6 and QB6 and your King is at your QB2. Then he moves (P–R7) and wins; and if your King were at Kt1, his King move would win. Now suppose your King were at Kt1 and his Pawn at his QB5 and QR5, you would draw by playing K–Kt2 and K–Kt1, waiting for him to commit himself. A striking consequence of these features is the following: 1k6, 8, P1P5, 8, 5ppp, 8, 6K1, 8.

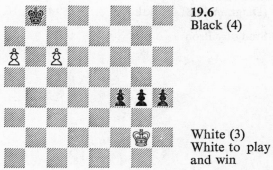

19.6
Black (4)

White (3)
White to play
and win

At first sight, it looks as if Black should win—indeed, if it were Black to move, Black would win by 1 ..., P–Kt6.

But White to move wins by 1   K–Kt1—only, therefore best! From Kt1 he can meet any pawn advance by opposing that Pawn with his King, e.g. 1   K–Kt1, P–Kt6; 2   K–Kt2. If 1 ... P–B6; 2   K–B2, etc.

In the art of losing moves, making the opponent move, Diagram 19.7 shows a neat device: (16, p4p2, p1p2k1p, 2P2P1P, 1PP2K2, 16.) 1 ... P–R5; 2   P×P, P–R4; leaving White to move and let the Black King in.

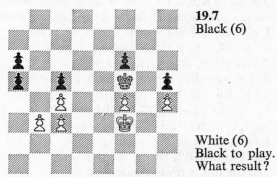

19.7
Black (6)

White (6)
Black to play.
What result?

The problem of losing a move acquires added interest when you learn that a Knight is incapable of losing a move.

On that theme here is a pretty endgame by that great composer Bron, which involves at least one of the devices that are included in technique, and in such a way as to transcend technique (Diagram 19.8: 4K1ktk, 7p, 8, 7P, 8, 4Kt3, 16.)

Study by Bron

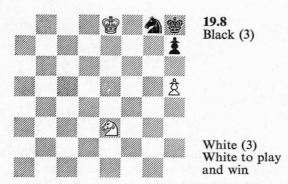

19.8
Black (3)

White (3)
White to play
and win

The problem is to win that Knight by *Zugzwang*. So we start by losing a move. 1   K–B7, Kt–R3 ch; 2   K–B8 (triangulation) and the Kt must return to Kt1; 3   Kt–Kt4 forces P–R3 (If 3 . . ., Kt–R3; 4   Kt–K5, wins). Now at this point I want to get my Knight to KKt6 when the White K is at B7 and the Black K is at KR2. If the K is at KR1 when I get there, it's no good, because he just moves to R2. As things are, I cannot (by Kt moves) bring that Kt to Kt6 at the right moment. Point of technique. A Knight cannot lose a move. But a King can. So what do I do? First, I take my Knight round to K8, in order to release my King: 4   K–B7, K–R2; 5   Kt–K3, K–R1; 6   Kt–Q5, K–R2; 7   Kt–B7, K–R1; 8   Kt–K8, KR2. That holds the Black Knight and King, while I take my King out for a further triangulation. 9   K–K6, K–R1; 10   K–Q6, K–R2; 11   K–Q7, K–R1; 12   K–K6, K–R2; 13   K–B7, K–R1. Now I've lost a move. So I take my Knight round the board again (Kt–B7, Kt–Q5, Kt–B4, Kt–Kt6) and when it arrives at KKt6, we find that the Black is at KR2. So the Black Knight has to move. I capture it and the rest is relatively easy technique.

This, surely, is the quintessence of technique, and its acme; too fine to be described as technical.

20 Endings—didactic and epicurean

(An edited version of a lecture to a meeting of The Chess End-Game Study Circle held on 30 December 1967 at The Times Hastings International Chess Congress.)

Let me tell you first how this topic came to be chosen. When John Roycroft approached me with flattering words, knowing full well that flattery will get you everywhere with me, it happened that I had been browsing in the back numbers of the old *Chess Amateur*. In the 1926 volume I found two thoughts, which I quote:

1 Chess is to be classed as a science rather than as an art ... but just as the philosopher evolves quite a poetry from mathematics and physics, so can the master-mind produce a thing of beauty in the game of chess
2 Problems are the poetry of chess, contrasted with its prose: or should we say the drama rather than the unwieldy epic. But like the modern play the problem tends to the presentation of climax only, a formal or thematic dynamic pattern to be appreciated aesthetically

Those two quotations do not exhaust thought—nor do I accept them completely. But when I tell you that they were written by an early teenager named Gerald Abrahams, who had just retired from problem composition in order to win some scholarships to a centre of chess, you will not blame me for making this my point of departure.

Forty-two years later I still regard chess as a science, and the composition of problems as an art; and that remains true whether the spectator requires to be immersed in the spirit of Dali or Picasso, or in the easier atmospheres of da Vinci or Rembrandt. But now I would restate any comparison of problems with poetry or drama. For the latter are nearer to life, and indeed science, than most chess problems are to chess. Chess problems, like much of music and ballet, are formal composition *sui generis*. Admittedly, the solver must have some grasp of the science of chess— but that assumption would only be relevant if the problemist were primarily concerned to test chess ability as such. Certainly, many of the early problems had that purpose—but it is long forgotten. The modern composer aims at producing an aesthetic effect. The solver, for his part, is not thinking quite like a chess-player—he is regrouping pieces in his mind, but over a very short range. As for the composer, he is creating a pattern, regardless of ease or difficulty. Tonight I distinguish between the game and the problem, treating the latter as the ballet rather than the drama. Between these two I place that most important *tertium quid*, the end-game study; and the question before the house is whether this is a manifestation of problem art or chess science or both.

Before I go further, let me illustrate what I apprehend the mental process to be in problem composition, and in the end-game as part of chess. I start with a problem (Diagram 20.1) that was composed by one of the greatest composers, A W Mongredien (1877–1954) who was also a fine chess-player. As a piece of play, this is quite meritorious. But Mongredien's values here are the forcing of a rearrangement of Black's pieces and the pretty set of moves which brings this about. All White's moves constitute a triangulation on three squares. And there's a prettiness, and a small intellectual pleasure, in triangulation (a *da capo* effect).

Many very good problems are much remoter than Mongredien's from practical chess. They involve such beauties as the neat change of mates, in the variations of the solution, from those latent but unachieved in the "set play." In contrast, the end-game composer is concerned with practical processes of winning a game or saving a game. (How different from this composer's purpose in the often very artistic help-mate or self-mate.) The examples in Diagrams 20.2 and 20.3 show the kind of affinity that

Problem by Mongredien

20.1
Black (11)

White (8)

Mate in 5.

1	Q–Kt2	B–R5
2	Q–R2	Q–K1
3	Q–R1	B–B3
4	Q–Kt2 and there is no defence	

A A Troitzky (*Novoye Vremya* 1895)

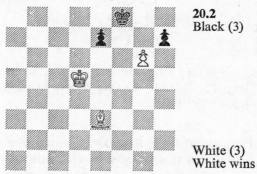

20.2
Black (3)

White (3)
White wins

1	B–R6 ch	K–Kt1
2	P–Kt7	K–B2
3	P=Q ch	K×Q
4	K–K6	K–R1
5	K–B7	P moves
6	B–Kt7	mate

If 2 . . . P–K4; 3 K–K6, P–K5; 4 K–B6 wins.
If 2 . . . P–K3 ch; 3 K–Q6, K–B2; 4 K–K5 wins.
N.B. The King must not capture the KP.

can exist between the game and the composed study, though I find it difficult to agree with Reinfeld that the Troitzky study actually assisted Tarrasch in discovering the winning method from position 3.

Vienna 1922

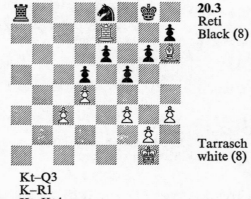

20.3
Reti
Black (8)

Tarrasch
white (8)

34	K–R2	Kt–Q3
35	R–Kt7 ch	K–R1
36	R–Q7	Kt–Kt4
37	K–Kt3	Kt×BP
38	K–B4	Kt–Kt4
39	K–K5	R–K1
40	K–B6	resigns

Because of the following line. 40 ..., K–Kt1; 41 R–Kt7 ch, K–R1; 42 R–Kt7, Kt–Q3; 43 R–Q7, Kt–Kt4; 44 K–B7, R–KKt1; 45 R–Q8.

Diagram 20.4 is a Selesniev stalemate idea which could have helped an old Russian master, Tchigorin; but he didn't see the device in play (Diagram 20.5); while Diagram 20.6 demonstrates awareness of the idea (not necessarily from the study) on the part of the modern Russian grandmaster Taimanov. Those examples justify two observations:

1 That players learn by the observation of ideas
2 That many chess "endings" are incidents from games where a player either saw, or failed to see, a continuation. (Remember Paulsen against Metger.)

Study by Selesnieff (*Deutsche Schachzeitung* 1918)

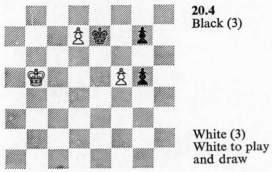

20.4
Black (3)

White (3)
White to play
and draw

	1	K–B6	K–Q1
	2	K–Q5	K×P
	3	K–K4	K–Q3
	4	K–B3	K–K4
	5	K–Kt4	K–B3
	6	K–R5	K×P

Stalemate

Ostend 1905

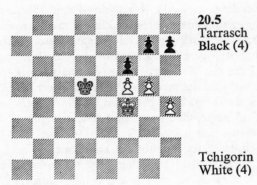

20.5
Tarrasch
Black (4)

Tchigorin
White (4)

White played 1 P×P P×P
             2 K–Kt4 K–K4 and Black won.
But White could draw as follows:
1 K–Kt4   K–K4
2 P–Kt6   P–R3
3 K–R5   K×P stalemate.

Championship of USSR 1967

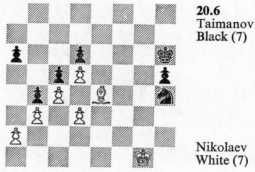

20.6
Taimanov
Black (7)

Nikolaev
White (7)

1	P–Q4	Kt–Kt3
2	P×P	P×P
3	B×Kt	K×B

Now White is able, by timely sacrifice of the QP, to capture the KRP and gain the opposition at KB6. In due course he closes on the QBP: but Black, getting his King into the refuge of QR4, is stalemated.

It is believed, though there is disputation about sources, that such endings as Reti's K-catching-P and the so-called Saavedra ending, and some studies by Lasker, were inspired by incidents of play—ideas stepping from the game into the frame.

Similarly, the compositions of such as Reti and Mattison and Havel are the fine perceptions of fine players. And it is to be suspected that the great research composers Rinck, Troitzky, and all those others, have been formidable players interested in the practical game. (We know that Selesniev played in tournaments with distinction.)

In contrast, let me show an end-game in which the composers seem to have forgotten that they were playing chess. Diagram 20.7 is a study, if that is the proper word, by Korolkov and Dolukhanov. Observe that Black has just failed to win a Rook and Knight—but don't lose interest, White now produces better chess than he had previously played. In the solution we reach the kind of mate that problemists like, and I think I should be right in saying that the two Russians composed a pretty problem.

"Problem" by Korolkov and Dolukhanov

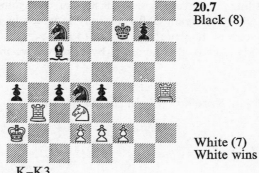

20.7
Black (8)

White (7)
White wins

1	Kt–K5 ch	K–K3
2	R–Kt6	K×Kt
3	P–K3	Kt–B4
4	R×B	Kt–Q4
5	P–B4 ch	P×P e.p.
6	P–Q4 ch	P×P e.p.
7	R–K4 ch	K×R
8	R–K6 mate	

On the same reasoning I say that some of Kipping's problems were end-game studies. C S Kipping was a problem composer who had a sense of chess realism. Diagram 20.8 is a problem that could be an end-game. The key is nice practical chess—but it's what we lawyers, having forgotten Euclid, call a "short point."

Problem by E S Kipping

20.8
Black (6)

White (3)

Mate in 3. Key 1, B–B4.

However, to return to our Russians, let no one think that I am belittling that very great master of end-game composition, Korolkov. Diagram 20.9 is a study in which he conjures all the resources of fine practical chess to make an instructive study— a study that is also favoured by whatever we mean by beauty.

Study by Korolkov (*Shakhmatny Listok* 1930)

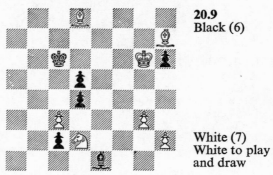

20.9
Black (6)

White (7)
White to play
and draw

1	Kt–Kt3	P–Q6
2	B–Kt5	P×B
3	K–R6!	P=Q
4	Kt×Q	P–Q7
5	Kt–Kt3	P=Q
6	B–B2	Q–Kt5
7	B–B5	Q–Q8 (if Q–QR5; 8 B–Q7 ch)
8	B–B2 and draws. The Q is dominated.	

Korolkov, in another mood, also provides us with another value—humour in chess. I defy any player not to laugh as he solves Diagram 20.10, but let us classify it as a problem. Without insisting on severe realism, I would suggest that the end-game study, being didactic, must be closely related to practicality. (In other words, the coefficient of teaching must always be important.) Beauty can be achieved—in echo variations, in thematic repetition, and so on. The fine composer contrives to give those values to didactic studies.

By Korolkov (Shakhmat v SSSR 1940)

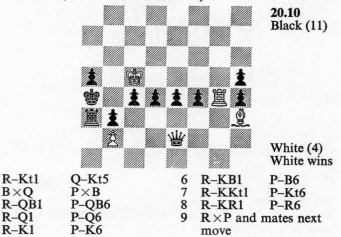

20.10
Black (11)

White (4)
White wins

1	R–Kt1	Q–Kt5	
2	B×Q	P×B	
3	R–QB1	P–QB6	
4	R–Q1	P–Q6	
5	R–K1	P–K6	
6	R–KB1	P–B6	
7	R–KKt1	P–Kt6	
8	R–KR1	P–R6	
9	R×P and mates next move		

I find great utility and great beauty in the study in Diagram 20.11 by Troitzky, though I lack the time to give a philosophic analysis of the beauty. However, here is one thought: I suggest that one element of beauty at least is in the intellectual satisfaction of a convincing solution where, before the thing is demonstrated, it seems wild and improbable; the solution brings order out of chaos. Let Kasparian demonstrate this (Diagram 20.12). Another of the greatest is Kubbel. Few, if any, of his studies are other than lifelike. Diagram 20.13 is one that has an amusing historical epilogue. The study is useful, as one sees at first glance. Over half a century after composition, which was in 1914, two Kazakhstan players arrived at the position in Diagram 20.14. The putative winner was, between moves 5 and 8, wasting time. It is told that, during the adjournment, someone showed him the Kubbel, and on his return to the board he applied the teaching. In Diagram 20.15 Kubbel is showing, in a quite practical setting, the beauty that seems to attach to unexpected play to empty squares. How valuable an awareness of empty squares can be is shown in the "study" in Diagram 20.16 from actual play, which brings me back to the observation that chess studies seem to step from the game into the frame.

By Troitzky (*Deutsche Schachzeitung* 1906)

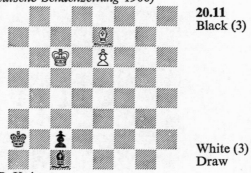

20.11
Black (3)

White (3)
Draw

1	B–Kt4	B–Kt4
2	B–Q2	B×B
3	P–K7	P=Q ch

4   K–Q7 and, as Black has no checks, White promotes and draws.
(4 . . . B–B5 just fails to win.)

Study by Kasparian (1966)

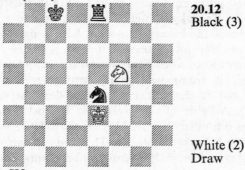

20.12
Black (3)

White (2)
Draw

1	Kt–Kt7	R–K2
2	Kt–B5	R–K3
3	Kt–Kt7	R–KKt3
4	Kt–B5	R–Kt5
5	Kt–R6	R–R5
6	Kt–B5	R–Kt5
7	Kt–R6	R–Kt3
8	Kt–B5	R–K3
9	Kt–Kt7	R–K2
10	Kt–B5	R–K1
11	Kt–Kt7	R–K2
12	Kt–B5 drawn	

Study by Kubbel (*Rigaer Tageblatt* 1914)

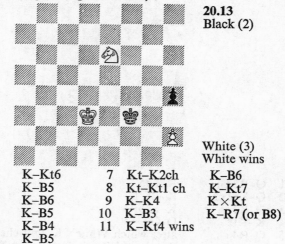

20.13
Black (2)

White (3)
White wins

1	P–R3	K–Kt6	7	Kt–K2ch	K–B6
2	Kt–Kt5	K–B5	8	Kt–Kt1 ch	K–Kt7
3	Kt–K4	K–B6	9	K–K4	K×Kt
4	K–Q4	K–B5	10	K–B3	K–R7 (or B8)
5	K–Q5	K–B4	11	K–Kt4 wins	
6	Kt–B3!	K–B5			

(Championship of Kazakhstan 1966)

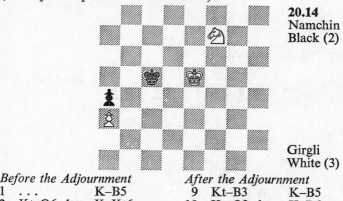

20.14
Namchin
Black (2)

Girgli
White (3)

Before the Adjournment

1	. . .	K–B5
2	Kt–Q6 ch	K–Kt6
3	Kt–Kt5	K–B5
4	Kt–Q4	K–B4
5	K–K4	K–B5
6	K–K3	K–B6
7	K–K4	K–B5
8	K–K5	K–B4

After the Adjournment

9	Kt–B3	K–B5
10	Kt–Q2 ch	K–B6
11	Kt–Kt1 ch	K–Kt7
12	K–Q4	K×Kt
14	K–B3 resigns	

Well played, Kubbel.

By Kubbel (*Shakhmatry Listok* 1924)

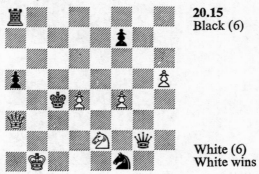

20.15
Black (6)

White (6)
White wins

1	Q–R2 ch	K–Kt5
2	Q–Kt2 ch	K–B5
3	Q–B2 ch	K–Kt5
4	K–Kt2	Q–Q4
5	Q–R4 ch	after which White's Knight checks win the Queen and Rook, leaving the White pawns to win.

Combination from actual play

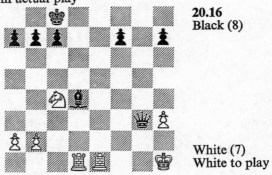

20.16
Black (8)

White (7)
White to play

1	R–K8 ch	K–Q2
2	R–K3	Q–R5
3	R × B ch	Q × R
4	R–Q3! wins	

From my own experience in the early 1920s here (Diagram 20.17) is one example. I sent this, with other pieces of play, to T R Dawson, and he described them as elegant compositions.

G Abrahams (Actual Play 1922)

20.17
Black (6)

White (6)
White to play

(Black has just played R–R8)

1	P×B	R×R ch		
2	K–Kt2	R–Q8		
3	P–B7	R–Q1		
4	Kt–K5	R–KB1		

5 P–R6 executing a *Zugzwang*.
If 2 ..., R×Kt; 3 P×P wins.

1	...	Q–B3 ch	4	K×Q	P×R=Q ch
2	K–Kt1	R–B8 ch	5	B–Kt1	Q–B6 mate
3	R×R	Q–R8 ch			

From a game at Valencia 1967

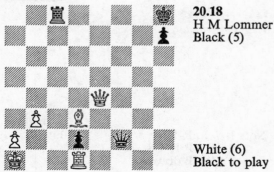

20.18
H M Lommer
Black (5)

White (6)
Black to play

That fine composer Lommer has profited from his own play. Diagram 20.18 is his actual play, and Diagram 20.19 the study. But, with respect to my valued friend Lommer, the study adds little except polish.

Study by Lommer (1967)

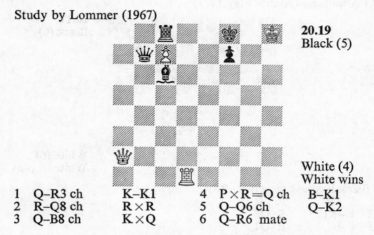

20.19
Black (5)

White (4)
White wins

1	Q–R3 ch	K–K1	4	P×R=Q ch	B–K1
2	R–Q8 ch	R×R	5	Q–Q6 ch	Q–K2
3	Q–B8 ch	K×Q	6	Q–R6 mate	

Again, an example worthy of the Russian composers is surely the end-game in Diagram 20.20 played between two grandmasters of the practical game.

Played *c* 1950

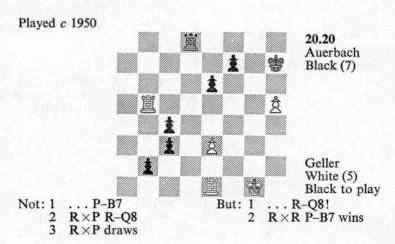

20.20
Auerbach
Black (7)

Geller
White (5)
Black to play

Not:	1	... P–B7	But:	1	... R–Q8!
	2	R×P R–Q8		2	R×R P–B7 wins
	3	R×P draws			

Also from grandmaster play, but less spectacular, is the "empty square" play (Diagram 20.21) of Smyslov against Mikenas. Diagram 20.22 is a study, which also appears, according to Darga, to have come up as a possibility in a grandmaster game. In actual play the solution could easily be missed. 1 BQ7 is the only move. The element of uniqueness is, surely, one of the "aesthetic values."

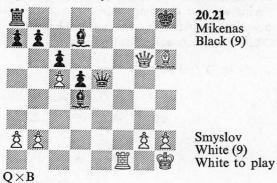

20.21
Mikenas
Black (9)

Smyslov
White (9)
White to play

27	B–K3	Q×B
28	Q–R5 ch	K–Kt1
29	Q–B7 ch	with perpetual check

(If 27 . . . B×B
    28   R–B7 wins)

Study by O Frinck

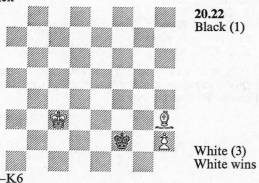

20.22
Black (1)

White (3)
White wins

1	B–Q7	K–K6
2	P–R4	K–K5 (if K–B5; 3 K–Q4 wins)
3	P–R5	K–K4
4	P–R6	K–B3
5	B–K8	wins

Simplicity is also an aesthetic virtue. Elegant and instructive is the study in Diagram 20.23 by David Joseph. Coincidentally Botvinnik discovered this side-step in a 1946 simultaneous display (Diagram 20.24). Also in point is the famous Joseph ending. In one form there was play ending with a check on b6, to which the best reply was K–Kt1 (Diagram 20.25). But I leave to the reader to decide whether the simple idea for exploiting this position is so beautiful in itself that the uncomplicated edition in Diagram 20.26 is the more aesthetically desirable.

Study by D Joseph

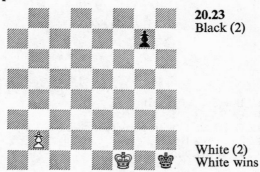

20.23
Black (2)

White (2)
White wins

1	K–B2	K–R7
2	K–B3	K–R6
3	K–B4	K–R5
4	P–Kt4	P–Kt4 ch
5	K–K3!	wins

1 P–Kt4, P–Kt4 only draws. Note that the principle operating on this study does not work if the White Pawn is at QR2. The difference is worth studying.

Botvinnik
(Study based on a position reached in a Simultaneous Display 1946)

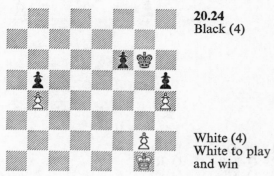

20.24
Black (4)

White (4)
White to play
and win

1	K–B2	K–B4
2	K–B3	K–K4
3	P–Kt4	P×P ch
4	K×P	K–K5
5	P–R5	P–B4 ch
6	K–R3!	P–B5
7	P–R6	P–B6
8	P–R7	P–B7
9	K–Kt2 wins	

Study by Joseph
A Czech Version (*Ceskoslovenska Republika* 1923)

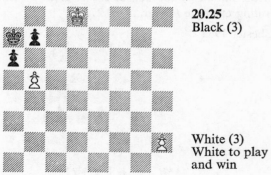

20.25
Black (3)

White (3)
White to play
and win

1–P–Kt6 ch–K–Kt1!
Forces White to find the pretty win shown in Diagram 20.26.

G

Study by Joseph (*BCM* 1922)

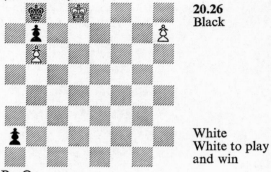

20.26
Black

White
White to play
and win

1	P=Q	P=Q
2	Q–Kt8	Q–R7
3	Q–K8	Q–R5
4	Q–K5 ch	K–R1
5	Q–R8	wins

Note that
2 Q–B8 is met by Q–R6
3 Q–K8, Q–K3 ch draws
Also 2 Q–Q8, Q–Kt2 draws.

The Joseph study causes me to say, first, that economy is a value and, second, that unexpected *dénouements* (from the chess player's point of view) are almost always of aesthetic value. In point are those long-distance stalemates, and mates or stalemates in the middle of the board. I take great pleasure in a relatively trifling example (Diagram 20.27).

Chester 1934

20.27
Golombek
Black (5)

Abrahams
White (3)
White to play

1	K–Q4	R–R4	4	R×P ch	K×R
2	R–B2 ch	K–Kt5		Stalemate	
3	P–B3	P–B5			

And Golombek hated me, not without justification. But long analysis has failed to find a winning line for Black.

In conclusion, of dominations, staircase effects, underpromotions, and a hundred other ideas, let me say, first, that they all belong to practical chess, and, second, that they all have the aesthetic value of pattern, of theme revealed, in many cases echoed so as to give additional pleasure, and one other common factor, the pleasure: stimulation in intellectual conflict resolved. The notion of conflict inspires me to quote, from a composer who has been accused of surrealism, a particularly natural sequence of play and counterplay, with a neat finish (Diagram 20.28).

Study by Birnov

20.28
Black (4)

White (5)
White wins

1	B–B7 (threatening P–Q5)	K×P
2	B–R3	B–KKt2
3	B–Kt2 ch	K–K5
4	B×B	But this is not the end.
4	...	B–B6 ch
5	K–B2	B–KR4
6	B–Kt3 (an Echo)	K–B4
7	B–B2 ch	K–Kt4
8	B–B8	B×P
9	B–K7 ch	K–R4
10	B–Q1 mate	

By way of postscript, let me add two of my own efforts, in one of which the didactic is emphasised, in the other the epicurean (Diagrams 20.29 and 20.30).

When not to take a pawn

20.29
Abrahams
Black (4)

Mühring
White (3)
Black to play

Hastings 1947

1	...	R–Q7 (Sealed move—and only)
2	R×P	K–B6
3	R–R3 ch	K–K7
4	P–R4	P–K6
5	P–R5	R–Q1
6	R–R2 ch	K–Q8
7	R–R2	P–K7
8	R–R1 ch	K–Q7
9	R–R2 ch	K–K6
10	R–R3 ch	R–Q6 wins

Championship of Lancashire 1948

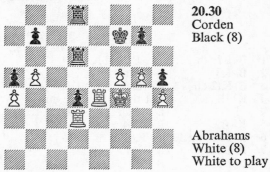

20.30
Corden
Black (8)

Abrahams
White (8)
White to play

1	P–Kt6 ch	K–B3
2	R–Q1	P–Q6 (to answer QR–K1 with R–Q5)
3	R×P	P–Kt3
4	R–Q5	R(1)–Q2
5	R–K8	*Zugzwang*

In my references to art and science I am following a distinction drawn by the late Professor Samuel Alexander—I paraphrase. "In the presentations (e.g. experiments and hypotheses) of science, the form is controlled by the material that is under investigation. In the presentations of art (which have been called ideal experiments) the mind of the experimenter is relatively free from that control." Applying this thought: the game is rigidly scientific—the board controls the player. In the problem, the mind of the composer (or solver) is creating effects relatively free from the purposes of the game. The end-game, in my submission, is certainly a field for aesthetic activity, but that should be subordinate to its function as a discipline (a teaching) determined by the practical necessities of the game. It is of interest to note that Russian experts (without stating a philosophy of the subject) have criticised Birnov and others for being unrealistic—in my terms, making problems rather than studies.

Part Five

A TALENT OF JEWS

21 Why are Jews good at chess?

When Sholom Aleychem's unfortunate chess player, Reuben Sholemov Rubinstein, was asked by the Czar of Russia where he had acquired his skill at chess, he replied: *"Es geht bei uns beyerusha"* (It runs in our family). That conversation (staged in the period of Nicholas I) took place before the scientists had become unanimously dogmatic against the transmission of acquired characteristics down the generations.

They hold, nowadays, that what a father acquired, in his life-time, in the way of skill does not get registered among his chromosomes: so it is not transmitted. If his son becomes good at the same subject that's because the "general factor" of intelligence in that family has always been such as to lend itself to that activity; or else the boy learnt when very young at his father's breakfast table what other children learn later in life. So he had a start. And there is a mystical school that talks of modifications, rather than transmissions. All of which is very orthodox scientific protocol about which I can only say: *Credat Judaeus Weissman, non ego.*

Prior to scientific pronouncements are, I think, certain accepted facts that require to be explained. One intransigent, and accepted, fact is that a disproportionately large number of Jews are endowed with greater mental aptitude than the European average. This could be the result of circumstantial selection. This group favours intellect. Their "general factor" at least is high. But, in addition, they furnish many prodigies in many subjects, the most specific of which are music, chess and, a third that often goes unnoticed, linguistic ability. Experts will tell you that of chess ability the Jews do not hold, and do not claim, a monopoly. Jewish Socialist egalitarians in Israel make strong disclaimers. In Israel a number of people actually succeed in being very bad at the

201

game. (They have the legitimate explanation that Israel has been heavily engaged in other directions.) Outside Israel the rolls of honour in the chess world include the names of many gentiles. Two gentiles at least, in our time, have been claimants to the Arch-Gaonate, even to the title of the greatest ever. I refer to the Cuban Capablanca, and the Slav Alekhine. Behind them in time looms the shadow of Irish American Morphy. (The Jewish challenger is Lasker.) At a lower level there have been gentile prodigies like the Spanish Pomar, and (greater) the Mexican Torre. Also, among the masses of masters that now exist, must be counted a large number of really Slavonic Slavs: as well as a miscellany of representatives of other groups, Latin, Teuton, and (not least in quality) Anglo-Saxon.

But when this is said, what does it amount to? A mitigation of, an apology for, a commentary on, the overwhelming fact that the chess world is, and has been for a century, a Jewish world. Even in Moscow—capital of chess and capital of the Slav lands that are so rich in chess ability—the majority of the great names are Jewish names. The Jewish majority in Slav chess is not so great as it was in the old days when, although chess was a social asset in Russia—a must for Russian officers—yet the Russian masses were not sophisticated enough to be interested in it. In those days—and even up to the time of the Second World War—the great tournaments of the world were so Jewish that any orthodox player in a tournament of twelve masters could have impressed a minyon (a quorum of ten for prayers) had he been needful of it—though he might have had to teach an occasional member the Aleph-Beth. There were even tournaments, with a Rubinstein and a Chajes, where one might have organised a Blatt (literally, a leaf as in *Schachblatt* or *Schachmatry Listok*—a study of the folios of the Talmud).

Certainly, in the late nineteenth century there was an immense preponderance of Jewry in the upper ranks of chess mastery. The names of Steinitz, Lasker, Tarrasch, Schlechter, Gunsberg, and a score of others, are only challenged by one Slav, Tchigorin, two or three British players, notably Blackburne, the American Marshall, and an American meteor, Pillsbury. In the first quarter of this century, the dominant names were still Jewish: Rubinstein,

Nimzovitch, Tartakover, Janowsky, Bernstein, Reti, Breyer, and a host of others; but with world supremacy falling, in the twenties, to two non-Jews, Capablanca and Alekhine. In the thirties, Flohr and Kashdan, Reshevsky (a prodigy with retained powers) Reuben Fine and the emerging Botvinnik were great Jewish names. Then, after the Second World War, the Slavs took over. At Tel Aviv, in 1964, many East European teams contained sufficient non-Jews to remind us of Holocaust. But the might of Russian chess, and Yugoslav chess, and Czech chess, included Jewish talent. Outside the Slav lands American chess and South American chess (recruited from European refugees) has been largely Jewish. (The Olympiad at Buenos Aires in 1939 left many East European players in South America.) In the world Championship Botvinnik (a not-quite crypto-Jew) prevailed for long, and was all but successfully challenged by a non-crypto-Jew, Bronstein (who later endeared himself to his masters by writing anti-Israel propaganda in the Russian press). He was later defeated by, and in turn defeated, a very amiable and talented Slav named Smyslov (alleged to have had a Jewish grandmother) —whose style and personality are greatly reminiscent of Rubinstein—and eventually decisively defeated by Tal, a young Jew with the intense brilliance that used to mark the Iluyim. Unhappily that flame diminished. Since then Spassky claims a Jewish grandmother, and Jewry claims Fischer.

From this review, one thought may emerge: that the Jewish Yerusha is not a long one. How good they were before the nineteenth century we do not know. Historians tell an old story of a Jew who recognised his son in the person of the Pope (Anacletus II) by reason of a winning opening move which the latter made. This story implies an unsophisticated chess equipment. A good Hebrew poem about chess is attributed to Abraham Ibn Ezra (twelfth century). We know little of play in those days. Rabbis in the middle ages were doubtful about the respectability of the game. According to the best later opinion it may be played, and played on the Sabbath; but is specially recommended to women. (Incidentally, the best woman player of this century so far—the late Vera Menchik—was Slavonic not Jewish. Her successor, Goprandashvili, is Georgian.)

Moses Mendelssohn, great Rabbi, great philosopher, owed his friendship with Lessing to chess. But he said of the game: *"Fur eine Partie zu viel Ernst; fur Ernst zu viel Partie"*—which I judge to be a tolerable excuse for losing games of chess.

Substantially, the Jewish performance seems to coincide with the immersion, in the mid-nineteenth century, of the pent-up Jewish energies of East Europe into the activities of the Western World. When the Jew began showing himself good at whatever occupation one allowed him to undertake, he demonstrated, at the same time, his skill at chess. (In many cases, in the Eastern Ghetto, it was his only possible livelihood and is comparable to the boxing skill of the Negro who finds no other vocation available to him.)

Wie es christelt sich, so es jüdelt sich. In the lands where chess was valued, Jews valued it too. That is, perhaps, an explanation of the relative scarcity of Jews on the highest levels of English chess. (Also in England other careers were open to Jewish talents.) In the nineteenth century Steinitz and Loewenthal lived here as representatives of European chess. But they did not at first represent Anglo-Jewry. Forty years ago, when a Jewish club made an effort in Manchester, a good deal of competence emerged but only one real player, David Joseph—who, however, did not maintain an active interest in the game. Out of Manchester, but independently, came a non-Jewish Jew (if I may use the expression) the redoubtable Victor Wahltuch. In the London of the twenties, the Goldstein brothers were strong, and Victor Buerger was of master-strength. A native of Latvia, but educated in England, Buerger also played Rugby, and is the only good chess player I know who has ridden in a steeplechase. From the 1920s (a vintage period of chess talent in England) there survive Harry Golombek (thrice British champion) and myself, and (if I may say so) we two almost exhausted, for a long time, the important native Anglo-Jewish contribution above the Baal Habatishe level. Other names in recent English chess history are Klein, Konig, and List—three brilliant refugee players. Further, Yanowski is the name of an excellent Canadian master, the son of a Hebrew teacher, who showed himself capable of winning the British Championship and of a first-class Honours BCL at Oxford.

Dr Fazekas, a medical man from Ruthenia, also won the British title. [Since the above was first written there have emerged William Hartston, the nephew of a Rabbi, and Jonathan Mestel, the son of an Astro-physicist—two players of great talent.]

In contrast, as we have seen, in lands where chess is popular Jews took the lead at least a century ago and kept it. The subsequent elective affinity of Jew with chess does invite some conjecture as to the reason for their striking dominance in this field—for the Neshomah Yeserah that they seem to inject into it.

Let me mention a few aspects of the matter. First, the Jews produce, more than any other group, the pure intellectual—the type, which, when it plunges into chess, produces Sholom Aleychem's watchmaker Reuben Sholomov Rubinstein, or the real-life Yeshivah bochur who was Akiva Rubinstein. Second, Jews are competent hard-working people; and competence and hard work go a long way in chess. Third, they love learning and the speculative. Among gentiles the Slavs are similar to them in this. Every reader of Russian literature from any period knows Russia to be rich in *Luftmenschen*: moongazers, who only in this last decade have contrived to convert their sky wandering into practical space travel.

Fourth, the Jew matures fairly early. Educationalists will agree with me, I think, when I say that the Jewish boy of fourteen is likely to be intellectually mature and creative. If precocious children learn chess, then they have a flying start. What can, in later life, only be laboriously learnt is really mastered if, early in life, the transition is made from struggling with the medium to free expression in it. So music, so languages (of which music and chess are instances) are to be mastered early in life; or, thereafter, only with great difficulty.

This brings me to the last, and, I think, the most important feature of the psychological phenomenon, which is skill at chess. I have mentioned Jewish linguistic skill and have suggested that chess is a "language." Everyone knows that there are stages in the learning of language in which the mind is tested as to its capacity. The infant experiences this transition, who develops from recognising the sound "chair," through reflexes conditioned by the banging of his head, to an ability to say effortlessly: "I want to sit on that chair." Similarly, the student of French passes from a parrot-knowledge of a few phrases about the pen of his aunt's gardener, to an ability to write, or speak, or at least translate, sentences about what one wants for breakfast, or the relation of the Latin spirit to the Saxon. So, in chess, there is a stage at which knowledge that a Knight on KB3 can capture a Pawn on K5 is transcended in the awareness of a long series of captures, recaptures, threats and defences that may be initiated by this capture. I suggest that this transition is psychologically similar to the transition from the psittacic knowledge of a few words in a language to the ability to express thoughts freely in that language; or from the playing of scales to the performing of a solo.

If this comparison is justified, then, perhaps, my further suggestion is justified, that Jewish skill in chess is cognate to that Jewish skill—so basic, so universal as to go unnoticed—which is Jewish skill in languages. The ability of the Cheder Ingel to translate himself into Yeshivah Bochur by coping with a page of unpointed, unpunctuated, Aramaic; the skill that enables the Yeshivah Bochur to teach himself German; the skill that makes the immigrant Jew achieve quickly a better accidence and syntax than is possessed of the slum dwellers among whom he trades; that specific creativity is also available to make the pieces of the chessboard into servants rather than masters, into the means of expression rather than the difficult symbols of an unknown tongue.

When the difficulties of elementary technique are transcended, then, in music, one is a performer, not a scraper; in words a speaker, not a half-mute stammerer; in chess a chess player, not a child playing with chess pieces as with toys.

Jews, I think, have this capacity to move quickly from the elementary technique involved in means of expression, to the free expression of ideas in the mastered medium. What scientific problems of transmission are involved in this is beyond my scope. I throw in the odd fact that some good Jewish chess players spring from apparently unclever parents; and so do some Jews who are great in other spheres. On the other hand, Jewish lions breed Jewish lions. Dr Snow's theory of a "gene pool" would account for both facts. Whence this pool of talent or genius? Have the Jews always had a great mental ability of the kind that I have described? Or is this an effect developing from centuries of intellectual activity? Possibly a survival of the fittest (for difficult survival).

Appropriately in very recent years the interest of young Jews (not all of them children of scholars) has become intense in the fields of "control theory" and, significantly, "communication theory;" which owe so much to the Jewish Norbert Wiener. They have completed a circle for us by programming computers to play chess.

Phenomena such as these seem to justify (in the general field) a belief that the Jewish group is characterised by psychologica- factors which enable the young to learn rapidly and perform impressively. What secrets of biological transmission are involved are, so far, beyond biology.

To recapitulate: there seems to emerge from a group of people much involved with problems of adjustment, with the learning of languages quickly, with the acquisition of skills in all aspects of life, a number of young people who show talent, even genius, in music, in control theory, in most of the sciences, including the science of chess. Does this not suggest thoughts about Yerusha which would intrigue the shade of Weissman?

22 From Passover to Tabernacles

By Sholom Aleychem (translated by Gerald Abrahams)

[Before reading the following story I should like readers to know that the name Rubinstein is as coincidental here as the fact that the author's real name was the good chess name—Rabinovitch.

Sholom Aleychem wrote this story in the very early years of this century, just before Akiva Rubinstein ascended to celebrity.]

It was a good bit after midnight at the mid-winter party. Supper was over, and the big table declared that appetites had been satisfied. From little green tables, chalk-marked and covered with scattered cards, jolly Aces and Kings were beckoning. Another session of vingt-et-un or preference, or euchre, was tempting indeed. But how could one? It was so late. So we just sat about, smoking, drinking black coffee, and talking scandal. When the topics ran out, someone threw in a word about chess, and others joined in. The idea was to arouse the interest of one of the company, a chess enthusiast named Rubinstein.

Rubinstein is what is meant by a "dangerous chess player." To play chess he'll walk ten miles, go without food and drink and forget about sleep. In the proper sense, an "awful player." About his chess there are anecdotes galore. That he will play a game against himself for a whole night. That he has had three divorces because of chess. That he once got lost for three years by reason of chess. In short, Rubinstein stands for chess and chess means Rubinstein. And Rubinstein enjoys a talk about chess in the way that an alcoholic enjoys a talk about good drink.

If you look at Rubinstein, what strikes you first is his extraordinarily big forehead, high and broad and round. I mean with statuesque curve. Also fantastically big eyes, round and black—

but cold. In body he is dry, meagre. But he has a voice like a bell—a fine bass note. When Rubinstein is in conversation you only hear Rubinstein.

Now, as you'd expect when the talk got to chess, Rubinstein showed signs of life. He knitted a brow, looked profoundly at his empty coffee-cup, sniffed as if speculating whether the flavour was of soap or dishwater, and finally gave utterance, a thundering peal, directed at everyone and at nobody in particular.

"Ladies and gentlemen, if you do want to hear a nice tale about a chess player, sit yourselves down and I'll tell you an historic story."

"A tale about a chess player—an historic story." Our hostess (possessed of the good hostess's fear that her guests might drift away) was all agog. Excellent. "Tell the maid to close the piano and please close the door, and let us have a few more chairs. Sit down please everybody. Mr Rubinstein will tell us a story of a chess player—an historic story."

And Rubinstein perpended the newly lit cigar, with which our host had honoured him, contemplating it from all sides, as if he were estimating the cost; wrinkled and knotted his immense forehead, as if he were saying: "Yes, you have the appearance of a cigar, but you taste like a besom." After which inspection, he plunged into narrative.

"That I myself am an enthusiastic chess player, that our whole family, in fact, consists of natural chess players, that, ladies and gentlemen, I need hardly tell you. You know it yourself. The name Rubinstein is not unknown. And I'd like to wager that you can't show me a Rubinstein who isn't a chess player."

"I know a Rubinstein, an agent who calls on me every week, who, apart from life insurance, doesn't know anything at all. An absolute ass."

The interrupter was one of the guests, a young man with a pointed skull and gold spectacles, who fancied himself wise and witty. But Rubinstein was undisturbed. With his cold black eyes he dissected the young man, and said, in his deep voice:

"Probably not one of our Rubinsteins. A real Rubinstein is by nature a chess player. That is as true in the nature of things as it is true in the nature of things that idiots like to make silly jokes.

"Such a real Rubinstein was my grandfather, Reuben Rubinstein. I tell you of him because he was the chess player *par excellence*. As far as he was concerned the world could turn upside down while he was playing. People came from far and wide to play him. Landowners, counts, personalities came, though he himself was only a watchmaker. A humble craftsman I may say, but a good one; an artist at his work. But because his essence was chess, he had great difficulties; no real living; hardly managed to find a crust of bread.

"Well, one day, there happened an event. To the door of my grandfather's little house, drove up a magnificent equipage, a carriage with a string of fiery horses. And there alighted from the carriage a *poritz*, a magnate with two attendants, and decorated from top to bottom with orders and medals—a personality.

"He burst in tempestuously: 'Whereabouts is the Jew, Reuben Rubinstein?'

"My grandfather (may he forgive me for saying so) was at first almost frightened out of his wits. But pulling himself together, he managed to say: 'I am the Jew, Reuben Rubinstein. How can I be of service?'

"The 'personality' was satisfied.

"'If you are the Jew, Reuben Rubinstein, I'm delighted. Tell them to put on the samovar, and produce the board. You and I will play some chess. I've heard,' he added, 'that you play very well, and that no one has ever mated you.'

"So spoke the magnate (evidently a lover of chess), and sat down to play with my grandfather: one game after another; game after game. Meanwhile the samovar came to the boil. Tea was served—naturally, on a tray, with confectionery, and a variety of eatables. My grandmother managed this somehow though she hadn't a *groschen* in her purse. And outside, around the equipage, the whole town had gathered. A small thing—a magnate was in the house of Reuben the watchmaker. Obviously, the town was full of explanations. This one said it was an officer from the government with an inspection order relating to counterfeit money. Another said that an informer had been at work, and that a scandal, a defamation, an affaire was developing. To look inside (and see the personality playing chess with my grand-father) that nobody dared. The idea could not occur to any-body.

"And what results, you may ask, was the personality achieving? Although he was playing not badly—indeed one can say he was playing quite well—he was being subjected by my grandfather to mate, after mate, after mate. And the more he lost, the more excited he became; and the more excited he became the more he lost. And my grandfather? His face was untroubled. Just as if he was playing with anyone at all. But the great one was undoubtedly thoroughly upset. What do you think? Nobody likes losing. And particularly to whom? To a Jew! But what could he say? There was nothing to be said. The man was playing too well. As the world has it: 'If he can do it, nothing else matters.'

"And you must appreciate, ladies and gentlemen, that a real chess player is much more concerned with the play than with the result. To the real chess player, there are no players—only the game. I wonder if you understand that."

"We can't swim, but we understand swimming," put in our young wit—as usual in the wrong place. And Rubinstein, the enthusiast for chess, surveyed him with his cold eyes, and said: "Yes, it's obvious that you understand swimming." After which he took a puff at his cigar, and resumed.

"Well, as all things come to an end, so this chess playing came to an end. The magnate arose, fastened his tunic meticulously, extended two fingers to my grandfather, and spoke:

" 'Listen, Reuben Rubinstein, you have beaten me, and I must admit that you are the best chess player, not only in my province, but in the whole country, perhaps in the whole world, and I reckon myself fortunate to have had the honour and pleasure of playing with the greatest chess player in the world. Be assured,' he added, 'that from today, your name will be even greater than it was. I will communicate it to the ministers, mention it in the palace. . . .'

"Hearing such words—'ministers, mention in the palace'—my grandfather timidly asked: 'Who, then, are you, My Lord?' The great one laughs, sticks out his chest with all the medals and says, 'I am the Governor.' My grandfather was horror-stricken. Had he known who was playing with him he would have played differently. But what can one do? One can't alter the past. Meanwhile the Governor bade a very friendly goodbye, went out to his equipage, installed himself, and away.

"Naturally, the crowd, at long last, fell on my grandfather—'Who was it?' And when he told them it was the Governor: 'What was the Governor doing here?' And when my grandfather made it clear that the Governor had only come on account of chess, there was a great deal of expectoration and exorcism, and a pouring of the contents of bad dreams onto the heads of various enemies. And so the crowd melted, gossipped, gossipped and forgot. And my grandfather also forgot. He had other things to think about, other games of chess, to say nothing of his living, such as it was. A Jew has to worry, struggle along, keep looking for a bit of bread.

"But there came a day, a long time after. I can't tell you how long had elapsed. I only know that it was the eve of Passover. And in my grandfather's house there was, so far, nothing for the holy days—not even a bit of Matzoh.

"Children, of course, in plenty, this one requiring a shirt, that one a pair of boots. Things were bad. He sat, poor man, bent in three, with the little glass stuck in his eye, fiddled with a watch that had decided not to go, and thought: 'From whence will come my help?'

"Suddenly, the door opened, and in came two gendarmes, and addressed my grandfather: 'If you please. . . .'

"The thought flashed across his mind (my grandfather was a man of strange ideas) that perhaps they were from the Governor. Could there by any doubt about it? Perhaps he wanted to reward him, to make him happy. It had happened so often that, through an accident, a trifle, a magnate would take a Jew and shower him with wealth, making him happy for generations.

"As it happens, in this case, no such thing. They apologised, and asked him would he put himself to the trouble of taking himself to—guess where?—to St Petersburg.

" 'What's it about?'

"They don't know. They have received, they say, a document from St Petersburg, on which was written an order: forthwith to produce the Jew Reuben Rubinstein in St Petersburg. There must be some reason.

" 'Admit it, old man, what tricks have you been up to?' My grandfather swears that he can't conjure the wildest nothing or anything. In his whole life, he says, he hasn't even killed a fly. The whole town will answer for him. "But it's like talking to a wall. They order him to go. And how? By the 'route'—that is with the chain-gang. Because it says in the order 'produce' and how can one 'produce' anyone except by the 'route' and in shackles. And it says 'forthwith.' That means the sooner the better.

"So, without much ado, they took my grandfather, stood on no ceremony, shackled him hand and foot, along with all the thieves, and conducted him 'by stages.' And what, in those days, was implied in 'going by stage' I won't try to describe to you. If a refined man set out in such company, he was not likely to survive the journey. There were no trains, no paved highways. People went down like flies. More than half died on the way, and the rest arrived exhausted, broken, exposed—cripples. Fortunately my grandfather was of a constitution like mine, dry and tough. But basically a good Jew. Also with a thinking mind, pious and philosophical. 'A man only dies once,' he said, 'not twice. And if a man is destined to live no one will deprive him of his life.' And why this dwelling on life and death. Because there was an atmosphere of prison, of Siberia, of even worse. When he left he not only said goodbye to his wife and children, but to the whole town and forever; and he asked for a copy of the last rites, and the prayers of the dying. They tried to comfort him. The whole town saw him off (as if it were a funeral) and tears flowed copiously and without cease.

"To tell you everything that my grandfather suffered on that journey I would require not one night, but three nights, which would be a pity. The time could be better used for playing chess. In short I can only tell you that the journey dragged out the whole summer, from Passover to nearly Pentecost, because the route, you must know, has its 'points.' And at every point where the gang stopped, they kept the convicts, sometimes a week, sometimes two weeks, sometimes more, until a new party of thieves and rogues could be assembled, and then they were driven on. And even when, after great sufferings, plagues and exhaustions, they arrived at happy Saint Petersburg, do you think it was over? If you do, you are wrong.

"First they put my grandfather in a dungeon—that is a kind of dark room where you haven't space to sit or lie, walk or stand."

"A good place in which to play chess," suggested the young wit.

"And in which to make idle jokes," replied Rubinstein. "In the dungeon," he continued, "my grandfather really began to say goodbye to life: recited by heart the prayer for the dying, saw the angel of death and felt that, any moment, his soul was departing before they could bring him to trial, and he actually prayed for a quick release.

"His only faint hope lay in his home town. He was sure the town would not keep quiet. There would be advocates—rich Jews who would pull string, invokes protective clauses, and if bribery was necessary, bribe, in order to extricate an innocent Jew from a misfortune, from a defamation.

"And he was not wrong. In fact, from the first day when they took him away, and right through the summer, the whole town made desperate efforts. They went to advocates, invoked protections, bribed, poured money out—but nothing helped. People took their money, but said it was impossible to promise to do anything for my grandfather. And they explained this logically. In the case of a thief or other kind of ordinary law-breaker, it's easy to extricate him with money. You can classify him because you know what he is—a thief who stole a couple of horses, a miscreant who set fire to a house. But in the case of a man like my grandfather who never stole anything, and never set anything on fire, who knows what kind of criminal he is? Perhaps a 'political.' In those days a 'political' was worse than a murderer who'd exterminated a whole province. To go and plead on behalf of a 'political' was dangerous. The very word must not be spoken aloud, but whispered in the dark. Though how could Reuben Rubinstein the watchmaker get involved as a political? Still, there you are. A Jew with an inquiring mind—a philosopher.

"However, as I said before, everything comes to an end. So

there came a day when the gates of imprisonment were opened.
Two gendarmes, armed to the teeth, took my grandfather,
barely alive, put him into a carriage, and away.

"Where? He didn't even ask. To trial? Let it be so. To the
scaffold? So be it. As long as the thing has an end. And he
imagined himself on trial. As soon as they brought him before the
tribunal and said to him: 'Reuben Reubinstein, confess,' he would
answer, 'I confess, I am a Jew, and a poor watchmaker, and I
live by the work of my hands, and I have never stolen, or swindled,
or insulted anyone, and God is my witness. And if you wish to
punish me, punish me; but first take my life, it is in your hands.'

"So my grandfather disputed with the tribunal in his mind, and
the carriage rolled up to a kind of fortress, and my grandfather
was ordered to alight. He alighted and they led him into a room,
and then into another room, and they ordered him to undress—
undress down to his shirt. He didn't understand the purpose.
But when a gendarme tells you to undress, you can't be obstinate.
Then they asked him (forgive me, ladies and gentlemen) to
remove his shirt as well. He removed his shirt, and they led
him into a bath. But what a bath! And they washed him and
rubbed him and swilled him. Then they dressed him, and they
travelled with him further: they travelled and travelled and travelled. And he thought: 'Lord, what's going to happen to me?'
And he tried to remember the stories that he once read about
Spain and Portugal. But he couldn't remember having read of
quite such an occurrence as giving a prisoner a bath before
taking him to trial. And as he was thinking, the carriage drove
up to a palace surrounded by iron railings with golden points
and on every point an eagle. And they led him in among generals
with golden epaulettes and medals, and they told him not to be
afraid, he was to be presented to the Czar. And he must look
straight ahead, not utter any unnecessary word, not complain
of anything, just answer: 'yes' where yes was required; 'no'
where 'no' was required. And before he could give a thought to
where in the world he was, he found himself standing in a painted
room, with delightful pictures and golden chairs, and standing
opposite him was a tall man with side-whiskers.

"The man with the side-whiskers (it was Czar Nicholas I)

took my grandfather in with a glance: and there took place the following conversation:

Czar: What is your name?
Grandfather: Reuben Sholimov Rubinstein.
Czar: How old are you?
Grandfather: Fifty-seven.
Czar: Where did you learn to play chess?
Grandfather: It runs in the family.
Czar: They tell me you're the best player in my country. I congratulate you.

"At that point grandfather Rubinstein wanted to say that he only wished he wasn't the best player in the country. But the Czar would doubtless have asked what was the trouble and my grandfather would have given him an account of how not to treat a famous chess player whom the Czar wished to see.

"If this questioning had taken place, grandfather Rubinstein would certainly have been able to give an answer. Only at this point the Czar made a gesture with his hand. Whereupon generals sprang into action. The same gendarmes conducted my grandfather back into the palace, and from the palace he was allowed to go free—but he was told that he must immediately return home because he could not be allowed to stay.

"How he got home—don't ask. So long as he got out alive. He got home punctually for Tabernacles. That's all."

23 Day out in the life of an Ilui

(Tel Aviv 1964)*

"And there came down a troop of Prophets. . . ." Right out of
Samuel into the Sheraton Hotel at Tel Aviv. Only that grotesque,
"aesthetic," inner wall, with its strange figures and its numerous
holes, so suggestive of biblical crudities, made the procession
plausible in time or place. Prophets? Essenes? Chassidim?
Were they not too well arrayed, too clean? Too occidental?
No fringes showing. Beards and earlocks, yes; but tidy enough
to make a beatnik sick. Good European suits—no robes, no
kapotes; stetsons rather than streimels. One sensed a collection
of scrubbed BBC Batlonim, waiting to play in Dybbuk. But the
cognoscenti knew that the boys of Bene Berak had come to town.

Specifically, they had come from their Yeshivoth to watch the
Chess Olympiad at the Sheraton. Students of Halacha will tell
you that chess is respectable. Rabbis allow it to be played even
on the Sabbath, though there is opinion that it is more of a
pastime for women. In any case, "what Jew doesn't understand
chess?"

But their polyglot leader, the Ilui (genius), a serious-faced man
of twenty-eight, with the placid, stockbroking, appearance that
so often distinguishes real brilliance from pseudo, and no apparent
evidence of 6000 days and nights of learning, made it clear that
he was more than a Kibitzer of chess. I think he was concerned
to prove, if only to himself, that, if you can understand a Pilpul
or a difficult Tosafot or Yerushalmi, you can understand any
mental process that a human being can follow. Only his method
of organising a test was spectacular.

I met him while he was testing his form, not unerratically, on a
nondescript Hungarian. Since Hungarian was as unknown to

217

him as to everyone except his opponent, he had time for talk
with me, whom he knew from Rabbinical associations. After
mutual expressions of esteem he asked me (in discreet Hebrew)
if I could indicate some really strong Goyim. "What about this
fellow? He's eating you up. The lion of Babylon, right out of
Baba Mezia." He was unimpressed by my ostentatious display
of learning. "This is no *Grossmeister*." (As if any Hungarian
can be less.) "Chaver, would you include among Goyim the
Russian Jews? Apart from those, they've massacred Jewish
chess out of Europe." He did not answer that directly. But with a
gesture he sent out a couple of quiet spies, and resigned politely
to the Hungarian, who had been planning a forced win in 120.

The next incident is so well attested that it actually took place,
though it went unreported because incredible. The language was
Yiddish—I translate.

"Grandmaster Botvinnik, be so good as to play chess with me;
and I'll do to you what you did to Khrushchev."

Everybody knows that Botvinnik is one of the most imperturb-
able men in the history of chess, and one of the smoothest.
This he proved by saying politely, in a Yiddish-accented German
(what Jew doesn't know German?), that he was tired and preoccupied. A spy had meanwhile located Boleslavski.

"Grandmaster Boleslavski. Play. . . .' The same invitation,
the same terrible threat. Boleslavski "made like" a polite passer-by
"who doesn't know from anything." That, may I add, is the normal expression of Boleslavski and many other grandmasters.
But cheerful, English-speaking, Spassky saw a humorous situation. "Do you speak English? Well I'll take you on."

The scene in the press room was for epic. On one side of a low
table sat the Ilui, in a semicircle of awe-stricken beards and
earlocks. Who doesn't know Spasski? The latter, on the other
side of a small board, was not lacking in moral support. On his
left Botvinnik; on his right Geller; on the flanks mixed Hun-
garians and Yugoslavs. In a far wing Reshevsky, animated by
orthodoxy, I think, jeered at Spassky a little—sufficiently to
annoy him. For my part, I did not think that my Ilui would be
morally ruined by a defeat. Nevertheless, I like to think that the
good conservative Yiddish advice that I gave him stood him in

good stead: "Don't rely on miracles, friend; say a few prayers."
He smiled like a gladiator, and murmured something about a lion
coming up from Babylon.

Spassky was taking liberties. 1   P–QR3 is playable. (Anderssen
played it.) But 2   P–KR3 made it clear that he had in mind other
sport than chess. The hands of the Ilui, with each several finger
suggesting an argument, as at the Talmud table, hovered anxiously
over the small board. But every time the board was visible his
position had improved. When a stupid Kibitzer said to Reshevsky:
"He knows his way better in the gemara," Sam replied: "He
knows his way round a chessboard."

To cut a long game short (and how I regret that nobody made a
score) Spassky, mobilising late, suddenly found that he wasn't
doing so well. Accordingly, a Queen's side demonstration, where
the other was castled but safe. With new-found vigour, and
impressive parade, the grandmaster violently threatened nothing
at all. Too inexperienced to know any defence to this, Black
organised a small sacrificial King's side attack, and looked oddly
disappointed when his opponent resigned, and actually called for
a round of applause. After that, in a daze, he found himself with
White, and soon being offered a draw. Then Spassky set to work
on the stunned Ilui, and won. Honour was satisfied. A nondescript
Pole supervened; and the crowd dispersed. (That game was a
draw—beards of opposite colour.)

I don't claim to know whether the Spassky incident softened up
the Jewish Russians. Coincidentally, grandmaster Stein lost in
the next round to a Canadian millionaire (non-Jewish). And
there were other Russian losses. Had USA included Fischer and
Evans and Lombardy that team might have won the Olympiad;
and Ben Gurion, who gave the prize in Russian, would have
had to speak English.

As for the one-night hero, I met him hours later. "Master,
I'm proud of you. You showed the lion of Babylon that it was
only a fox."

His answer I find endearing. "Chaver, when the Lord wishes it,
a broomstick can shoot."

Soon after this, having declined a set of blindfold games, I
introduced him to Alexander, explaining the meaning of the word

"wrangler." He spent the rest of the Olympiad posing, to Alexander, who shares my affection for him, a series of good mathematical problems. After all, if you can learn Talmud you can learn anything.

Part Six
SLAVONIC NIGHTS

24 The capital of chess

The chess player approaches Moscow rather as a pilgrim approaches Mecca or Rome. He expects to see chessboard pattern on the pavement, Staunton pattern houses, to make Knight moves through chess cathedrals and to receive a blessing from Botvinnik. But when I got to Moscow my imaginings of hierarchy were dwarfed by the realisation of a fact which hitherto I had only known verbally—that Moscow loves chess; and that is a much more important fact than that Moscow organises chess superbly. The organisers of chess in Russia, generally, receive a support from the public comparable to the support for British football or American baseball; and that is why Russia produces, and will go on producing, the Stanley Matthews and the Babe Ruths of the chessboard.

In Russian chess a Communist theorist might well find a good example of the quantitative as matrix of the qualitative. If sufficient people watch and study chess with sufficient enthusiasm, it is only to be expected that a high standard is likely to emerge. Certainly the probabilities are that way. The Russians were always fond of chess; and Russia was a chess country back in 1851 when Petroff and Jaenisch were invited to the London tournament (Jaenisch could not leave his military academy, and Petroff arrived too late). The officers of the Czarist Army were encouraged to play chess as well as to fight duels. But they were a privileged order. It is different now. In the twenty-round finals of the Championship of the Soviet Armed Forces I saw a Russian sailor named Kondratyev disposing very quickly of what appeared to be an admiral; and the two were on the friendliest of terms.

At the Women's World Championship, which I attended as observer, the crowds were enormous, and many among them played better than most of the participants. (The opinion of the boys in the back room was that the women played chess rather worse than I spoke Russian; that, however, may be an exaggeration.) At all events, the large hall in which the tournament was played was always completely crowded by the end of the evening. It accommodated the better part of a thousand people. Red Army generals and shop-assistants with their fiancées, to say nothing of school children, sat and looked at the exhibition boards as one watches a cinema screen, with the difference that they were all analysing quietly and the total effect was what the officials in charge described as Slishkom Shum. When bad moves were made—and many of the moves made in that tournament could only be explained on medical grounds—there were audible groans. The Russians have a good word to describe this kind of barracking. The spectator is a *bolelchik*—a sufferer; it takes very little to make him feel ill. Nevertheless, he comes again and asks for more. Given a nation populated by long-suffering enthusiasts such as this, it is not surprising that the organisation of Russian chess has achieved so much.

But there are other factors. In the Soviet Union, it must be understood, sport and education are the only things that are recognised as legitimately competitive. Sport canalises and sublimates the kind of ferocity that expresses itself in the American capitalistic "cannibal" (I take the word from *Pravda*). So it comes about that there is a committee directly responsible to the Supreme Council called the Sports Committee. This Sports Committee is the parent body of state sports committees, town sports committees, district sports committees, to the infinitesimal. From the other side (if it is the other side) the trade unions all have their sports organisations: and these ensure, not only the organisation of teams (Dynamo, Energy, Bolshevik, being typical names of trade union sports sections) but they also see to it that no worker loses pay once his entry to a competition is approved; that no worker loses pay through taking time off for training; and that if a worker's sport activity entails substitute labour, the sportsman will not be left without a job when he has finished his training or his tournament.

I cannot help feeling that it would be a good thing for British chess, and for British sport and British education, if our trade unions—

which are now our only surviving capitalists—took some cognisance of this benevolent aspect of their Soviet opposite numbers. The Soviet trade union has, among other things, succeeded in preserving amateur status for the players of many games at levels of professional excellence. In some cases the amateur appearance wears thin, as when a master or grandmaster gets himself paid as an expert under the direct employ of a sports committee. Then he becomes in effect a chess journalist. I would observe, in passing, that this makes the standard of chess journalism, like sports journalism in general, very high in the Soviet Union. They produce sports papers and bulletins of tournaments with remarkable speed, accuracy and a high standard of criticism. I did observe one or two tendencies to gloss (rather than conceal) some of the vagaries of the Soviet women players; but I felt rather compensated when I read a review of one of Miss Tranmer's games by Flohr, in which he said that the spectators might have thought that Capablanca was playing Miss Tranmer's pieces until a bishop unaccountably disappeared.

On the whole, I decline to withhold my admiration for Soviet chess organisation simply because the fans prefer Russians to win, and because some of the writers try not to offend against this fan-like jingoism. Certainly the organisation of a tournament is most scrupulously fair. It seems to be common experience that, when a Russian has decided on the interpretation of his agreement, then he fulfils his conception of the agreement generously and without reservation. In the case of chess organisation there is little scope for ambiguity. In that direction, therefore, the Russian shows himself reasonably fair minded and not lacking in generosity. As for the hospitality that surrounds the Russian organisation of competitions, I can testify to its warmth and abundance.

In conclusion, I think it is important to observe—what is not generally recognised—that Soviet organisers have not allowed any confusion between the average of play and the standard. The qualitative that emerges from the quantitative is of high quality. It may surprise British readers to learn that in the Soviet Union where there are so many hundreds of thousands of keen chess players, the sports committee had, up till January 1950, only vouchsafed the title of master to sixty-three persons—not

H

a great number when one considers the extent of the territory. (I, myself, met a good player from a Tatar Republic, who told me there were players of his strength in remote places like Uzbekistan.) Before a first-class player achieves master strength he has to achieve the status of candidate for master; and he has to do several good performances before, from that chrysalis, he emerges into the butterfly aristocrat which a chess master is in Russia.

For my part, I know no Soviet master who is not in my opinion a genuine master. British players do, however, tend to ridicule the sub-classification of grandmaster. This is a title awarded to the winners of Soviet championships, and to those who win matches against them. In January 1950 there were eleven grandmasters. That the class is not easy to get into is evidenced by the fact that when grandmaster Levenfisch was doing very badly, and was challenged by Alatortzev to a match, he defeated Alatortzev by a score in the neighbourhood of 7–1, so that Alatortzev remained only a master. In the month of my visit the grandmasters were rather glad of their titles because the Soviet authorities declared four Russian ladies to be masters, who hitherto were not seriously regarded in the Pyervoi Rasryad. Had time permitted I could have organised a successful strike among the non-grandmasters. But as for the higher classification, I take the view that the expression "gross" in *Grossmeister* is as supererogatory; as the "gross" in "gross negligence." So long as the reigning world champion continues not to be negligent I do not begrudge him the added epithet. But I view with concern the possibility that grandmasters will multiply, and that we shall be compelled to cope with great-grandmasters. And who knows what other avatar. (That situation is now in being.)

25 Laughter and the Russian Gods

The important word in "cult of personality" is "cult," because it conveys the melancholy lesson that among the hardened atheists, the finally, inexorably, godless, there is a reversion to the worship of human beings, including inhuman beings.

So it comes about that Vladimir Iljitch Ulianoff, the worst waiter that ever slopped coffee in an East End Cocoa-room, lies embalmed in a Moscow mausoleum; and, outside, in a temperature lower than Russian political morality, people stand in queue on the solid snow waiting to file past the creator of their world. They say he looks very self-satisfied. (Perhaps he's right.) For my part, I have not seen him; because when a female interpreter woke me at nine a.m. with an invitation to join a *delegazia* that had permission to jump the queue, I replied irately that I had come to Moscow to see live Russians not dead Russians; and that I would see live Russians by appointment between three p.m. and four a.m., which is the Russian chess master's working day. The desiccated hag replied with some spirit: "It is not right to laugh at Lenin."

Nor was it right to laugh at Stalin. And I am a witness, from more than one standpoint, that the Russians did not laugh at Stalin; for exactly the same reason that made it impossible for them to laugh at Lenin. They loved him. Nay, more—they adored him.

It came about while I was there (December 1949 and January 1950), that out of a frozen sky thundered the declaration of the Praesidium: "Tomorrow will be officially recognised as the seventieth birthday of our great leader Comrade Stalin." The date was between the Western Christmas and the Eastern Christmas. (I have never discovered whether that fact is accidental.)

Planning there evidently was. The loudspeakers were immediately at full screech in the seventy languages of the Union. And suddenly, the clear sky of a Moscow midwinter night was filled with immense barrage balloons. Each balloon was adorned with an enormous portrait of the head of Stalin, grinning abominably. Batteries of searchlights, working with better precision than the Slavs are normally capable of, spotlighted that grin. I was reminded of a line in Shakespeare: "portrait of a blinking idiot." Unfortunately not true—and not funny. Certainly, in the crowded streets, the only laughter was hysterical joy, and most of it was tears. I found myself conjuring—though with a sense of blasphemy —the tearful joy of the London crowds at the Jubilee of King George V. Whether the comparison be true or false, I am still convinced that the emotion of those Russian crowds (allowing for "tear leaders") was completely sincere, completely unrehearsed, was genuine devotion.

The next day I sought refuge in the Tretiakovsky Gallery—the Moscow Tate. But what an escape. Cold-blooded officials had gone through the gallery removing from the walls every single picture of the ordinary collection. These they had stacked in the basement. Nor was that a crime, because, since the last days of the Ikons, the best Russian painters have been house-painters. What, then, was the crime? That every yard, every inch, every acre, of wall-space in that large building was covered with hideous portraits of Stalin, grinning, as always, abominably. (Who said that art is the laughter of the gods?) I contemplated Stalin in heights ranging from twenty-four feet down to a mere seven feet; diminished, again, in occasional group photographs where he was shown with Roosevelt, with Churchill, with Voroshilov. Perhaps for reasons of perspective, they did not show him with Ribbentrop. I saw Stalin eating, drinking, walking, riding, sleeping, orating, doing every possible act that can be spectated. The body drawing was good, but the sentimentalisation of the face in every single picture was such that, had Stalin known as much about art as he claimed to know about literature, philology, physics, philosophy, history and the rest, he would undoubtedly have had all the artists shot. For all I know perhaps he did. But here, again, one thing I can attest: the Russian spectators were happy without reservation; were delightedly telling each other the history that lay behind each particular picture; and their tears flowed like vodka in the Kremlin.

Nor were the Stalin-lovers only to be found in the toiling masses, as the Russians describe their crowds. I glimpsed it high up. I had been to watch the chess championship of the Red Army. Enjoying, as I did, the hospitality that the Capital Town of Chess extends to visiting chess players, I found myself having tea with some very high brass, including a general. In conversation, I was inquiring whether any of the leading Russian Marshals, Zhukov, Koniev and others, were strong chess players. The general said he had heard that some of them were very good. A sycophant sitting by him whispered, with lowered head: "Does Stalin play chess?" The general discreetly whispered back: "He has never actually been seen to play, but his interest in the game is so intense that we think he plays a very fine game indeed." I ventured a bold suggestion: "Tactically, perhaps, rather than strategically?" The general had all the smoothness of Russian diplomacy, which is very smooth indeed when it wants to be. "You mustn't take me into detail; I am very bad at chess. Let me get you some more cakes."

On the way home the interpreter asked: "What was that about Stalin?" "Little mother, I had it in mind that no Russian chess player is so defective in strategic insight as to have made the pact of 1939, which, you may remember, cost you twenty-five million Russian lives." She replied, "You are making a joke! We do not make jokes about Stalin." Her speech accelerated into declamation. "Stalin with us is not an ordinary statesman, like Churchill or Roosevelt or Attlee or Truman. He is everything to us. He is our comfort in defeat and our hope in victory. He is the embodiment of our ideals. We love him." Apologetically —for a guest should not appear inhospitable—I was suggesting that I'd like to watch her lighting a candle to Stalin in one of the better-class anti-god museums, when that godless woman turned my humour into embarrassment by bursting into copious tears.

Incidents like these make me think that the staged performances which led, years later, to the disinterment of the Georgian brigand prove little about the Russian people. If they prove anything, it is, surely, that the enemies who have lip-serviced a great villain take about five years to summon up the courage finally to vent on his corpse the hatred that they suppressed in his lifetime. Stalin, however, was lucky; luckier, for example, than Trotsky. Stalin may have died naturally (and only been disinterred) because his successor was Khrushchev. Trotsky fared worse because Lenin's throne was seized by Stalin.

Of them all Lenin remains untroubled, probably still self-satisfied. And if the Russians need somebody to love—as they do—the old waiter is always there for them. Blood that the tyrants have spilled has never stopped a Russian from loving a tyrant. That is why Russia has never really had a revolution.

Part Seven

FORGET-ME-NOTS

26 History of the Abrahams defence

Harry Golombek, who remembers the days before the flood, wrote recently in *The Times*:

> Many wrong attributions of openings depend on national-istic considerations. Thus the Russians call the Pirc Defence after one of their players, Ufimtsev, and the Abrahams variation, a complicated line in the Half-Slav Defence, which is rightly called after the Liverpool player, Gerald Abrahams, who worked out the whole line and played it in a number of tournaments in this country before the Second World War, suffers a change every country in which it is being played. In Germany they call it the Klaus Junge variation, after a talented young player who was killed in the last days of the Second World War; in the Netherlands it is known as the Noteboom variation.

January 1925 was a great month in my life. Early in that month I won an open Scholarship to Wadham College, Oxford, and on the thirty-first I defeated the invincible Dr Holmes—Amos Burn's favourite pupil (incidentally, a great ophthalmologist). Holmes as Black always played a sort of Slav formation:

1 P–Q4, P–Q4; 2 P–QB4, P–K3; 3 Kt–QB3, *P–QB3*.

Against him I had Black—a colour with which I have had a higher percentage of success than is thought normal. He played QP,—and in playing that third move I was indulging curiosity— or was it a refined sadism?—using the man's own opening against him. All I knew about it was that Holmes's opponents seemed always to play 4 P–K3, thus saving Black from the Pillsbury attack (the pinning of the KKt).

233

On this occasion perhaps Holmes was experimenting. He played 4 Kt–B3; and I decided to capture the Pawn and make him fight for its recapture. I saw some intriguing lines. In the struggle I worked out the whole variation.

I do not give that game here, because one or two Knight moves were introduced which prevent the simple form from being seen. But in November of 1925 I played the uninterrupted line in a match between Oxford and London University, against a player named Allcock. Here is the text.

White Allcock	Black Abrahams
1 P–Q4	P–Q4
2 P–QB4	P–K3
3 Kt–QB3	P–QB3
4 Kt–B3	P × P
5 P–K3	P–QKt4
6 P–QR4	B–Kt5

This starts the novelty: Holmes had told me that he expected 6 . . . P–Kt5, which is quite playable.

7   B–Q2

The only way to force the eventual recapture of the Pawn. It is arguable that 7   B–K2, abandoning the Pawn, is better.

7 . . .	P–QR4!
8 P × P	B × Kt
9 B × B	

Not 9   P × B. The KtP is a weapon.

| 9   . . . | P × P |
| 10   P–QKt3 | |

Regaining the Pawn. Of course P–Kt5 is unplayable because the RP is pinned.

10 . . .	B–Kt2
11 P × P	P–Kt5
12 B–Q2	(B–Kt2 is probably better Kt–KB3)
12 . . .	Kt–KB3
13 B–Q3	Kt–K5 (analysed below)
14 Q–B2	P–B4
15 Kt–K5	0–0
16 P–B3?	Q–R5 ch and won quickly

Before analysis of the critical thirteenth move let me mention an

amusing continuation against Fairhurst at Ramsgate (1929)
(Fairhurst had played 7   B–Kt2).

15	0–0	Kt–Q2
16	Kt–K5	Kt × Kt
17	P × Kt	0–0
18	QR–Q1	Q–R5
19	P–Kt3	Kt–Kt4 Not difficult, but pretty
20	P–B3	B × P!

To revert to the history: I played this defence throughout my
Oxford days—and it was seen, and liked, by Willy Winter, who
appreciated that, in an end-game, Black's Queen side Pawns
should prove better than White's centre Pawns. (This I have
often been able to demonstrate.) He played it in a match against
the promising, but ill-fated, Dutchman, Noteboom. In turn,
Noteboom adopted it, and it became known as Noteboom's
Defence. Later, it seems that the Germans captured it when they
aggressed into Holland, and they awarded it as a decoration to
some Totenkopf.

The line of play is good, if Black can solve, on the thirteenth
move, the problems set by White's projected advance. Dr Euwe
has suggested 13 ..., B–K5. But I dislike the idea of losing
that dynamic piece.

Certainly Kt–K5 is rendered "difficult" by 14 Q–R4 ch.
If then Kt–Q2; 15 Kt–K5 with pressure. If, instead 14 B–B3,
15 QB2, P–B4; 16 Kt–K5 gaining tempo.

Also 14 ..., K–B1 and 14 ..., K–K2 seem unnatural.
And 14 ..., Q–Q2 is met by Q–B2 with threat of Kt–K5.
(Have I, then, in Q–R4 ch, found the refutation of my own defence
I refer to my earlier narrative.) Well, it had a good life!

However, in minor company I have tried 13 ..., QKt–Q2
and 13 ..., 0–0 (one does not die of King's side attacks,
except one's own), White having played 7 B–Kt2.

I won a game in Manchester with the continuation: 13 ...,
0–0; 14 Q–B2, QKt–Q2; 15 P–K4, P–K4?

I query it because 16 P–Q5 puts Black into restriction.
He must try Q–B2, followed by R–K1, and Kt–B4. When that is
done he will be threatening P–R5, but the prospects are not clear.
What happened in Manchester was that my opponent could not

resist the Pawn offer. There followed 16 P×P, Kt–B4;
17 R–Q1, KKt×P; 18 B×Kt, B×B; 19 R×Q, B×Q, and
the Queen's side pawns promoted themselves to victory.

A subtler line of thought is the following. White can, in the
main line, save a move ingeniously. Instead of 11 P×P, try
11 P–Q5. If now Kt–KB3, which seems indicated:

12 P×P	P–Kt5
13 B×Kt	(not losing tempo)
13 ...	Q×B (P×B is unattractive)
14 Q–R4 ch	K–B1 (seems better than Kt–Q2)
15 Kt–Q4	P×P
16 Q–Kt5	B–B3

17 Q–Kt6 with an attack—(threats include R×P, and after
R×R, Q×Kt ch followed by Q×P ch). One suggestion for
preventing this attack is to answer P–Q5, not with Kt–KB3, but
with P–B3.

Obviously, there is still much to analyse—suffice it to boast
quietly that "the thoughts of youth" in 1925 were "long long
thoughts."

Worth mentioning is a by-product: opponents tend to avoid
my variation by playing 4 P–K3. That, I have found, makes
playable the Stonewall Defence: 4 ..., P–KB4; 5 Kt–B3,
B–Q3; 6 B–Q3, Kt–KR3 (so as to enable the recapture of the
Queen's Pawn with the King's Pawn. After that 0–0. And development of the Queen's Knight via Q2 to KB3.

The White-squared Bishop sometimes comes to life on the
Queen's side. But it also has a possible future on the King's side
(arriving via Q2, K1, at R4).

Another by-product is 4 P–K4, which invites 4 ..., P×P;
5 Kt×P, B–Kt5ch; 6 B–Q2, Q×P. Very risky, I prefer 4 ...,
B–Kt5 leading to a good form of the French.

Needless to say, life is more complex than these simple plans
seem to suggest. But I cordially recommend the line of thought.

27   My favourite game

My particular sack is not full of the scalps of the great. But a good game of chess does not depend for its value on the status of the opponent: only on how he played. If he plays well, he makes your win more meritorious. Exploiting that principle, I can boast of a few games that may well be of permanent value, and that allow me the luxurious thought: *Et ego in Arcadia fui.* My own valuation of this one is enhanced by the fact that it is one of a few of mine that opponents enjoyed losing as much as I enjoyed winning them.

The early attack (Diagram 27.1) leads to a fairly obvious sacrifice which my opponent had anticipated and thought he could cope with. But behind that there's a deeper, better, sacrifice of an altogether different type. The first sacrifice is a typical blow against a fianchetto defence system—which is not hard to analyse up to the return of the gift.

The later sacrifice, which I had seen as part of the movement, is necessary in order to prevent equalisation. It came as a great surprise to my strong opponent who had been preoccupied with a clever line.

My opponent was the late Edmund Spencer of Liverpool—a man who is remembered with affection by all players who ever met him, and who is remarkable in that his strength developed in what should have been middle life. When he died, lamentably early, in the 1930s, at about 53, he was at his best, and of recognised master status.

This game was played in 1930. I had the White pieces. The opening moves were as follows:

1	P–Q4	P–Q4
2	P–QB4	P–QB3
3	Kt–KB3	Kt–KB3

4	Kt–B3	P–KKt3
5	B–B4	B–Kt2
6	P–K3	0–0
7	B–Q3	P–QKt3

This is a slight error of order. Better is QKt–Q2. Now with 8 Kt–K5 I am able to give a shape to the game. (He cannot reply with QKt–Q2.)

8	Kt–K5	B–Kt2
9	P×P	P×P
10	P–KR4	P–KR3

This results in the position in Diagram 27.1 (rkt1q1rk1, pb2ppb1, 1p3ktpp, 3pKt3, 3P1B1P, 2KtBP3, PP3PP1, R2QK2R).

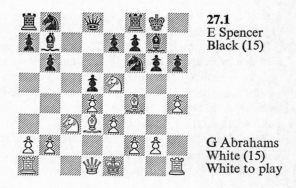

27.1
E Spencer
Black (15)

G Abrahams
White (15)
White to play

This P–KR3 is made in reliance on quite a clever defensive method which only fails against an extraordinary sacrifice. The decision was a difficult one because 10 ..., P–KR4 invites P–KKt4. So does Kt–R4. Best was probably QKt–Q2; then, after 11 P–R5, Kt×Kt; 12 P (or B) × Kt, Kt–K5 and there are defences. However, the game proceeded:

10	...	P–KR3
11	P–R5	P–KKt4
12	B×P	The obvious sacrifice
12	...	P×B
13	P–R6	B×P

My opponent had expected equality after this. Interesting is:

13	...	B–R1
14	P–R7 ch	K–Kt2
15	P–KB4	P×P
16	Q–B3	the theme song of this game. Black would be

helpless. To resume:

| 13 | ... | B×P |
| 14 | R×B | K–Kt2 |

With this, Black is threatening R–R1. (My opponent had thought about

15	R–R7 ch	Kt×R
16	Q–R5	P–B4
17	Q–Kt6 ch	K–R1
18	B×P	R×B
19	Q×R	Q–Kt1

and decided he could hold the attack.) I myself had rejected R–R7 ch because of K–Kt1, ignoring it. Also I had a preconceived idea. What my opponent had not seen is a move that the late Emanuel Lasker described as one of the best sacrifices in the history of chess. After:

| 14 | ... | K–Kt2 |
| 15 | P–B4! | K×R |

There is nothing better. If 15 ..., P×P my reply would be 16 Q–B3 leaving the Rook *en prise*. When one gives a gift one gives it. After:

| 15 | ... | K×R |
| 16 | P×P ch | K×P |

observe that if K–Kt2 one variation is:

17	P×Kt ch	K×P
18	Q–B3 ch	K–K3
19	Q–B5 ch	K–Q3
20	Kt–Kt5	mate

In answer to K×P, I played:

17	Q–B3 a quiet move:
17	...	K–R3 Best. If:
17	...	Kt–R4
18	Q–B5 ch	K–R3
19	Kt×P ch	K–Kt2

20	Q–Kt6	mate. After:
17	...	K–R3
18	Q–B4 ch	K–Kt2
19	Q–Kt5 ch	K–R1
20	0–0–0	and my opponent resigned.

The late Znosko-Borovski, who printed the game in *Novoye Vremya*, wanted to know why 0–0–0 is a better move than K–K2. I told him that I always wanted to demonstrate that castling is an attacking move, not a defensive one.

Against that same opponent I played innumerable games, and I don't think I won the majority. But a few of those that I did win I am proud of, and feel justified in publishing. Here is one from 1925:

White	Black
G Abrahams	E Spencer
1 P–Q4	Kt–KB3
2 P–QB4	P–K3
3 P–QR3	

One of my contributions to Opening Theory? But I've not used it much. It could be loss of tempo: but that would need demonstrating.

3 ...	P–Q4
4 Kt–QB3	P×P

His idea is to weaken my centre; but I think he loses tempo.

5 P–K3	P–B4
6 Kt–B3	Kt–B3
7 B×P	P×P
8 P×P	B–K2
9 0–0	0–0
10 P–QKt4	P–QKt3
11 B–Kt2	B–Kt2
12 Q–Q3	R–QB1
13 QR–Q1	Q–Q3
14 KR–K1	Q–B5

Underestimating my next move.

15 P–Q5	P×P

(If KR–Q1, 17 QB1)

16 Kt×P	Kt×Kt

17	B × Kt	KR–Q1
18	Kt–K5	

This gives me remarkable control of the board.

18	...	Kt × Kt
19	B × Kt	Q–Kt5
20	P–R3	Q–R4
21	Q–KKt3	P–Kt3 (B–B1 is necessary)

Diagram 27.2: 2rr2k1, pb2bp1p, 1p4p1, 3BB2q, 1P6, P5QP, 5PP1, 3RR1K1.

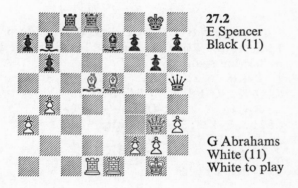

27.2
E Spencer
Black (11)

G Abrahams
White (11)
White to play

22	B × P ch	K × B
23	Q–Kt3 ch	K–B1
24	B–Kt7 ch	K × B
25	R × B ch	K–R3
26	R × R	R × R
27	R × B	

And White won easily.

Note a piece of chess chance. Had my Queen been at QR2 Black could now win by:

26	...	R–B8 ch
27	K–R2	R–R8 ch
28	K × R	Q × P ch forcing mate

Coincidentally, in the same year, against the same opponent, I achieved the ending in Diagram 27.3 (6k1, q1B2ppp, p7, 1p6, 5P2, 1B 3QKP, Pr6, 8).

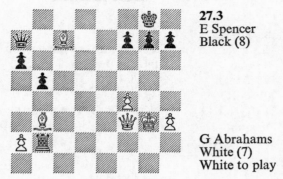

27.3
E Spencer
Black (8)

G Abrahams
White (7)
White to play

These are two of many endings (referred to previously) which I sent to the *Chess Amateur*, where the editor published them as "elegant studies."

1 B–Kt6   Q–Kt1
(if Q–K2; Q–R8 ch, Q–B1; B × P ch wins)
2 B–Q4   R–Q7
(if 2 . . . R–Kt8; 3   Q–Kt4 wins)
3 B × P ch   K–B1
4 B–B5 ch   K × B
5 Q–Kt3 ch wins

28   A score of
my scores

Chess is strictly a Science, however inexact. To the playing of the game (in contrast to the composition of problems and studies) all aesthetic factors are irrelevant. If a player seeks to make his product a thing of beauty he is to be condemned as a strainer after effects, a player to the gallery. Far better to accept the classification given by Diderot: be a good pusher of wood.

Nevertheless, for the spectator—and the player is also a spectator—there can be conjured an aesthetic experience. A fine piece of chess, with dramatic movements, convincing *dénouement*, makes the master into an artist *malgré lui*—a fate shared by scientists in more than one field.

In collecting, therefore, a few specimens of my more interesting performances, I have had in mind the epicurean appeal more than the didactic content. I also have it in mind that the muse of chess is a comic muse. Amusement ranges from the French sense of the word—pleased appreciation of the expected being fulfilled, or of the unexpected supervening. Occasionally the surprise produces a more hilarious reaction, comparable to that of the visitor to the zoo when for the first time he sees a secretary bird, or a giraffe engaged in eating, and declares that there's no such animal. Be, then, amused.

MY BEST SCHOOLBOY GAME

In this game, played in Liverpool in 1924, Rubinstein was playing simultaneously against four opponents.

WHITE	BLACK	WHITE	BLACK
A Rubinstein	G Abrahams	A Rubinstein	G Abrahams
1 P–Q4	P–Q4	10 P–KR3	P–QB4
2 Kt–KB3	Kt–KB3	11 B–K2	P–B5
3 B–B4	B–B4	12 Q–B2	P–QKt4
4 P–K3	P–K3	13 P–K4	P × P
5 P–QB3	QKt–Q2	14 Kt × P	Kt–Q4!
6 Q–Kt3	Q–B1	15 Kt–Q6 ch	B × Kt
7 QKt–Q2	B–K2	16 B × B	Q–B3
8 Kt–KR4	B–Kt3	17 B–Kt3	Kt–K6!
9 Kt × B	RP × Kt	18 P × Kt	Q × P

The idea latent in the position at move 14. I value this game because move 17 . . . (a sacrifice, which is not a checking move, on an empty square) is hard to see. Tarrasch failed to see Kt × P (e3) when Yates threatened it.

19 0–0–0	Q × B	28 RP × P	P × P
20 Q–K4	0–0	29 K–B2	P–KB3
21 QR–KKt1	Kt–B3	30 KP × P	R × P
22 Q–B3	Q × Q	31 R–R2	P × P
23 B × Q	QR–Kt1	32 K × P	R(B3)–Kt3
24 P–K4	P–QR4	33 P–Kt4	R × P
25 P–K5	Kt–Q4	34 R–QB2	R–Kt6 ch
26 B × Kt	P × B	35 K–Q2	R–Q6 ch
27 P–QR3	P–Kt5	36 Resigns	

(Reprinted, first eighteen moves, from the *Chess Amateur*)

MY IDEA OF AN "EVERGREEN"

Queen's Indian Defence, played in Nottingham in 1936.

WHITE	BLACK	WHITE	BLACK
Abrahams	Zukerman	Abrahams	Zukerman
1 P–Q4	Kt–KB3	3 Kt–QB3	B–Kt2
2 P–QB4	P–QKt3	4 P–KB3	P–QB4

5	P–Q5	P–Q3	7	...	P–KKt3
6	B–KKt5	QKt–Q2	8	KKt–K2	B–Kt2
7	P–K3		9	P–KR4	P–QR3

Better than P–K4, because it
leaves lines open.

10	Kt–Kt3	P–KR4

Compromising, but, were it not for White's combination (move
12 et seq), adequate.

11	B–K2—Not	B–Q3,	12	P–B4!	

because of Kt–K4

12	...	P–B3

11...		Kt–R2	13	Q–B2	KKt–B1

I am very proud of this idea.

If K–B2; 14 Q × P ch. My opponent did not see this. His choice
of move was "judgement."

14	B–Q3	K–B2	15	0–0	

Alekhine said that castles is an attacking move.

15	...	Q–K1	18	R–B7	Kt–K4
16	P–B5	P × B	19	QR–B1	
17	P × P ch	K–Kt1			

At this point I could regain my piece with R × B ch, followed
by Kt–B5 ch and P–Kt7. But a good sacrificer hates recapturing.

19	...	B–B1

Forced: if e.g. Kt × B;   20 Kt–B5, B–B3; 21   Kt–K4 wins.

20	B–B5	P × P	21	B × B	P × Kt

Black's defence, removing a Knight, is the best possible. But one
Knight survives.

22	B–K6	Kt × B	24	Kt–Q5	QR–R2
23	P × Kt	R–R3			

If 24 ... Kt × KtP; 25 Q–B5 maintains the pressure.

25	Kt–B4	K–R1	27	Kt × RP	Kt × R
26	Q–B5	Q–QB1	28	KtP × Kt	Q–KB1

If, 28 ... R × P, 29   Q–R3

29	Kt × B	K × Kt	33	P–K4	K–Kt2
30	R–B4	R–Kt3	34	Q–R7 ch	K–B3
31	R–R4	R–R1	35	R–B4 ch	K × P
32	Q–R5	K–B3	36	Q–R3 ch	

Forces mate in 6 and remains a Rook down.

Black's last alternative is 33 . . . , Q–B1. There follows:

34	Q–B3 ch, K–Kt2;	39	P–K5! My intended line
35	Q–B3 ch, R–B3;		has been demonstrated success-
36	Q × P ch, R–Kt3;		ful in all variations (see *The*
37	Q–B3 ch, R–B3;		*Chess Mind*).
38	Q–KR3, Q–R1; (best)		

This, perhaps my best, and certainly my best-known game, is clouded for me by the memory of my opponent. He was a charming Polish Jewish émigré to Paris (where he won the Championship from Tartakover). He there studied medicine while earning a living as a chess player. He qualified by 1940, but committed suicide when the Germans entered Paris.

AN IMMORTAL

Liverpool 1930.

WHITE	BLACK	WHITE	BLACK
Abrahams	Thynne	Abrahams	Thynne
1 P–Q4	Kt–KB3	13 K–B1	
2 P–QB4	P–K3	So as to make possible	
3 Kt–QB3	P–Q4	Kt–K5.	
4 B–Kt5	B–K2	13 . . .	P–KR3
5 P–K3	QKt–Q2	14 P–KR4	P × Kt
6 Kt–B3	0–0	15 P × P	P–K4
7 R–B1	P–B3	16 P × Kt	Q × P
8 Q–B2	R–K1	17 Q–R7 ch	K–B1
9 B–Q3	P × P	18 Kt–R4	Kt–Kt3
10 B × BP	Kt–Q4	Preventing the threatened	
11 Kt–K4	B × B	Kt–B5.	
12 Kt(K4) × B	Kt(Q4)–B3	19 P × P	Q × P
	(best)		

Here is a fine example of luck in chess. [We have good luck, never bad luck: "We should have seen it."] Black's alternative 19 . . . R × P leaves me still trying to win. But my opponent has been digging a pit for me. He expected B × Pch.

In answer to Q × P I had been saving something up. In fact I'd

invited an old gentleman who was pottering towards the door, to
stay, because in a few minutes I'd have a good move for him to
see.

20 Q–Kt8 ch

And the rest is history.

20 ...   K–K2

If K × Q; 21 Kt–Kt6 forces mate.

| 21 | Q × P ch | K–Q1 | 23 | Kt–Kt6 | Q–B3 |
| 22 | R–Q1 ch | B–Q2 | 24 | Q × R ch | Resigns |

AN EARLY ENDGAME

November 1923.

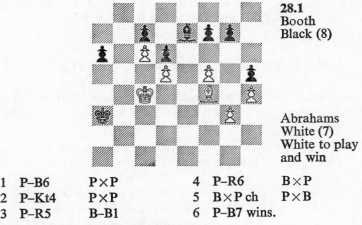

28.1
Booth
Black (8)

Abrahams
White (7)
White to play
and win

1	P–B6	P × P	4	P–R6	B × P
2	P–Kt4	P × P	5	B × P ch	P × B
3	P–R5	B–B1	6	P–B7 wins.	

Note that if 1 P–Kt4, P–B3 draws.

A GOOD SKITTLE

I call this a skittle. It was played at high speed in a league match
in 1929.

WHITE	BLACK	WHITE	BLACK
E Fish	G Abrahams	E Fish	G Abrahams
1 P–Q4	P–Q4	3 Kt–KB3	Kt–KB3
2 P–QB4	P–K3	4 B–Kt5	P–KR3

At that time I was experimenting with the idea 5 B–R4, P–KKt4; 6 B–Kt3, Kt–K5; 7 P–K3, P–KR4; 8 P–KR3, Kt × B with advantage.

But my opponent made a much better move. Nevertheless the idea is an adverse criticism of White's move of QB before QKt.

5	B × Kt	Q × B	
6	Kt–B3	B–Kt5	
7	Q–Kt3	Kt–B3	
8	P–QR3	B–R4	
9	P–K3	0–0	
10	B–Q3	P–K4	
11	P × QP	P × P	
12	P × P	R–K1 ch	
13	K–B1	Q × Kt	
14	P × Q	B–R6 ch	
15	K–Kt1	Kt × P	
16	Q–Q1	R–K8 ch	
17	B–B1	R × B ch	
18	Q × R	Kt × P mate	

Note that if at move 13 White plays B–K2, 13 . . ., R × B ch; 14 K × R, Q × Kt ch wins two pieces for a Rook.

SKITTLE AGAINST AN IMMORTAL

Less impressive, but more amusing, is the following disaster that befell a press room grandmaster in skittles. *Queens' Gambit Declined.*

	WHITE	BLACK		WHITE	BLACK
	Grandmaster	G Abrahams		Grandmaster	G Abrahams
1	P–Q4	P–Q4	7	B × P	B × Kt ch
2	P–QB4	P–K3	8	P × B	Q × Q ch
3	Kt–QB3	P–QB3	9	K × Q	B–K3
4	P–K4	B–Kt5	10	R–Kt1	Kt–QR3
5	B–Q3	P–K4	11	R × P	castles! ch
6	P × KP	P × KP		Resigns	

MY SHORTEST GAME

Centre Counter. This game was played twice.

WHITE BLACK
G Abrahams   W R Thomas (1923 Championship of Liverpool)

G Abrahams   A H Crothers (1925 Championship of Oxford-shire)

WHITE	BLACK	WHITE	BLACK
1 P–K4	P–Q4	4 P–Q4	Kt–KB3
2 P×P	Q×P	5 B–Q2	Kt–QB3
3 Kt–QB3	Q–QR4		

Normal is 5 ..., P–B3. But the text had the support of no less than Mieses. (Against Mieses I played, and won, my longest game—well over 100 moves—at Bournemouth in 1939.)

6 B–QKt5   B–Q2

Missing the point: 6..., P–K3 is no better. 6..., Q–Kt3 is "only, therefore, best."

7 Kt–Q5	QKt–Kt5	8 B×Kt	Resigns

CAISSA FAVOURS THE BRAVE

Liverpool 1929.

WHITE	BLACK	WHITE	BLACK
G Abrahams	E Collé	G Abrahams	E Collé
1 P–Q4	Kt–KB3	6 Q–B2	0–0
2 Kt–KB3	P–K3	(Inviting an attack.)	
3 P–QB4	P–QKt3	7 P–K4	P–Q3
4 B–Kt5	B–K2	8 R–Q1	KKt–Q2
5 Kt–B3	B–Kt2	9 P–KR4	P–KB3
		10 P–K5	BP×P

If P×B, White gets a fine attack. Thus: 10 ... P×B; 11 P×KtP, P–Kt3 (if P–KR3; 12 R×P); 12 B–Q3, Q–K1; 13 R–R6, K–Kt2; 14 Kt–R4, B×P; 15 R×RP ch. Collé thought for half an hour before deciding not to risk this.

11 B–Q3	P–R3	16 Kt–Kt5	Kt–B3
12 B–K4	Kt–QB3	17 Q×P ch	K–Kt1
13 B×P	P×B	18 Kt×P	Kt–K1
14 B×Kt	B×B	19 R–Q3	B–B3
15 Q–Kt6 ch	K–R1	20 Q×R ch	Resigns

MISOGYNY

Canterbury 1930.

WHITE	BLACK	WHITE	BLACK
V Menchik	G Abrahams	V Menchik	G Abrahams
1 P–Q4	P–Q4	5 QKt–Q2	KKt–B3
2 P–QB4	P–K3	6 B–Q3	B–Q3
		(The experts prefer B–K2.)	
3 Kt–KB3	P–QB3	7 0–0	0–0
4 P–K3	QKt–Q2	8 P–K4	P–K4

Had White's Knight stood on QB3, this would have been
dangerous because, after exchanges (on d 5) B × P ch is a threat.

| 9 R–K1 | P × KP | 10 QKt × P | |

Probably B × P is better. The retention of the Bishop costs tempo.

10 ...	Kt × Kt	13 Kt–Q2	Q–R5
11 B × Kt	P–KB4	14 Kt–B1	Kt–B3
12 B–B2	P–K5	15 Q–Q2	P–KR3
		Keeping the Queen out.	
16 P–QKt3	B–Q2	17 B–Kt2	B–K1
		An interesting manoeuvre.	
18 P–KR3	B–Kt3	22 R–K2	B × B
19 P–Q5	P–B5	23 R × B	P × P ch
20 P × P	QR–Q1	24 K–R1	
21 Q–R5	P–K6		

If R × P P–QKt3.

| 24 ... | P–B6 | | |

Threatening P × P ch followed by Q–K5 ch.

25 Q–KB5	P × P ch	29 R × R	R × R
26 K × P	P–KR4	30 R–Q1	Q–Kt4 ch
27 Q–K6 ch	K–R2	31 K–R1	Kt–B7 mate
28 R × P	Kt–K5		

SERGEANT NOT "FELL"

Hastings 1932.

WHITE	BLACK	WHITE	BLACK
G Abrahams	E G Sergeant	G Abrahams	E G Sergeant
1 P–Q4	P–Q4	16 Kt–K5	R–KB1
2 P–QB4	P–K3	17 P–Kt4	0–0–0
3 Kt–QB3	Kt–KB3	18 P–Kt5	P × P
4 B–Kt5	QKt–Q2	19 P × P	Kt–K5
5 P–K3	P–B3	20 B × Kt	P × B
6 Kt–B3	Q–R4	21 Kt–B4	Q × RP

The Cambridge Springs.

7 B × Kt	Kt × B	22 R–KB2	Q–R3
8 B–Q3	B–Kt5	23 Q–Kt3	K–Kt1
9 0–0		24 R–R2	Q–Kt4

Sacrificing for Tempo.

9 ...	B × Kt	25 Q–R3	Q–R3
10 P × B	Q × BP	26 Q–Kt3	Q–Kt4
11 P–B5	Kt–Q2	27 Q–B2	P–K4
12 R–B1	Q–R4	28 R–Kt1	B–K3
13 Kt–KKt5			

Aiming really at K5.

The Queen has no escape.

13 ...	Kt–B3	29 R × Q	P × R
14 P–B4	P–KR3	30 Kt × P	B × R
15 Kt–B3	B–Q2	31 Q × B	P–B3
		32 Kt–B7	R–Q2
		33 P–Kt6	Resigns

STING IN THE TAIL

London 1946.

WHITE	BLACK	WHITE	BLACK
G Abrahams	W Winter	G Abrahams	W Winter
1 P–K4	P–QB4	3 B–Kt2	
2 P–QKt4	P × P	One of my "contributions."	

I had won with this line against Mieses at Blackpool. Probably an improvement on the "book" P–QR3. May I add that I had frequently opened with what I called the Yokohama attack (1P–QKt4) so this play suited my then style. Winter, in this game, counter-attacks well.

3	...	P–Q4	20	Q–Kt3	B × R
4	P × P	Q × P			
5	P–QB4	P × P e.p.			
6	Kt × P	Q–Q1			
7	Kt–B3	Kt–KB3	21	RP × B	Q–K5
8	P–Q4	P–K3	22	Q–Kt4	K–Kt2
9	B–Q3	B–K2	23	Kt–K7	B–R3
10	0–0	0–0	24	R–K1	Q–Q6
11	R–K1	Kt–B3	25	Q–Q6	Q–B5
12	R–K3	Kt–Q4	26	B–B5	R–KB1
13	Kt × Kt	P × Kt	27	Kt × QP	KR–K1
14	Kt–K5	B–Kt4	28	Q–B6 ch	K–Kt1
15	R–Kt3	P–KKt3	29	R × R ch	R × R
16	B–R3	R–K1	30	B–B8	Resigns
17	B–Kt5	B–B5			
18	B × Kt	P × B			
19	Kt × QBP	Q–R5			

At that time of my life, I still regarded the loss of the exchange as an advantage.

If K × B; 31 Q–R8 mate. If R × B; 31 Kt–K7 mate.

I explained B–B8 by saying that Winter was threatening Q–B8 ch followed by Q–R3 ch, and that had to be prevented. I had an argument with Bernstein. He had just played his subtle end-game against Prins. I said that his was the best ending in the tournament. He insisted that mine was. The argument is of theoretical interest, and the distinction to be drawn between the "subtle" and the "sharp." (I have published Bernstein's ending in *The Chess Mind*.)

IMPRUDENT OR IMPUDENT?

An amusing game, played in Nottingham in 1936, showing the success of a possibly unsound sacrifice.

WHITE	BLACK	WHITE	BLACK
R Coggan	G Abrahams	R Coggan	G Abrahams
1 P–Q4	P–Q4	13 R–K1	B × P ch
2 Kt–KB3	P–QB4	14 K–B1	
3 P–K3	Kt–QB3	(If 14 Kt × B, QR–K1 wins.)	
4 P–QB3	P–K3	14 ... QR–K1	
5 QKt–Q2	P × P	15 Q–R3	R × R ch
6 KP × P	B–Q3	16 Kt × R	Kt–K5
7 B–Q3	P–KB4	17 QKt–B3	Kt × QP!
8 Q–K2	Kt–KB3	18 P × Kt	Q–B5 ch
(Sacrifice for tempo.)		19 Kt–Q3	Q × Kt ch
↓9 B × P	0–0	20 K–K1	Kt–Kt6
10 B × KP ch	B × B	Resigns	
11 Q × B ch	K–R1	(If 21 P × Kt, R–K1 ch;	
12 0–0	Q–B2	22 Kt–K5, B × P ch wins.)	

TRIUMPH OF THE UNCONVENTIONAL

Margate 1939.

WHITE	BLACK	WHITE	BLACK
G Abrahams	Opocensky	G Abrahams	Opocensky
1 P–K4	P–K3	12 P–KR4	P–QKt3
2 P–Q4	P–Q4	13 P × P	R–Kt1
3 Kt–QB3	B–QKt5	14 P–R4	R × P
4 P–K5	P–QB4	15 B–Kt5	KKt–K2
5 Q–Kt4	K–B1	16 0–0	P–QR3
6 P–QR3	B–R4	17 P–B4	P × B
7 P × P	B × Kt ch	An echo from 1936	
8 P × B	P–B3	18 RP × P	Q–Kt5
9 Kt–B3	Kt–B3	19 B–R3	Q × BP
10 Q–KB4	Q–R4	20 Q × Q	P × Q
11 B–Kt2	P–KB4	21 P × Kt	R × P
The "frog pond" voted unani-		22 KR–Q1	K–K1
mously for B–Q2 until Capa-		23 B × Kt	K × B
blanca, passing, said "B–Kt2,		24 R–R7 ch	K–K1
that's a good move!"		25 Kt–Kt5	Resigns

SICILY AGAINST SPAIN

London 1946.

WHITE	BLACK	WHITE	BLACK
A Medina	G Abrahams	A Medina	G Abrahams
1 P–K4	P–QB4		

I never lose with Sicilian, because I very rarely play it.

2	Kt–KB3	Kt–QB3	22	Kt–B3	R–Kt1	
3	P–Q4	P × P	23	R–B2	Kt–Q2	
4	Kt × P	Kt–KB3	24	R–K2	B × Kt	
5	Kt–QB3	P–Q3	25	Q × B	Q × QP	
6	Kt–Kt3	P–KKt3	26	B–R6	P–K4	
7	P–KB3	B–Kt2	27	R–Q2	Q–K3	
8	B–K3	0–0	28	P–KB4	P–B3	
9	Q–Q2	B–K3	(Inviting an attack.)			
10	Kt–Q5	B × Kt	29	P–B5	P × P	
11	P × B	Kt–K4	30	Q–Kt3 ch	K–B2	
12	P–QB4	Q–Q2	31	Q–Kt7 ch	K–K1	
13	Kt–Q4	QR–B1	32	Q–R8 ch	K–K2	
14	R–B1	P–QR3	33	Q × RP ch	K–Q1	
15	B–K2	P–QKt4	34	B–K3	P–Q4	
16	P × P	R × R ch	35	Q–R8 ch	K–B2	
17	Q × R	P × P	36	Q–R3	P–Q5	
(Inviting 18 B × P, Q–Kt2;			37	B–B2	P–B6	
19 B–B6, Q–R3 with attack.)			38	P × P	R–Kt8 ch	
18	0–0	R–B1	39	B–K1	R × B ch	
19	Q–Q2	Kt–B5	40	K–B2	R–K6	
20	B × Kt	P × B	41	Q–R8	R × P	
21	Kt–K2	Q–Kt2		Resigns		

KING IN THE CORNER

Canterbury 1930.

WHITE	BLACK	WHITE	BLACK
G Abrahams	H E Price	G Abrahams	H E Price
1 P–Q4	P–Q4	3 Kt–QB3	Kt–KB3
2 P–QB4	P–K3	4 B–Kt5	QKt–Q2

5	P–K3	B–K2	19	P × BP	P × P
6	Kt–B3	0–0	20	K–K2	B–B3
7	R–B1	P–B3	21	Q–Kt6	Q–K1
8	Q–B2	Kt–K5	22	R–R2	Q × Q

5 P–K3　　B–K2
6 Kt–B3　0–0
7 R–B1　　P–B3
8 Q–B2　　Kt–K5
9 P–KR4　P–KB4

My opponent was a fighter.

10 B–KB4　QKt–B3
11 P–R5　　Kt—Kt5
12 Kt × Kt　BP × Kt
13 Kt–K5　Kt × Kt
14 B × Kt　B–Kt5 ch
15 K–Q1　　B–Q3
16 P–KB4

Highly speculative, but necessary.

16 ...　　　P × P e.p.
17 B–Q3　　B × B
18 B × P ch　K–R1

19 P × BP　P × P
20 K–K2　　B–B3
21 Q–Kt6　Q–K1
22 R–R2　　Q × Q

A mistake. My opponent was not expecting me to imprison my Bishop at R7.

23 P × Q　　B–Kt4
24 R–KKt1　R–B4
25 P–B4　　R–Kt4
26 K–Q1　　B–R3
27 R × B　　R × P
28 K–B1　　R × P
29 K–Kt1　R–K7
30 R–R5　　P–K4
31 P–B5　　B × P ch
32 R × B　　R–KR7
33 R(Kt1)–B1　Resigns

The threat for many moves was to double Rooks on the KR file. This never happened.

ICELANDER SHOWS SANGFROID

Hastings 1947.

WHITE	BLACK	WHITE	BLACK
Gudmundssen	Abrahams	Gudmundssen	Abrahams
1 P–Q4	P–Q4	9 P × B	P × P
2 Kt–KB3	Kt–KB3	10 B × P	Q–B2
3 P–QB4	P–K3	11 Q–Q3	QKt–Q2
4 Kt–QB3	B–Kt5	12 B–KKt5	P–K4
5 P–K3	0–0	13 P × P	Kt × P
6 B–Q3	P–B4	14 Kt × Kt	Q × Kt ch
7 P–QR3	P × QP	15 Q–K3	Q–B2
8 KP × P	B × Kt ch	16 B × Kt	Q × B

17	B × P	B–Kt5	19	Q–R6 ch	K–Kt1
18	B × R	K × B	20	Q–Kt5 ch	K–B1
				Drawn

17   B × P   B–Kt5

18   B × R   K × B

19   Q–R6 ch   K–Kt1

20   Q–Kt5 ch   K–B1

Drawn

A "SUEZ"

Bad Gastein 1948.

WHITE	BLACK
G Abrahams	Canal
1 Kt–KB3	P–Q4
2 P–B4	P–QB3
3 P–Q4	Kt–B3
4 Kt–B3	P × P

WHITE	BLACK
G Abrahams	Canal
5 P–QR4	

More effective here than against my own variation.

5   ...   B–B4

6   Kt–R4

Animadverted on by the critics; but it has point. (6   Kt–K5 is good.)

6   ...   B–Q2

7   P–KKt3   Q–R4

My very strong opponent chooses a bad square for his Queen.

8 B–Q2	P–K3
9 P–K4	Q–Kt3
10 Kt–B3	B–Kt5
11 P–K5	Kt–Q4
12 B × P	0–0
13 P–R5	Q–B2

If 13   ..., B × P; 14   R × B, Q × B; 15   Kt × Kt wins.

14 0–0	Kt × Kt
15 P × Kt	B × RP

(15 ... B–K2 is better.)

16 Kt–Kt5	B–K1
17 Q–R5	P–R3
18 Kt–K4	

Sacrificing for a tremendous attack.

18   ...   P–B4

19 B × P ch	K–R1
20 Q–R4	P × Kt
21 B × P	B–B2
22 B–B5	B–R4

Ingenuity of desperation.

(If 23   Q × B, R × B; 24   Q × R, P × B).

23 B × P ch	K × B
24 Q–Kt5 ch	K–B2
25 P–K6 ch	K–K1
26 Q × B ch	K–K2
27 Q–R4 ch	R–B3

(If K–Q3, 28   P–K7, Q × P; 29   Q–B4 ch.)

28   Q–Kt5   Resigns

(If Kt–Q2 simplest is 29 P × Kt, QR–KB1; 30   KR–K1.)

The moral of this story is that even so great a player as Canal cannot afford to make a bad move. By putting his KB out of play he gave me the opportunity for successful aggression.

AN AMUSING GAME BY TELEPHONE (1952)

WHITE	BLACK	WHITE	BLACK
R Morry	G Abrahams	R Morry	G Abrahams
(Birmingham)	(Manchester)	(Birmingham)	(Manchester)
1 P–Q4	P–Q4	3 Kt–QB3	P–QB3
2 P–QB4	P–K3	4 P × P	KP × P
			Black is now free.
5 Kt–B3	Kt–B3	10 Kt–B3	Kt–K5
6 B–Kt5	P–KR3	11 R–QB1	B–KB4
7 B–R4	Q–R4	12 P–K3	Kt–Q2
8 Q–R4	Q × Q	13 B–K2	
9 Kt × Q	B–Kt5 ch		
		If 13 B–Q3, P–KKt4 wins a piece.	
13 ...	Kt × Kt	16 K–Q2	Kt–R5
14 P × Kt	B–R6	17 QR–KKt1	
15 R–Q1	Kt–Kt3		
		Forced clearance.	
17 ...	B–Kt7	26 K–R2	B–R4
18 P–B4	B–B6 ch	27 K–Kt2	B–B6 ch
19 K–B1	B–QKt5	28 K–R2	P–QR4
20 P × P	Kt–B6	29 Kt–K5	P–R5
21 B–Q1	P × P	30 B × QP	B–R4
22 K–Kt2	0–0	31 B × P ch	K–R2
23 B–QKt3	Kt–K7	32 Kt–B4	R × Kt
24 R–Q1	KR–B1	33 B × R	R–QB1
25 P–QR3	B–B6 ch	34 B–Q3	

I

Relied on.

34	...	B × B	35	R × B	R–B8
				Resigns	

R–Q1 loses a piece. R × R also loses a piece, but Black has to play carefully to win.

SACRIFICIAL PEAK

French Defence, Bad Gastein 1948.

WHITE	BLACK	WHITE	BLACK
G Abrahams	S Toth	G Abrahams	S Toth
1 P–K4	P–K3	3 Kt–Q2	Kt–QB3
2 P–Q4	P–Q4	4 P–QB3	Kt–B3

This makes Black's third move pointless. Better is 4 . . . , P–K4.

5 P–K5	Kt–Q2	8 QKt–B3	P–QR3
6 B–Q3	Kt–K2	9 Kt–K2	P–KR4
7 P–KB4	P–QB4		

Defensively intended.

| 10 0–0 | P–KKt3 | 11 P–KKt3 | |

Against the threat of P–R5, followed by Kt–B4.

11 ...	P–QKt4	13 P × KtP	RP × P
12 P–QR4	R–QKt1	14 P–QKt4!	

Alexander wrote of this move: "An exceedingly ingenious 'Abrahams special.' I am not sure whether it is worth two exclamation marks or one query." I, who am grudging of exclamation marks only ask for one. If I can't sacrifice a piece in a position like this, when can I afford it?

14 ...	P × KtP	16 B–Q2	B × P
15 P × P	Kt–QB3		

Better than Kt × P. He wants to play Q–K2 without impeding the Bishop.

| 17 B × B | Kt × B | 18 B × KKtP | |

The reason why move 14 merits an exclamation mark.

| 18 | ... | P × B | 20 | Q × P ch | Q–B2 |
| 19 | Q–Kt1 | Q–K2 | | | |

Better is K–Q1. Then R–R7 is unplayable because of Kt–B1.
But 21 Kt–Kt5, Kt–B1; 22 Kt–B7 ch, K–B2; 23 R–R7 ch,
R–Kt2; 24 R × R ch, B × R; 25 Q–Kt1 leaves plenty of attack.

21	Q–Kt1	Kt–QB3	24	Kt × Kt	P × Kt
22	Kt–R4	Kt–K2	25	R × P	Q–Kt1
23	P–B5	Kt × BP			The only square.

26	R–R7	P–R5

Counter attack. Typical in an open game.

27	Kt–B4	P × P	30	P–K6	R–B8 ch
28	P–R3	R–R3	31	K–Kt2	R–B7 ch
29	Q–Kt4	R–QB3	32	K–B3	Kt–B4

After 32 P–Kt7; 33 P × Kt leads to mate. The text by blocking the
Queen's line creates a threat.

| 33 | KR–B7 | R–Kt3 | 35 | P × Kt | R × KP |
| 34 | R–KKt7 | Q–R1 | 36 | Q × P ch | Resigns |

The Bad Gastein organisers promised me a Brilliancy Prize for
this; but all I got was a free copy of the Tournament book.

MY COUNTER—GRÜNFELD

Bad Gastein 1948.

WHITE	BLACK	WHITE	BLACK
G Abrahams	E Gereben	G Abrahams	E Gereben
1 P–Q4	Kt–KB3	3 Kt–QB3	P–Q4
2 P–QB4	P–KKt3	4 B–B4	

This introduces a sequence which I tried against Flohr in 1939.
Flohr commended it. I think it looks "natural," and that is
very often a good basis for judgement in chess.

| 4 | ... | B–Kt2 | 6 | B–K5! | QKt–Q2 |
| 5 | P–K3 | 0–0 | | | |

Gereben (which name happens to be Hungarian for Grünfeld)

felt that P×P or P–B3 or P–K3 left White far too much play.

7	P×P	Kt×B	
8	P×Kt	Kt–Q2	
9	P–B4	P–QB3	
10	P×P	P×P	
11	B–B4	Q–Kt3	
12	Q–K2	Kt–B4	
13	Kt–B3	R–Kt1	
14	0–0–0		

This is a defensive move. Let me quote the Tournament book: "*In die offene Linie hinein zu rochieren bekundet grossen Mut, welchen Meister Abrahams in reichlichem Masse sein eigen nennt.*"

14	...	P–QR4
15	R–Q2	P–R5
16	Kt–Q4	B–Q2

(P–R6 is defensible with P–Kt3 if necessary.)

17	P–R4	Q–R4

Black does not realise that my attack is better than his.

18	P–R5	P–R6
19	P×KtP	

The book says: *Weiss kennt keine Gespensterfurcht.*

19	...	P×P ch
20	K–Kt1	RP×P

(If Q×Kt; 21 P×BP ch wins)

21	R–B2	P–K3

(To stop in some variations P–K6)

22	P–Kt4	R–Kt5
23	Q–R2	R–R1
24	P–B5	Threatening mate, in effect.
24	...	KP×P
25	P×P	Kt–K5

(Now both the defenders of QR2 are attacked.)

26	P–B6	

(I should have played Q–R7 ch first. That has the advantage of being unanswerable.)

26	...	Kt–Kt4
27	P×B	B–R6

(Ingenious, but only delays the end.)

28	Q–B4	R×B
29	R×B	Kt×R
30	Q–R6	P–B3
31	Q–R8 ch	

(Not P–K6 because of Q–R4.)

31	...	K–B2
32	Q–R7	R–KKt1
33	P–K6 ch	K–K2
34	Q×R	Resigns

A NICE QUIET GAME

Most of my sacrifices have been for time. This game, played in Nottingham in 1954, shows a sacrifice for space.

WHITE	BLACK	WHITE	BLACK
G Abrahams	L W Barden	G Abrahams	L W Barden
1 Kt–KB3	Kt–KB3	4 P–K4	P–Q3
2 P–B4	P–KKt3	5 P–Q4	0–0
3 Kt–B3	B–Kt2	6 P–KR3	P–B4

White now has the Maroczy formation against the Sicilian—if he wants it.

7 P–Q5	P–K3	9 B–Kt5	Kt–B3
8 P × P	P × P	10 P–K5	

A sacrifice for space!

10 ...	P × P	11 B–Q3	Q–Kt3

A difficult decision. If 11 ..., Kt–QKt5; 12 B–K4 (not Kt × P, because of Q–Q5).

12 0–0	P–K5

A thrust for freedom.

13 Kt × P	Kt × Kt	15 R–Kt1	Q × R
14 B × Kt	Q × P	16 Q–Q3	

A move which attacks nothing, but leaves Black without scope.
16 ... Q–R4 *en route* for QB2.

17 Q–Q6	R–K1	22 Q–B7 ch	K–R1
18 B × Kt	Q–R3	23 B–B6	B × B
19 Kt–K5	P × B	24 Q × B ch	K–Kt1
20 P–B4	Q–R6	25 Kt–Kt4	P–R3
21 Q–B7	B–QR3	26 Q × KtP ch	Resigns

MY MOST IMPORTANT BAD GAME

A radio match played in 1946.

WHITE	BLACK	WHITE	BLACK
V Ragosin	G Abrahams	V Ragosin	G Abrahams
(USSR)	(UK)	(USSR)	(UK)
1 P–Q4	P–Q4	6 B–K2	Defends against
2 P–QB4	P–K3	Abrahams' Defence by ignoring
3 Kt–QB3	P–QB3	the Pawn loss.
4 Kt–KB3	P × P	6 ...	QKt–Q2
5 P–K4	P–QKt4		

Not good. Better are Kt–B3 and B–Kt5.

7	0–0	B–Kt2
8	P–Q5!	Kt–B4
9	P × BP	B × P
10	Kt–Q4	Q–Q2
11	Kt × B	Q × Kt
12	P–QR4	R–Q1
13	P × P	Q–Kt2

At this stage I felt like the phototographer's daughter—under-developed and over-exposed.

14	Q–B2	Kt–Kt6
15	R–R6	Kt–B3
16	B–K3	B–B4
17	B × B	Kt × B
18	R–B6	Kt–Kt6
19	B × P	Kt–Q5
20	Q–R4	0–0

One exchange I can't win.

21	R–R6	Q–Kt1

Russian commentators praise this move.

22 P–B4 (Kt–Kt5 was threatened.)

22	...	P–KKt4

23 P–K5 I was worried by the possibility of 23 B–Q5! Years later the Russian commentators discovered it.

23	...	Kt–R4
24	P–KKt3	K–R1
25	Q–Q1	Kt–Kt2
26	Q–Kt4	P × P
27	Q × P	Kt(5)–B4
28	Kt–K2	Kt–R4

(Inviting Q–Kt5, Q × P.)

29	Q–K4	R–Kt1
30	B–Q3	R–Kt4
31	R–B6	R–Q4!
32	KR–B1	K–Kt2
33	P–Kt6	

To deprive the Queen of a square.

33	...	P × P

34	R–B7	P–Kt4	44	K × Kt	R–Q8 ch
35	R(1)–B6	Q–Q1	45	K–K2	R–KR8
36	R–B8	Q–R4	46	K–K3	R × P
37	Kt–B4	Kt × Kt	47	P–Kt3	R–R4
38	Q × Kt	Q–K8 ch	48	R–B7	R–Kt4
39	B–B1	Q–K6 ch	49	K–B4	R–Q4
40	Q × Q	Kt × Q	50	K–K4	P–R4
41	R–Q6	KR × KP	51	P–QKt4	R–Kt4
42	R × R	R × R	52	K–B4	R–Kt5 ch
43	R–B3	Kt × B	53	Resigns	

The Russians "damned me with faint praise"—called me "an excellent tactician." With the White pieces I won a pawn, but oniy managed to draw.

AN EXPERIMENT

Played at Bognor 1962

WHITE	BLACK
G Abrahams	P N Lee

	WHITE	BLACK
1	P–Q4	P–Q4
2	P–QB4	P–K3
3	Kt–QB3	Kt–KB3
4	B–Kt5	QKt–Q2
5	P–K3	B–K2
6	Kt–B3	0–0
7	R–B1	P–B3
8	B–Q3	P × P

9 B–Kt1 ! ? Working on the principle that a Gambit is a sacrifice. Whether White gets enough value for his pawn is debatable. This game only proves that it gives a strong opponent (Mr Lee was later British Champion) some problems to solve.

9	...	Kt–Q4
10	P–KR4	P–KB4
		Stonewalling
11	P–K4	Kt × Kt
12	R × Kt	P–Kt4
13	R–K3	P–B5

A difficult decision

After 13 ... Kt–B3; perhaps 14 B × Kt, B × B; 15 P–K5, B–K2; 16 P–KKt4. But this is speculative.

14	R–K2	Q–K1		23	B×Kt	R×B
15	P–K5	B–Kt5 ch		24	B–Kt6	Q–Kt5
16	K–B1	Q–R4		25	P–R5	R×Kt

Counterattacking ingeniously.

Forced: R–R4 was threatened.

17	Q–B1	B–Kt2		26	P×R	Q×BP
18	P–R3	B–R4		27	B–K4	Q–B2
19	B–K4	Kt–Kt3		28	R–K3	R–KB1
20	B×KBP	Kt–Q4		29	R–KB3	Q–Q2
21	B–Kt3	P–KR3				

He intended P–Kt4. White's next move prevents it.

A mistake—Q–K2 is necessary, but Black stands badly.

| 22 | Q–B2 | Kt–B5 | | 30 | B–R7 ch, resigns | |